A Guerrilla Guide to Refusal

A Guerrilla Guide to Refusal

Andrew Culp

University of Minnesota Press
Minneapolis
London

The University of Minnesota Press gratefully acknowledges the financial assistance provided for the publication of this book by the California Institute of the Arts School of Critical Studies.

Portions of chapters 1 and 2 were previously published in "Confronting Connectivity: Feminist Challenges to the Metropolis," *Communication and Critical/ Cultural Studies* 13, no. 2 (2016): 166–83; copyright the National Communication Association; reprinted by permission of Informa UK Limited, trading as Taylor & Francis Group, www.tandfonline.com, on behalf of the National Communication Association; all rights reserved. Portions of chapter 3 were previously published in "Afro-Pessimism and Non-Philosophy at the Zero Point of Subjectivity, History, and Aesthetics," in *The Big No*, ed. Kennan Ferguson (Minneapolis: University of Minnesota Press, 2022).

Copyright 2022 by the Regents of the University of Minnesota

All rights reserved. No part of this publication may be reproduced, stored in a retrieval system, or transmitted, in any form or by any means, electronic, mechanical, photocopying, recording, or otherwise, without the prior written permission of the publisher.

Published by the University of Minnesota Press
111 Third Avenue South, Suite 290
Minneapolis, MN 55401–2520
http://www.upress.umn.edu

ISBN 978-1-5179-0522-4 (hc)
ISBN 978-1-5179-0523-1 (pb)

Library of Congress record available at https://lccn.loc.gov/2021054543.

The University of Minnesota is an equal-opportunity educator and employer.

UMP LSI

Contents

Introduction: Underground Philosophy   1

Part I. Anonymity   31
1. The Guerrilla Force of Liberation   35
2. Propaganda of the Deed   47
3. The Voice of Bullets and Bombs   51
4. Messages without a Sender   54
5. The Sprawl   60
6. The Politics of Asymmetry   64

Part II. Criminality   75
7. Society with Sexual Characteristics   79
8. Excitement and Exposure   83
9. A Heart That Burns and Burns   92
10. We Are Bad, but We Could Be Worse   94
11. We Don't   101
12. Making Illness into a Weapon   103

Part III. Fugitivity   109
13. Uprising   113
14. Self-Abolition   117
15. Searing Flesh   129
16. Captive Media   132
17. Black Out   139
18. Trapped between Withdrawal and Hypervisibility   144

Conclusion: Communism at the End of the World   155

Acknowledgments   169
Notes   171
Index   205

Introduction
Underground Philosophy

The most important movements now pose no demands. In their midst are those who refuse labels. Joining them together is the notion that there can be no political solution. Their ranks swell in the riots that now fill the streets, reverberate through the prisons, and simmer in refugee detention centers. The passion is felt in the red hot rage of radical queers who respond by bashing back. It has spread like wildfire before. Just a decade before, the movements of the squares toppled many governments. And it continues daily in those who insist that Black lives matter. What is most curious of all is that, in the midst of so much refusal, so many of their hearts are still moved by the language of "revolution."

Change is coming. But as Gil Scott-Heron said, the revolution will not be televised. It will not ask for time at the next presidential debate. It will not be interviewed on the front page of your favorite news site. Though they might try, it will not be included in any party's platform. Even those grassroots organizations "working at the neighborhood level" will not recognize it. It is the politics of the unseen. This book is for them.

Chaos Reigns

We live in an era of dissolution. As with any period, its social character is defined largely by its media forms. Whereas a century ago the world was taken to be a cinematic projection of a strip of individual celluloid frames, today we are blown to bits, thought to be acting out the programming of hidden codes. Time is now tracked to the 1/705,600,000th of a second, each division called a "flick," a portmanteau of the cinematic frame and computer-instruction-cycle tick. All user actions are tracked, fed into an adaptive system to maximize certain outcomes (demographics, geography, behavior, virality, attention, retention, revenue). This obsessive cutting up and tracking of time is done for a very specific purpose: *prediction*.[1] As a consequence, the future is colonized through a whole range of technical mechanisms, from financial capital to securitized governance.[2] Everyone now suffers its combined effect (though, as always, unevenly). While the modern era was plagued by misery and early consumerism bred boredom, today "We Are All Very Anxious."[3]

As the French collective Tiqqun argues, the motivating fiction of our age is cybernetic, enraptured by the idea of biological, physical, and social behaviors as all "integrally programmed and reprogrammable."[4] A dream born during the Second World War, it imagines the world through the screen of a mechanical dialectic of recognition, approximating Henri Saint-Simon's utopia of "replacing the government of persons with the administration of things."[5] The politicians are replaced by the managers, who in turn see themselves as pilots, transforming the art of government from the guiding of souls to a science of navigating inhuman forces.[6] Charles Babbage dubbed his forerunner to the computer the "difference engine." Indeed, today's difference engines operate a control grid that runs the new information society: "Every real integration is based on a prior differentiation. . . . The homogeneous, the mélange, the syncretic, is entropy. Only *union in diversity* is creative. It increases complexity, it leads to higher levels of organization."[7]

Social solidarities are being strained to their limit by a digital system that disaggregates identity. Categories of social belonging like race, gender, and class are now treated as a matter of psychological perception to be surveyed and charted. For example, pioneering cybernetician Karl Deutsch used the race riots of 1968 to spearhead the transformation of politics into data science: race was merely a set of communication differentials residing in wealth, geography, language, and attitudes.[8] So, even in an era of resurgent identity politics, their success remains reported through "objective measures" of public opinion that say less than nothing. All the while, the world has become transfixed by figures who delight in cynical piety, who use words frivolously to influence public perceptions or simply troll, leaving it to their opponents to feel obligated to use words seriously.[9] No wonder faith in solutions has dissolved.[10] The few who still present solutions are self-professed "disruptors" hawking a technical fix. Crisis serves as the motor for both the state and capital now more than ever.

The social categories of identity were sliced up for a purpose: so they could be synthesized higher up. With the rise of informationalization, computer-driven capitalism was able to promote integration of even some of the most unwanted subjects.[11] The digital logic of differentiation has fueled an overall shift of the leading capitalist economies toward strategies of flexible accumulation since the 1970s. This regime of accumulation builds on the already-existing infrastructure of capitalist modernization that used the architecture of the factory as a diagram for all sectors of society. But informationalization provoked a passage in the leading architectures of society away from the self-contained walls of the factory to the open system of the network.[12]

The effects have been drastic. Rather than a small set of institutions determining the direction of the whole in the last instance ("as goes the military, so goes the nation"), every part is now governed according to whatever patterns emerge from the distributed system. Yet the managers of society are not so cold-hearted mathematicians as to let whatever comes out the other side of their differential equations rule us all, argues Gilles Châtelet; they wield it offensively in *a microphysics of obedience* that "dissolve[s] certain global entities defined through solidarities which are refractory to homogenization."[13] After being split into a thousand points of light, society is reconstituted through the seemingly "self-organizing" differential relations of politics, economics, and communication.[14] The first is a political arithmetic registering citizen-panelists through their joyous expression of an "average opinion" to be surveyed through polls and the ballot (black) box. [15] The second is the economics of mercantile empiricism, which slices the social body into numbers and thinly disarticulates it until it is nothing but a fluid mass of particles that obey the laws of envy and attraction.[16] Third, a neurocratic behaviorism floods the communication channels of humans, animals, and machines, understanding them as nothing but thermostats that will shift predictably in response to environmental "inputs" and require constant external stimuli to continue operating.[17]

Post-Foucauldian governmentality scholars put it in plainer language, arguing that governance has shifted from producing good citizens to a far more atmospheric environmental governance that patterns subjects' space of potential to guarantee virtuous outcomes from virtuous and unvirtuous subjects alike.[18] Michel Foucault himself uncovered how *policy and political economy grew out of the police,* leading him to denounce all three.[19] His spirit has been resurrected in recent years through the words "we are ungovernable" emblazoned on banners.

Failing to account for these shifts, most political thought is still trapped in the outdated nineteenth-century political framework of recognition. It remains tied up in monarchic court drama played out through new communication technologies, "public spheres" of radio, TV, and now the internet. As long as the dialectic of recognition remains, the sovereign view of power persists, even after we have cut the head off the king. And with it, an outmoded politics quibbles over who gets to pose for the next state portrait as power has spread elsewhere.

Central to the operation of the dialectic of recognition is the transformation of people into *subjects*. No matter how much philosophers have tried to abstract the term, the meaning of the subject retains its Latin roots—*sub-jectus,* to be brought under—designating the power afforded to a person by virtue of subordination to another. Its image is a portrait of "the one" who recognizes the superiority of "the other."[20] As liberalism triumphantly pulls this chain of causation through politics, only two positions become possible for subjects: either as agents enacting their will on the world or as impotent victims of another's agency. Justice then makes its appearance through the politics of recognition, seeking representation and integration within a political system previously characterized by disregard and exclusion.[21]

The poisoned path to freedom offered by the politics of recognition begins with subjects being told to constitute themselves as subjugated groups, submitting themselves to the dominant order by first taking a seat in the back (promised a chance to be the ones issuing orders one day). Their acceptance is then determined by national debates over just how much assimilation is necessary until their pledge of allegiance can be taken as true, with diehard nativists sticking to the position that even the most bombastic displays of patriotism are not enough. Outlining its impact on Indigenous peoples' over the last century in Canada, Glen Coulthard argues that the politics of recognition reproduces "the very configurations of colonial, racist, patriarchal state power" they sought to overcome.[22]

Under Ground

Conceptually, this book proposes a different path, one outlined in the ideas of Gilles Deleuze and Félix Guattari. But forty years after they published *A Thousand Plateaus* (the second volume of *Capitalism and Schizophrenia*), it seems that most readers have gotten lost along the way. Many lose their place and get their heads trapped in the clouds after the first two lines: "The two of us wrote *Anti-Oedipus* together. Since each of us was several, there was already quite a crowd."[23]

The shock of the opening stops liberals in their tracks, who pause to delight in its seeming defense of plurality. Starry-eyed cosmopolitans quickly join the party, incapable of turning down an opportunity to stare deeply into the universe in the search for new cosmic bodies. Speaking "Deleuze and Guattari" like an incantation, they wax poetically about the human body not being a single self-contained organism but a complex ecosystem, whose population includes not just a number of organs, but a substantial amount of liquids and other organic matter made up of a great variety of molecules, themselves serving as a habitat for communities of microorganisms residing within the skin, mouth, lungs, eyelids, gut, and reproductive system. Too many stop there, sufficiently amazed by the sudden multiplication to take this rather simple shift in perspective as the most important trick in the book.

To read their book as a trip through the kaleidoscopic complexity of the world is to miss the point. Deleuze and Guattari themselves state as much a few pages later (for the precious few still reading that far): "In truth, it is not enough to say, 'Long live the multiple!' . . . The multiple *must be made*."²⁴ They follow this up with an even more scandalous statement on method: multiplication is not the result of adding new dimensions to the world (as in tacking an *s* on everything as a suffix or increasing the number of viewing angles), but of *subtracting from it!*

Subtraction is the political science of the underground. Deleuze and Guattari define it precisely as the operation of "n-1."²⁵ With it, they propose a two-step process of first locating the determinates that hold a system together and then, second, subtracting a dimension from the system, pushing it into crisis. The two-step process of subtraction is strategic, not moral or ponderous. It is not transfixed by earthly appearances. It fragments the world, frustrating synthesis, tearing down the cybernetic perch of angels (human, animal, or machine) that might offer a unified synoptic view.²⁶ If it is trapped in the world of representation, it is only as a partisan operating behind enemy lines. And partisans respond tactically, appropriating the most cutting-edge technology like the Bonnot Gang did with automobiles and repeating rifles. The point is neither to sing like a mystic about the "rhapsody of sensations" nor to stand in judgement, which would only fuel the cheap self-righteousness of legislative philosophers instead of making incursions under the cover of night.²⁷

The Political Aesthetics of Imperceptibility

"Visibility is a trap," Foucault warns in *Discipline and Punish*.²⁸ "It summons surveillance and the law, it provokes voyeurism, fetishism, the colonial/imperial appetite for possession."²⁹ This is why, after gathering a crowd and declaring their intention to proceed by any means necessary, Deleuze and Guattari outline another dictum of the philosophy of subtraction: "Prevent recognition."³⁰ How? By becoming imperceptible.

The politics of imperceptibility partakes in "larval warfare." *Larva* is Latin for "mask," as Nandita Biswas Mellamphy reminds us, echoing words of René Descartes and Friedrich Nietzsche that presage a warfare fought by constantly changing masks: "Larvatus prodeo [I advance masked]" (Descartes); "whatever is profound loves masks," and "every philosophy also conceals a philosophy; every opinion is also a lurking-place; every word is also a mask" (Nietzsche).[31] Specifying the operation, they single out a process that will act as a recurring lever throughout the rest of the book: "To make ourselves unrecognizable, to render imperceptible."[32] And the process of rendering imperceptible takes aim not at "ourselves," "but what makes us act, feel, and think."[33]

Deleuze and Guattari additionally mention imperceptibility two more times in the opening chapter. First, as an aesthetic critique of mimicry: the "vapid idea" of producing an "image of the world" as a mimetic *imago*, that **imā* copy of *āgō* objects, plants, and things.[34] Imperceptibility is a movement without such an image; a process by which a book, an animal, a fictional character, or a bar of music breaks with the world to fabricate something new. Even similarity, such as a crocodile's resemblance to a tree trunk, reproduces nothing of the original and merely uses appearances as a trick to conceal its obvious incomparability. Taken methodologically, imperceptibility operates without the descriptive, documentary, and sociological modes. The point is to circumvent representational approaches that echo of the world as it is (or was) or outline an ideal future to be imitated. Imperceptibility as a mode produces events without an image, those types of events in which the sudden invasion of something unrecognizable forces a rupture. In brief, the imperceptible is arrival of the alien.

Second, Deleuze and Guattari introduce imperceptibility as a political goal.[35] As unwavering critics of the state, they condemn the unparalleled violence it marshals and how it chokes off thought. This puts them at odds with most modern political thought, which advances the liberal incrementalist accumulation of reforms and the revolutionary break in an effort to salvage the old sovereign state. But even a revolutionary break is not radical enough for Deleuze and Guattari, who disparage it as still too caught up in how states pass from one form to another (from kingdom's court of reason to empire's functionaries of thought, or even to a constitutional republic of minds) to avoid dethroning politics.[36] The failure of previous revolutions is not that they have insufficiently wielded power, parties, and the state, but that they have proven incapable of breaking with them (hence the failure of state socialism ever bringing about communism or withering away of the state and private property, and neoliberalism's ostensibly minimal state larding up agrobusiness subsidies and police budgets).

In contrast, imperceptibility promises a political rupture that breaks apart the state's "pretension to be a world order, and to root man."[37] To achieve this goal, imperceptibility must function as a movement, not a model.[38] Here, the imperceptible is that which interrupts simulations, short-circuits diagrams, and evades representations, not as something ineffable, but as the abstraction of movement itself, the abstraction of an antipolitics that arrives from the outside to disrupt, receding before it can be captured and put to work for the benefit of the state. Enunciated formally in the politics of aesthetics, "imperceptibility" names the relationship to the outside (the incomprehensible) defined precisely as the refusal to create a new image of statecraft.[39]

Imperceptibility winds through the rest of *Thousand Plateaus* like Ariadne's thread. The first stitch appears with the imperative to "become clandestine" to escape "the head" and "dismantle the face" (of the imperialist state, white supremacy, phallic misogyny, and so much more).[40] The second move of the needle strikes like an anonymous "arrow crossing the void" with the force of an impenetrable forgetting that explodes everything it crosses without even being known—"a becoming only for one who knows how to be nobody, to no longer be anybody."[41] Here, its destructive force is unlike that of other types of lines, such as molar "breaks" that separate rigid segments like the passage between forms of the state and molecular "cracks" that cause leaks in supple segments of quanta like the march of missives carried by electrons that feed cybernetic machines.[42] The "rupture" is, by contrast, the line of flight of a nonsegmentarity, "abstract, deadly and alive."[43] The third loop braids together everything that politicians fail to grasp from their viewpoint of organizations. Disability, feminism, youth in revolt, "changes in value," and May 1968 are all given as examples of a micropolitics that completely escapes politicians, except perhaps when it can be used to shore up their own position.[44] Imperceptibility in this case means denying legibility in a system that demands "measurable results for every action, like citing a policy change in exchange for a protest," Richard Gilman-Opalsky argues, as in refusing to take the bait of the social and political scientists who say that "the current Black-led revolt could only prove its worth if it changes laws."[45] No one believes that racism ends with the burning of a cop car, but (continues Gilman-Opalsky) with the suspension of the current reality in the situation of a revolt, people begin to experiment with their own powers. And the subsequent failures of Mohamed Morsi and Alexis Tsipras should cast doubt not on the potency of the revolts that proceeded their rise, but on the capacity of governments to save us.

The final moment in the "advances of the imperceptible" in the book is the "becoming-revolutionary" that underwrites the whole of the becoming plateau.[46] Such revolution is opposed to the macropolitics of winning a majority, pitting it against history itself.[47] It does not seek to throw off its imperceptibility, instead preferring to remain "relatively unformed," always arriving too early or too late to develop into a subject or a formation of subjects.[48] This is why Deleuze and Guattari offer horror fiction and music as examples, even in the context of politics: it is not that revolutionaries should write sci-fi like Muammar Gaddafi's dic-lit, but that aesthetic revolutions are far better at illustrating the shape, form, and movement of transformation than jurists ever will be.[49]

In two brief pages, "becoming-imperceptible" is outlined formally as a three-part process: "saturate, eliminate, put everything in."[50] Each step is tied to one of "the three virtues" corresponding to the three strata that Deleuze and Guattari say make up the earth (and their mode of expression): the anorganic (immaterial imperceptibility), organic (asignifying indiscernibility), and alloplastic (asubjective impersonality).[51]

Saturation evokes aesthetic richness and vivid excess, but ironically also works as a tactic of anonymity. Artist Hito Steyerl examines this dynamic in *How Not to Be Seen: A Fucking Didactic Educational .MOV File,* (a nod to a Monty Python sketch about camouflage).[52] Dispensing little practical advice, the film instead demonstrates the link between visual identification and military violence (How not to be seen? Become "a disappeared person" by virtue of being "an enemy of the state"). Her film presents an aesthetic world in which all the techniques of sight are used to make a subject into a target, and evading sight means eluding violence. Additive techniques such as face paint are paired with sarcastic suggestions like "live in a gated community." Steyerl gestures toward neither subjects nor objects, but a world: cybernetics. The primary operation in the cybernetic world is violence at a distance, spawning a general transformation in vision and reason.[53] In terms of vision, our world is now dominated by aesthetic models of interfaces that transform the visual for use as pattern-seeking sense organs, with networked sensors and cameras that practice autonomous observation, using sight as a negative feedback tool, like self-correcting torpedoes closing in on a target. In terms of reason, cognition now rules supreme through behaviorism (using interactivity, environment, and prediction to replace ontology, materiality, and description), psychology (relying on the perceptual, emotional, and affective), and biopolitics (resolving problems through population-level environmental actions).

Saturation reconfigures this world through the production of a new one "that can overlay the first one like a transparency."[54] This involves jamming the cybernetic infrastructure that makes our world. This was well understood by the Revolutionary Cells (RZ) group in Germany, which did not form an army like the Red Army Faction (RAF). They allowed anyone to take action on their behalf as long as it was anti-imperialist, anti-Zionist, and supported "the struggles of workers, wimmin, and youth."[55] Their actions were intentionally nonlethal, focusing on bombing symbols of authority, as well as materially disrupting nonhuman systems by distributing massive quantities of transit passes and food vouchers.[56] Despite their newspaper being banned, it still enjoyed a wider readership in the milieu.[57] The idea is to loosen the ties that bind everybody and everything to this world, not in an intersubjective loop, but at the material basement of what is taken as reality.

Elimination turns codes opaque as if hidden by a criminal underworld. This is found in the prescription "to paint oneself gray on gray" or "to be like everyone else."[58] Such neutralizations of resemblance and analogy are the strategic operations of nonexistence, a task clearly understood by theorists of digital subversion.[59] It is the trick of becoming indiscernible to those looking (such as the mechanical eye) while not actually going anywhere, which is to say, practicing non-existence rather than no-existence. The internet is awash with guides on how to disappear, none of which suggest vanishing, but instead outline procedures for manufacturing a complex set of false identities and leads to throw anyone off the trail, a process regularly suggested to women and gender-nonconforming people looking to get out of situations of domestic abuse. The key is obfuscation, hiding in plain sight through "the deliberate addition of ambiguous, confusing, or misleading information to interfere with surveillance and data collection."[60] Obfuscation is additive concealment, cloaking itself in added complexity. Core cases include airplanes seeming to multiply by releasing chaff, Twitter swarms and bots hijacking hashtags, numerous individuals donning a single outfit in concert to thwart detection, and hiding voice within a background of multiconversation babble tapes.[61]

Putting everything in is the fugitive gesture of leaving it all behind. It is described as the impersonal becoming of "no longer anything more than an abstract line."[62] This means not confusing identity for structural positions. Pure structure is found in the modernists and the avant-garde through abstraction.[63] There, the impersonal abstraction of "a season, a winter, a summer, an hour, a date" finds form in the hands of the Russian constructivists and the situationists, all finding in abstraction "a perfect individuality lacking nothing, even though this individuality is different from that of a thing or a subject" and their anonymous peers of "a climate, a wind, a fog, a swarm, a pack."[64] On the one hand, these abstractions expressed the same newfound movement of the railroad, assembly line, machinegun, and automobile, such as Étienne-Jules Marey's chronophotographic gun, Henri-Robert-Marcel Duchamp's *Nude Descending Stairs,* and Dziga Vertov's *Man with the Movie Camera.* On the other, subtractive abstractions spin off, like Paul Klee's black arrow or Fernand Deligny's wandering lines. But all these examples remain far too male and white.

An alternative is the opacity proposed by Martiniquan poet and philosopher Éduoard Glissant. Glissant defends unknowability in a colonial context that wields transparency like a scalpel.[65] He refuses the great Western anatomy experiment of slicing open plants, animals, stories, texts, and everything else it sees. Once underground, less conventional forces covertly emerge, queer ones, such as the criminal bond shared between the Black Panther Party and Jean Genet. Parallel to Genet's avant-garde boldness, the Panthers called Johnson and Nixon motherfuckers in public, brandished weapons in front of state buildings, and declared the revolution "by any means necessary." The latter were more successful than any performance artist in staging "poetical revolt," an "act" spotlighting "that the Blacks really existed."[66] Appreciating this from his own queer position in the underground, Genet argued that the Panthers "have no possibility for existence outside of their violence," characterizing their acts as practical, positive violence that constituted their being, without which they may cease to exist.[67]

And while imperceptibility plays a role in the rest of the plateau, it is through topics on which much ink has been spilled but without much progress. In particular, issues of drugs, becoming-women, and secrecy. Because of this, it may be best to answer them succinctly. Drugs: "too unwieldly to grasp the imperceptible" and too often lead to addiction, black holes, and lines of death.[68] Becoming-women: unconditional support for everything trans and queer, following the principle that there are "a thousand sexes, which are so many uncontrollable becomings," like Black anarchist Lucy Parsons, the original "girl with the bomb, the guardian of dynamite."[69] Secrecy: this has nothing to do with obscurantist writing or esoteric knowledge, only a secret that "has nothing to left to hide."[70]

From a Guerrilla Logic Point of View

Everything snaps into focus when *Thousand Plateaus* is read as a philosophy from a "guerrilla logic point of view," as its authors suggest.[71] Deleuze and Guattari trace their foremost political concept, the line of flight, back to incarcerated Black Panther George Jackson.[72] The line of flight, or *ligne de fuite* in French, refers to the vanishing point in three-dimensional perspective. When thought politically, it suggests the technique of concealment by hiding something outside of a line of sight, or more literally, by smuggling things over a horizon line. Taken tactically, it mocks warfare's outdated linear formation of firearms that expressed the attempts by Descartes, Thomas Hobbes, and Louis XIV to "reduce the world to order" "in a machine-like manner."[73] Those who follow lines of flight locate cleverly simple means for defeating expensive state projects like the Maginot Line by not even appearing on the front lines, and instead follow molecular lines taken from the life of testosterone or the fugitive lines of marronage.[74] Furthermore, even the rhizome lends heft to their friend Antonio Negri's quiet disdain for the hierarchical organization of the Red Brigades, of which Negri was falsely charged with heading, resulting in a four-year incarceration until he was smuggled out of the country by Guattari.[75] The dissident "autonomist" Italian Marxist tradition of which Negri was a part had created a non-Leninist underground, with Autonomia Operaia complementing Jackson as one of the only contemporary examples of nomadic politics.[76]

While cited only once, a single document anchors the subterranean philosophical logic of *Thousand Plateaus*: T. E. Lawrence's encyclopedia article on his theory of guerrilla warfare.[77] Citing Lawrence, Deleuze and Guattari argue that "guerrilla warfare explicitly aims for the *nonbattle*," in which "the concept of the nonbattle seems capable of expressing the speed of a flash attack, and the counterspeed of an immediate response."[78]

In a brief entry for *Encyclopedia Britannica*, Lawrence outlines the defeat of the well-provisioned army of the Ottoman Empire by the irregular forces of the Great Arab Revolt, in many ways setting the mold for fifty years of "revolutionary warfare," in which "inexpensive, easily fomented, and extremely difficult to counteract" tactics became "one of the most efficient weapons in the Communist arsenal."[79] The strategy was a result of a creative inversion of the accepted military doctrine of "absolute war" that made the Arab forces appear utterly incapable of waging war, as two things were true of them: they were unable to defend a point against conventional attack and unfit to form a line for an effective conventional attack on a position. Its theory developed around a single principle: the "unconscious habit of never engaging the enemy at all."[80]

Though garnering only one footnote, the principles of Lawrence's doctrine reverberate throughout the book, echoed in the core concepts of nearly every plateau. For instance, in the introduction to *Thousand Plateaus*, Deleuze and Guattari's rhizomatic attack on centralized models of organization echoes Lawrence's tactics ("plants, immobile as a whole, firm-rooted, nourished through long stems to the head" that know only three directives: "seek for the enemy's army, his center of power, and destroy it in battle").[81]

Lawrence's formulations haunt the text again and again: in plateau 2 on pack movement (a relay of raiding parties, "self-contained like ships" that could "cruise securely along the enemy's land-frontier," along the edge just out of sight, where they can "tap or raid" into the lines "easiest or most profitable, with a sure retreat always behind them"); plateau 3 on the material constitution of the earth (combining the three decisive "elements" of war: inorganic mathematics, organic bionomics, and alloplastic dietetics); plateaus 4 and 5 on linguistics and semiotics (constituting an unorthodox distribution of raiding parties with "no lines of communication or labor troops," whereby "maximum disorder was, in a real sense its equilibrium," for it was "impossible to mix or combine tribes, since they disliked or distrusted one another"); plateau 6 on lines (a curious "internal economy" of "maximum irregularity and articulation" that "could not hope for any *esprit de corps*" but whose "diversity threw the enemy intelligence off track"); plateau 7 on facility ("an influence, a thing invulnerable, intangible, without front or back, drifting about like a gas"); plateau 8 on conceptual rupture ("the capacity for mood," "the adjustment of spirit to the point where it becomes fit to exploit in action" as in a force "seldom to concern itself with what its men did, but much with what they thought"); plateau 9 on linearity and circulation (disarranging "the enemy organism" through the tactics of "always tip and run; not pushes, but strokes," never to "maintain or improve an advantage, but to move on and strike again somewhere else" using "the smallest force in the quickest time at the farthest place"); plateau

10 on imperceptibility and generalized secrecy ("a war of detachment: to contain the enemy by the silent threat of a vast unknown desert, not disclosing themselves till the moment of attack"); plateau 11 on repetition (refrains like "nothing material to lose" and "defend nothing and to shoot nothing"); plateaus 12 and 13 on the nomad war machine's nonbattles as a minoritarian force (following the rule of "never giving the enemy's soldier a target," the singular individual "at least equal to the product of a compound system of the same strength," their operations depending "entirely on quality, not on quantity," and thus securing victory through the intellectual superiority of "a just use of speed, concealment, accuracy"); plateau 14 on space ("an assiduous cultivation of desert-power" trading hitting power for space and time "like naval warfare, in their mobility, their ubiquity, their independence of bases and communications, in their ignoring of ground features, of strategic areas, of fixed directions, of fixed points"), and plateau 15 on summative rules: "Granted mobility, security (in the form of denying targets to the enemy), time, and doctrine (the idea to convert every subject to friendliness), victory will rest with the insurgents, for the algebraical factors are in the end decisive, and against them perfections of means and spirit struggle quite in vain."

A thinker of the raid and friend of the partisan, sworn enemy of armies and their battles, Deleuze further specifies his alignment in an essay on Lawrence (that draws out the other's shame as an Orientalist but ultimately fails to fully escape it himself).[82] This point of view surfaces in other places too, such as Deleuze's concluding line of the opening to his essay on control: "It's not a question of worrying or of hoping for the best, but of finding new weapons."[83] He takes seriously the idea of the partisan philosophy, trapped behind enemy lines working to expel an occupying enemy through sabotage, disruption, and theft.

Key here is Kimberly Mair's *Guerrilla Aesthetics* on the "scandal of negativity" in West Germany's Red Decade, including: the RAF; Kommune 1; 2 June Movement; and Revolutionary Cells.[84] The guerrillas' aesthetics, Mair argues, are negative disruptions of the senses achieved through the violent illegibility of their gestures.[85]

Their actions are not that of rational subjects outlining a positive program or founding a new sensorium. Rather, they further sharpen the spearhead of the avant-garde who transformed aesthetics into critique. Whereas their actions appear intentionally crazy to a Christian Democrat, they are perfectly perceptible in video artist Paul Ryan's framework of "Cybernetic Guerrilla Warfare."[86] Mair cites Herbert Marcuse on the negative function of art to explain the guerrilla's actions as ultimately performative, "naming the 'things that are absent, is breaking of the things that are; moreover, it is the ingression of a different order of things into the established one."[87] They constructed negative situations, with their most explosive actions paralleling performance art's dismantling of the rational subject, pushed the extreme with antihappenings, illness, and self-starvation.[88] In an example, the imprisoned RAF refused to speak, adopting a code of conduct stating: "Not a word to the pigs, in whatever guise they may appear, particularly as doctors."[89] And while their main weapons were guns and bombs, used in destroying symbols of power or ransoming those of the Nazi generation who were still in positions of authority, groups like the Revolutionary Cells did not shoot to kill. The violence of their actions reflected less a desire to hurt than a result of general disillusion with state politics and fantasies of social rebirth in the New Left.[90]

"War" and "Politics" as Analytics of Power

Near the beginning of his famous chapter on method in *The History of Sexuality*, Foucault posits that power can be coded as either "politics" or "war."[91] Criticizing the "politics" approach in a lecture, he explains that politics analyzes power through a "contract-oppression" schema inherited from seventeenth-century thinkers in which power is taken to be a "primal right" to enter into contracts, the legitimacy of which "becomes oppression" when the specified limits of that contract are overstepped.[92]

A contemporary example of the contract-oppression notion is the discourse of "police brutality." There is a stark difference between condemning "police brutality" and "the police." "Brutality" is an exception to the rule of force, implying that there is a norm of an appropriate amount of force that was surpassed. Even the police themselves oppose police brutality as they seek to shore up the routine violence at the core of their job. Brutality is thus a question of where the line should be drawn between necessary (as authorized by the social contract, delineated by law) and unnecessary violence. Even when the rhetoric is pushed to its breaking point, as abolitionists rightfully do by arguing that all policing is brutal, it still frames power as a juridical decision over limits to the use of force—treating power as nothing but a public courtroom for moderating the actions of various social factions through debates over where to draw the line between legitimate activity and oppression.

"Politics" and its contract-oppression model stands as the apogee of the metaphorization of war, rendering power seemingly bloodless by submitting the conflict of interests to the conventions of civil society. In Europe, the discourses of antimonarchist republicanism, colonial racialization, and the bourgeois adoption of liberalism all took up "politics" to replace an older analysis of the state as a force of domination. Under the sign of "politics," these new discourses imagined the state as serving as a mere vanishing mediator for the administration of things. Since then, nearly all critics of the state have ceased waging wars of annihilation against it and now instead make the case for how, under their leadership, they could enhance its potentiality, know-how, and universality.[93] This is how politics took the state to be both truth and agent of the universal, no longer perched on a throne overseeing a permanent internal war, but installed into the core of a dialectic that feeds on reconciling conflicts.[94] In sum, the great victory of "politics" is to make the state no longer the object of critique, but rather the thing to be conserved and perfected.[95]

The cybernetic way of *waging politics* can be found in the techniques of counterinsurgency. Official U.S. Army doctrine on counterinsurgency specifies victory not as defeating an armed opponent, but as "the acceptance of an authority by a society," which they call "legitimacy."[96] Practically, the doctrine guides operations to thwart certain strategic objectives, listed as:

Force significant political, economic, or religious change.

Overthrow the existing social order and reallocate power.

Generate resistance to outside occupiers or change within a society.

Nullify government control in an area.

Cause a region to secede.[97]

The military here is rather unconventional, as the counterinsurgency framework plays down its conventional offensive capacities of defeating enemies in combat, securing terrain, depriving resources, and occupying population centers and the defensive capacities of retaining terrain, protecting fighting forces, and developing more favorable conditions.[98] Rather, the military's most crucial role is found in "stability operations," not just as "security forces" to back up civil society, governance, and infrastructure, but also as "partners" in all aspects of the state.[99]

From the perspective of counterinsurgency, war is simply a form of statecraft that takes populations as its objects. And while the term "counterinsurgency" is new, the Stop LAPD Spying Coalition would call it "not a moment in time but a continuation of history."[100] Drawing on Simone Browne, the point is that cybernetic suspicious-behavior policing is nothing but a continuation of "slave patrols, indigenous extermination, lantern laws (forcing Black people to illuminate their bodies in public), infiltration of organized dissent, and enforcement of apartheid."[101] Police, policy, and political economy together take populations as their focus, inventing the modern categories of sex and race in the colonies, revealing a series of previously indiscernible fissures for power to use as leverage in reassembling the social.[102] Divulging its postwar cybernetic heritage, counterinsurgency describes its aim as population "control," which digitally generalizes social markings like sex and race into a near-infinite number of divisible cuts, systematizing power as a long chain of relatively coordinated nudges that transforms intervention into a general ecology of automatic background processes.[103]

Diving into the black box of control, U.S. Army counterinsurgency doctrine works from the assumption that "all population groups are controlled by some combination of consent and coercion" in which "policing power" is used as an example of a necessary use of coercion for all "legitimate government."[104] Beyond traditional means of governance, it also outlines a specific "indirect" method for disassembling a network of people to regain population control: "identify, separate, isolate, influence, and reintegrate."[105] In sum, counterinsurgency doctrine uses the military to manufacture political authoritarianism.

There is no clearer example of counterinsurgency's "waging politics" than the George Floyd uprising, in which it took less than three weeks for the explosive force of a Black uprising that laid siege to police precincts, corporate stores with high-tech surveillance programs, and gentrifying retail boutiques to be confined to a narrow set of budgetary policy demands. The conditions were ripe for the revolt to accelerate rather than diminish, as the governor of Minnesota disclosed that, even with the deployment of the National Guard, "we do not have the numbers" to even make arrests, as they were simply "trying to hold ground."[106] Such a defanging was the result of a "deliberate counterinsurgency operation," argues Martin Schoots-McAlpine, "combining the (sometimes coordinated) efforts of: various police forces, the capitalist media, the American military, nongovernmental organizations (NGOs), the Democrats, both state and federal governments, and other liberal establishment figures" to resolve the legitimacy crisis incited by the uprising.[107] Particularly powerful was the discourse of the "white" "outside agitator," a reiteration of a trope previously used against abolitionists such as Harriet Tubman, John Brown, and Frederick Douglass and the last century of red-baiting, effectively shifting the center of gravity of the uprising to self-styled "social justice" peace-broker activists, media personalities, professional NGO workers, and Democratic politicians.[108] This mirrors a method proposed in the U.S. counterinsurgency document: "to educate and empower the population to participate in legal methods of political discourse and dissent," targeting specific "factions from a population . . . to get them to see the benefit of participating in peaceful means to address their core grievances."[109] The law here is used to prevent radical change, bogging it down with the drudgery of civil society, electoralism, and political representation in which centralized forms of power prevail.

In contrast, "war" as analytics of power counters that "war continues to rage in all the mechanisms of power, even in the most regular."[110] War offers a "strategic model" of power that Foucault finds necessary, "not out of a speculative choice or theoretical preference," but because "the expression of war" has "gradually become invested in the order of political power" (and not the other way around).[111] War sees through the ruse of the juridical model of power. It fosters disinterest in the finer points of the law, unconcerned by nuance or instances in which the legal mechanisms may have worked to the interest of the downtrodden; it does not even condemn unjust governments, crimes, or violence if this means "referring them to a certain ideal schema."[112] This is because "war" refuses all claims of legitimacy or right, as it finds that even the most supposedly just law is "born of real battles, victories, massacres and consequences," "in burning towns and ravaged fields."[113] This is why we should never mistake the imagined battles of lawyers or politicians as war, but peer "beneath the forms of justice that have been instituted, the order that has been imposed, the forgotten past of real struggle, actual victories, and defeats, which may have been disguised but which remain profoundly inscribed" and instead rediscover "the blood that has dried in the codes."[114] What war offers is "a discourse in which truth functions exclusively as a weapon that is used to win an exclusively partisan victory."[115] On an expanded scale, "war is a general economy of weapons, an economy of armed people and disarmed people" along two poles: invasion and rebellion.[116] It refuses politics' coding of power as an unarmed civilian rivalry over the universality of the state.[117] Put succinctly, in an inversion of Carl von Clausewitz's famous dictum: politics is the continuation of war by other means.[118]

A war analysis does not mean adopting Mao's belief that "political power grows out of the barrel of the gun" and related Marxist-Leninist state philosophies that crudely try to monopolize the politics-as-war discourse. None think critically enough about sovereignty, all of them seeing the state as the prize to be won in war.

Of course they offer a variety of alibis, such as "the people," to justify their power grabs. Their commitment to the war analysis of power ends after they have seized the state, often retaining it in a degraded form to wage those campaigns of terror endemic to state socialism, resulting in gulags, genocides, and camps. Genet spoke the partisan truth of war as an analytic when he said that, "the day the Palestinians become an institution, I will no longer be on their side. The day they become a nation like other nations, I won't be there anymore."[119]

As the speculative sci-fi film *Born in Flames* attests, feminist revolutions are still necessary after socialist ones because the "social" in socialism explicitly targets queers and other "anti-social" minoritarians. Following its revolution, Cuba's first major raid was "the nights of the three P's," which targeted "pederasts, prostitutes, and pimps."[120] Homosexuals were incarcerated in sweltering labor camps that held tens of thousands, forced into "virilization treatments" to rid them of what was taken to be learned behavior and expelled from all levels of society, including the military, universities, the party, and government posts.[121] This was the case in nearly all socialist countries throughout the twentieth century, with queers being monitored, blackmailed, fired, arrested, and medicalized, except in those places so bold as to proclaim that socialism purged all social ills, so homosexuality did not even exist there.

There is an end to the long journey through war as an analytic: what I propose as *subtractive communism*. It does not blueprint the ideal society, which has gotten state "communists" only as far as authoritarian socialism. It instead casts its lot with the ungovernable. Its subtractive operations are the negation of cybernetic governance through the growth of the underground. Its underground world is made up of sex workers, convicts, and outcasts as seen through the eyes of Genet, *Der Eigene*, Lucía Sánchez Saornil, Pier Paolo Pasolini, Guy Hocquenghem, Françoise d'Eaubonne, Mario Mieli, Sylvia Rivera, Marsha P. Johnson, and Linda Evans. Any communism worth its name aligns with them, as even Huey P. Newton came to see by 1970, pondering in his famous letter whether "maybe a homosexual could be the most revolutionary."[122]

Against the state politicians' fair-weather use of war analysis,

Tiqqun proposes the conceptual framework of "diffuse guerrilla warfare."[123] It begins with "disseminating oneself in a multiplicity of foci, like so many *rifts* in the capitalist whole."[124] This shifts war from the defense of a collective subject (nation or people) to a struggle for autonomy. This difference was amplified during Italy's tumultuous Years of Lead, when numerous armed militants simply imitated the state while others spread the creativity of true guerrilla thinking without becoming guerrillas. These rifts were filled by "radio stations, bands, celebration, riots, and squats" that existed not as occupations, but as an empty architecture of indistinction, informality, and semisecrecy that became anonymous, "signed with fake names, a different one each time," and thus "unattributable, soluble in the sea of Autonomia."[125] These operations did not speak with the voice of a coherent subject, but rather their frequency and intensity formed a consistency that nonetheless, "like so many marks etched in the half-light," left but mere traces of authorship and thus constituted a multifaceted offensive "more formidable" than their hardened counterparts in the armed ranks of the Brigate Rosse and Prima Linea.[126] The noncoherence of the autonomous elements therefore outlined the struggle, which was not simply between revolutionary and conservative forces, but between different ways of doing politics. On one side was the coherence of the Italian state "derived from popular Italian perceptions that the authority of the state was genuine and effective and that it used morally correct means for reasonable and fair purposes," and on the other was a diffusion of fragmented appearances that formed "a certain intensity in the circulation of bodies between all of [its] points."[127]

A more contemporary example would be the vast network of "Antifa" activity with the dual precursors of German antifascism and the antiglobalization "black bloc." As nothing but a technique of negation, it has no organizational form, let alone formal coordination between actions, preventing it from boasting as parties do about membership numbers or programs for ruling society. This has not prevented conservatives (and liberals) from making it into a boogeyman, understanding antifa only from an authoritarian view of power that leads them to howl against billionaire funders, a unitary chain of command, and pending repressive legislation—the constitutive elements of their own political system. And unlike the parochial tradition of Autonomia, Antifa has been taken up by Black, Brown, Indigenous, queer, trans, disabled, poor, immigrant, and incarcerated people across the globe. This multiplicity grows out of anarchist and "New Left" currents whose slogans, posters, and other ephemera carry the battle beyond a struggle for control over the means of repression.

Turn-of-the century classical anarchism spoke in the fiery slogans: "Free the Class War Prisoners!" (International Workers of the World), "That which is maintained with blood and fire through blood and fire shall fall!" (Ricardo Flores Magón); "We are at war . . . but it isn't a war against another nation, but a never-ending war within our own country" (Marie Equi); "Everything that is beautiful and great is achieved by the dangerous march of humanity, and always against God, masters and government" (Virgilia D'Andrea).

The New Left, constituted in a time of global wars for independence, exclaimed: "Art is dead, burn the museums, baby!" (Up Against the Wall Motherfuckers); "Bring the war home" (Students for a Democratic Society); "Seja marginal, seja herói [be (a) marginal, be a hero]" (Brazil 1968), "Piece now"(Students for a Democratic Society National War Council); "The Indian Wars are not over" (Leonard Peltier Defense Committee).

New strands of war-fighting have appeared since in the rallying calls of: "ACT UP, fight back!" (ACT UP); "No justice, no peace" (Los Angeles riots); "They only call it class war when we fight back" (class-war anarchism); "The fourth world war" (Subcomandante Marcos); "Be gay, do crime" and "Stonewall was a riot" (Bash Back!); "We're here / we're queer / we're anarchists / we'll fuck you up," "hands up / shoot back," and "we cannot accept defeat / half of us are packing heat" (insurrectionary anarchism).

A Guerrilla Manual for a Nonfascist Life

Thousand Plateaus serves as a philosophical manual for irregular war without becoming an armed militant, a sort of *guerrilla-without-guerrillas*. Philosophers make poor combatants because, in "the struggle for legitimacy," the best make no claim on authority.[128] This is not to say that philosophy is useless. Lawrence, for instance, found his ally's situation "so weak physically that it could not let the metaphysical weapon rust unused."[129] Deleuze finds himself in a similar situation when explaining the title of a collection of his work, *Negotiations*. In the face of things with true power (religion, states, capitalism, science, the law, public opinion, television . . .), philosophy is not provisioned well enough to battle them head-on. But neither can philosophy engage them in civil discourse: it "can't converse with them"; "it's got nothing to tell them"; and "nothing to communicate."[130] All that philosophy can do is wage "a guerrilla campaign against them," negotiations in which words are wielded like weapons between hostile parties. [131]

In the situation of negotiations, counterinsurgency operations from the position of strength impose negotiations to deescalate conflict, manufacture compliance, and hide coercion in the neutral language of agreement. By contrast, philosophers working from a position of weakness use negotiations in bad faith. There are a number of texts to guide their operations, such as Foucault's famous "manual or guide" that prefaces *Anti-Oedipus*, Fred Moten and Stefano Harney's *Undercommons*, or the anonymously penned *Call* aimed "not to demonstrate, to argue, to convince."[132] The key? A nonfascist life: to dissolve the individual into a multiplication of action, thought, and desires without becoming enamored in power. At the heart of the *Undercommons*, there is an injunction to take up a maroon position against institutions (namely, the university), a concealed underground that is not only fugitive, but criminal.[133] And likewise, the *Call* is for a new beginning based on the withdrawal from the existing political coordinates and identities: "We contest nothing, we demand nothing; . . . we constitute ourselves as a *force*, as a *material* force, as an *autonomous* material force within the world civil war."[134] All of these culminate in the proposition that "on the one hand, we want to live communism; on the other, to spread anarchy."[135]

For some, this may still be too abstract. Thus debates within anarchist theory over the strategy of withdrawal serves as a final aid. Guerrilla philosophy wields abstraction like the *avant-garde*, which grew up "in the shadow of the anarchist movements" of the propaganda by the deed.[136] As neatly summarized by Jesse Cohn, its negotiation with power follows a doctrine of five "non-s":

> **Noncommunication:** a special affinity to the "destructive gesture" of the anarchist bomber, to "propaganda by the deed" as an alternative to propaganda by the word;
>
> **Nonsense:** a "resistance to representation" via absurdity or abstraction, the negation or emptying-out of meaning;
>
> **Nonutility:** a contempt for conceptions of art as having a use or purpose outside itself, rejected in favor of aesthetic "autonomy";
>
> **Noncollectivity:** a basic credo (despite the apparent diversity of the sects) of "aesthetic individualism," especially inspired by Max Stirner's egoism; and
>
> **Nonpopularity:** a repudiation of the popular and the accessible as hopelessly bourgeois and "corrupt."[137]

At first glance, this may appear to be a metaphorization of war. But is it not actually a distillation of the true principles behind the guerrilla, in which the intellect is the decisive weapon when otherwise outnumbered and outgunned?

Doing Philosophy for the Underground

With all of the qualification entailed by guerrilla-without-guerrillas, it is important not to downplay how Deleuze and Guattari supported comrades in arms both conceptually and practically. They write that the nomad war machine is "revived" by "insubordination, rioting, guerrilla warfare, or revolution as an act."[138] A young Guattari participated in clandestine work aiding Algerian independence and went on to instigate major actions in the revolutionary climate of 1968, including a series of occupations.[139] In the early 1970s, they worked with the Prison Information Group, helping publish an issue of its journal *The Intolerable* on the assassination of George Jackson, and would meet with Black Panthers while visiting the United States. Both were militant, life-long supporters of the Palestinian cause, with serious contributions, in addition to Deleuze's path-breaking conceptual work with Elias Sanbar that drew parallels between the decolonial liberation of the Palestinians and Native Americans.[140] While they were completing *Thousand Plateaus* in 1977, Toni Negri began living part of his time in Paris, spending weekends with Guattari and attending Deleuze's seminars at Vincennes.[141] That year Guattari became fast friends with the young radical Franco "Bifo" Berardi, who was living underground and was arrested that July. Guattari leapt into action, creating the Center for Initiatives for New Free Spaces (CINEL) to defend militants from prosecution, turning him into a movement celebrity in the streets of Bologna and Berlin.[142] Months later, Deleuze and Guattari mobilized in defense of Klaus Croissant, the lawyer for the RAF who was facing calls for extradition by the Western German state (and at the subsequent rally, Foucault was beaten so badly by the police that he suffered a broken rib).[143] And before the book was even completed, the Italian state escalated its repression with a series of arrests, sweeping up Negri and others as terrorists, almost immediately relegating Autonomia to "the Wax Museum of politics."[144]

Subtraction is how philosophy uses subterranean means for the guerrilla to go even further underground, like Negri's collaboration with Guattari on *Communists Like Us*, which grew out of their prison correspondence. Crafting a new "plague of dragons teeth, sown and nourished in the soil of confusion, social dissension, economic disruptions, etc., causing armed fanatics to spring up where peaceful peasants worked."[145] A place where the work is done is in figuring out how "guerrilla war is far more intellectual than a bayonet charge."[146]

Nearly half a century after the publication of *Thousand Plateaus*, a question remains: what are the new philosophical negotiations that revive the guerrilla-logic point of view? How has the militarization of the police and the politicization of the military shifted the strategic terrain? How must the analysis evolve to account for the surveillance of the American Muslim population at all levels of government, exchanges in which antigang police train with counterinsurgency military forces, and the military-policing coordination with nongovernmental organizations to control opposition?[147] And given that governments around the world are employing counterinsurgency techniques against radical politics, what can philosophy do to secure victory through intellectual superiority rather than combat force?

Can the proliferation of subterranean philosophy serve as a weapon of the weak? It is not strong enough to prop up a new government or design new models of society, or even the abstract principles for running either. But perhaps it does provide the means to communicate "nothing" to the forces of domination. There is nothing more important today than negotiating a release from all the intolerable things about this world—a process that will not occur in any legislature or town hall. The underground instead plants an explosive "nothing" behind the police lines waging annihilation against Blackness. Subtraction offers an alternative to simply multiplying the long chains of capital, the gender binary, and white lines of filiation. It does not play in the liberal game of exposure looking to dispute weak points in authoritarian paranoia, network echo chambers, or carceral aesthetics. For, in the end, it means not only intensifying the many forms of anger people feel, but also finding a way to negate the world behind them.

"Becoming-Imperceptible"

Part I of the present volume looks to the anonymity of techno-anarchism. It starts with my case for a form of communication dedicated to strategic-material interventions that I call "insinuation." This shift in perspective leads me to analyze the strategic principles behind the mid-century manuals on the guerrilla fighter, particularly the importance of specific ways of life, the decisiveness of terrain, and the necessity of camouflage. I contend that, while the era of the guerrilla is over, further abstraction of its elements helps outline a strategy for combating our cybernetic present: a politics of asymmetry that locates material vulnerabilities through the digital concepts of contingency, density, and clutter.

Part II explores the queer strategy of criminality. I open with the sexual attraction–repulsion dynamic made ubiquitous by digital devices and their underlying pornographic power of exposure. My journey continues with a trip through the queer-feminist refusal of interiority that builds on the work of Foucault, taking negative affects to be the consequence of bad encounters and not individual aberrations to be suffered in isolation. Affect here is treated not as a commodity to be accumulated, but as a political resource for feminist causes against the use of happiness to seal women in the sexual contract. An alternative appears in the work of Public Feelings and The Socialist Patients' Collective, who seek out ways to turn the illnesses caused by an exploitative society against its source.

Part III focuses on the fugitivity at the heart of Black study. In part circumscribed by my own structural positionality as a white academic dedicated to the politics of abolition, I look to whiteness's surveillance of Blackness. I forward the abolitionist cause through the method Christina Sharpe has called "Black annotation and redaction," looking to rehabilitate the older activist history of Twitter, turning it away from policing's prosecutorial function and toward anonymizing the actions of Black rebellion. The result is a form of media that I call "captive media," which captures Blackness by treating it as criminal, even when such media possession of the slave body is done by "allies" to publicize abuse. This is informed by vignettes on image techniques meant to evade further capture by despectacularizing Black death, such as cropping out bodies from scenes of violence. Whereas earlier theorists of photography such as Roland Barthes and Susan Sontag ponder how photography came to be seem as furnishing evidence, I trace photography's history of captivity and Black artistic efforts to frustrate its function. I find that the whiteness refracts the general condition of Blackness between two poles: hypervisibility and nothingness.

The present book concludes with a coda on communism. In it, I connect the project to ideas that motivate my wider body of work. This includes a number of themes introduced in my book *Dark Deleuze*, in which I argue for a conspiratorial communism to bring about the death of this world. Moreover, in the coda I elaborate on the anonymous forces that motivated each previous chapter: behind the anonymity of Part I is the force of insinuation; behind the criminality of Part II lurks affect; behind the fugitivity of Part III is the power of withdrawal. My contention is that the forces that subtend this world should not merely be indexed, they also serve as the means of its abolition. The subtractive spirit of communism burns with the hot fire of revolt sparked by secret complicities that smolder in the streets. It seeks not respite in distance, but a movement of separation whose intensive power brings the power of the outside to bear. It is less interested in communicating facts than the force of feelings, images, and slogans that evade capture. The task at hand, then, is not to describe these forces, but to put them to work, laboring under the realization that many others are doing the same, flourishing underground, transforming alienation into a shared cause, and refusing to treat infrastructure as neutral. What makes this cause distinct is its communist characteristic, in which the deepest analysis cuts across all causes, intersecting them with a common notion: "No one is free until everyone is free."

The unnamed narrator of Ralph Ellison's *Invisible Man* imagined such an underground. It is a situation that he found only after giving up on the old liberal story of uplift and fading into an ignored nook deep in the heart of the city:

> That is why I fight my battle with Monopolated Light & Power. The deeper reason, I mean: It allows me to feel my vital aliveness. I also fight them for taking so much of my money before I learned to protect myself. In my hole in the basement there are exactly 1,369 lights. I've wired the entire ceiling, every inch of it. And not with fluorescent bulbs, but with the older, more-expensive-to-operate kind, the filament type. An act of sabotage, you know. I've already begun to wire the wall. A junk man I know, a man of vision, has supplied me with wire and sockets. Nothing, storm or flood, must get in the way of our need for light and ever more and brighter light. The truth is the light and light is the truth. When I finish all four walls, then I'll start on the floor. Just how that will go, I don't know. Yet when you have lived invisible as long as I have you develop a certain ingenuity. I'll solve the problem.[148]

Part I
Anonymity

Manuals and guides inherently systematize.[1] The current guide is no exception. In classic figure-ground fashion, they generally describe a field alongside the conventional compendium of classified elements (edible plants, wild birds, or more recently, drones). Given the practical nature of guides, the field is treated technically as a strategic terrain with a variety of dimensions that will affect outcomes. For instance, *A Burglar's Guide to the City* surveys "lines of sight, potential hiding places, how shadows were cast at different times of day."[2] In short: the field offers a set of opportunities for expanding or diminishing power.

Even a cursory study of anonymity reveals something crucial: the importance of technical know-how. As anarchist Luigi Galleani said when denouncing the law, the power of anonymity "does not live in declarations," but "when one can exercise it."[3] This makes its closest analytic ally a military-strategic approach to power, which understands anonymity through the cruelty of the hunt. On the one side is the evolution of sovereignty, which can be traced from the prehistory of hunting cattle through the hunting of slaves, natives, Blacks, the poor, and foreigners to today.[4] These predatory hunters (like the police or lynch mobs) develop technology of anonymity that enhance tracking, territorial accumulation, and confinement.[5] On the other are those who evade capture. Their technologies of anonymity are practical devices born from very different circumstances. While the hunted are not constrained by the overriding need to identify, hold space, and fix things in place the same way as hunters, they are usually outmatched in material resources. Their technical intelligence is found in the hidden genius of the prison inventor, whose fabrications make something out of nothing.

The minoritarian guidelines to the game of war dictate that one should enter the field anonymously as a purely abstract figure, because to appear as a subject whose identity is known marks one for death before the battle has even begun. Through frogs' eyes, cybernetics researchers weaponized sight, associating the capacity of identification with the act of hunting (for a target).[6] The same basic algorithm computers use for sorting images also guides missile navigation systems, criminal-gait-analysis profiling, and all facial recognition software.[7] Figures of anonymity exploit the vulnerabilities created in these systems. The nameless narrator of Ralph Ellison's *Invisible Man*, for instance, testifies to becoming incognito after dissolving completely into white pathologization, concealing his Blackness like a fog. And hackers create cramped spaces of autonomy out of a world they do not own, in which identification is used as a weapon to name, track, and neutralize their power.[8] Anonymity thus serves as an aesthetic figure produced technostrategically by the field itself.

In his study of "improper names," Marco Deseriis outlines how social landscapes that rely on names as a form of identification have been hijacked. Examples include *noms de guerre*, networked names, and other multiple-use names like the Luddites, Luther Blissett, and Jane of the Abortion Counseling Services of Women's Liberation.[9] His argument is that they have at least three important uses: first as a medium for subaltern social groups to find each other and conceal their actions; second as symbolic power for those whose voices are crowded out by isolation or exclusion; and third as a mode of subjectivation that evaporates identity into difference.[10] Here, anonymity increases capacity by substituting subjection for an ever-shifting strategic position.

From the perspective of subtraction, the underground is not distant, esoteric, or hard to access. There are other spatial means to describe the terrain from which anonymity springs forth, as layered on top of this world, an expansion of what is already there, loops in its networked fabric, holes in a biopolitical fabric, or vacuoles of noncommunication. Each of them provides a different strategic angle of approach against the new Moloch created by cybernetics, which tried to mitigate the disaster of industrialization through the promise of connecting to anything at any time.[11] But in the process, it further proletarianized the world by concealing control behind slick telegraphic surfaces and sequestering away labor in an intensified global division.[12] Here, nature becomes pure spectacle through an environmental logic born out of the precise cybernetic thinking that produced the problem. The only resolution is to treat it as a new terrain of conflict.[13]

Chapter 1
The Guerrilla Force of Liberation

The urban guerrilla concept offers a powerful diagnostic for subversion. Today, the urban and the rural have been stitched into a dense fabric, neutralizing the separation between town and country that enabled millennia of peasant insurrections. Upon closer investigation, however, the historical record of urban guerrilla operations is also mixed at best, which renders it a bad model for political action. But the theory does signal fractures within the urban that can be exploited philosophically.

Mountains, jungles, and deserts are some of the oldest allies of the guerrilla fighter. But conditions began shifting in the middle of the twentieth century, as the distance-demolishing technologies of "bridges, all-weather roads, forest-felling, accurate maps, and the telegraph," as well as the "advanced techniques of defoliation, helicopters, airplanes, and modern satellite photography," changed everything.[1] It was not a totalizing shift, for there are still many small ponds across the globe in which guerrilla still swim, but self-sufficient sanctuaries based in a peasant way of life are quickly drying up as a resource.

Latin American theorists have been aware of this problem, as their thinner rural populations act differently than those in Asia, and they have designed their own liberation struggles accordingly.[2] Focoism, a largely failed project, was formulated after the Cuban Revolution to draw Mao's three-stage developmental model of guerrilla war into a single small nucleus of militants that leads by recruiting, organizing, and attacking in rural terrain while simultaneously forming a subservient nucleus of politics in the metropole.[3] Appropriations of focoism are often selective, generally retaining the theory of "armed propaganda" whereby militants do not wait for the right conditions to begin, but use armed struggle as a political expression that will itself ripen the conditions.

Following a line from Mao through the classic texts on the guerrilla, we find that it thought the key to victory was a rural population's semiautonomy from the politics of the metropole, a separation that hides and sustains the guerrilla. The basic requirement for this type of guerrilla war is a rural population, at least according to its theorists. As the Maoist maxim goes, "the guerrilla must move amongst the people as a fish swims in the sea." This gives the appearance of the guerrilla as an architect of insinuation who sharpens the people into a political force. But to clarify, the guerrilla neither takes the peasants' lead nor develops them into a revolutionary force—though both remain a strategic option—but uses rural areas and their residents for material support. What the rural enables is an autonomous way of life from which the guerrilla constructs a base. And because the base is independent, it provides a reliable means of subsistence and draws the enemy out into the countryside where the guerrilla's use of terrain is at its greatest advantage. The people are thus not the object of propaganda, but the cover used by the guerrilla to evade retaliation. And as a result of the guerrilla blending in with the rural population, the enemy is left with few options for identifying, containing, or eliminating the guerrilla. At their most drastic, commanders thus resort to "draining the pond to catch the fish."

Elevating the strategic role of the city due to its function as the seat of political power, the theory of the urban guerrilla marries armed propaganda with its political aim of political revolution. This theoretical shift, from the rural to the urban, is based on a strategic gamble: that the urban way of life, terrain, and camouflage are politically superior to their rural counterparts. Ultimately, guerrilla war is a clandestine operation premised on the power of escape, which serves as the decisive element in asymmetric warfare. Guerrilla logic distills escape in three basic principles for defeating a superior enemy: an autonomous way of life, the advantage of terrain, and indistinguishability. In particular, the urban guerrilla leverages contingency, density, and clutter. To capitalize on each of these weaknesses, the urban guerrilla utilizes them as both points of antagonism and forms of escape, raising withdrawal as the primary objective in the process of attack. And because the turbulent flows of modern cybernetic governance provides ample opportunities for escape, it offers its enemies the means for its own destruction. Escape is not the product of the guerrilla, as if they opened up escape routes; rather, the guerrilla is escape itself: an army in perpetual retreat that wields withdrawal as an offensive force. If the politics of the future is to avoid the same grisly fate of the guerrilla, however, it may employ escape like the guerrilla, but to bring life where the guerrilla too often only caused death.

The Guerrilla Way of Life

The success of the guerrilla depends on transforming anthropology into a weapon unto itself: "In revolutionary war the human is always superior to military hardware."[4] Guerrilla theorists depict this transformation in various mixtures of conservative and progressive forces. On the one hand, there are the conservative theorists, such as Mao, who imagine the guerrilla to spring from souls of an oppressed people like a natural reaction to an exterior threat that enables a nation "inferior in arms and military equipment" to turn their "conditions of terrain, climate, and society in general" against an imperialist oppressor as "obstacles to his progress," used "to advantage by those who oppose him."[5] On the other, there are progressivists, such as Ernesto "Che" Guevara, who see the guerrilla as an agent not of solidarity, but of creative evolution in the human condition, where the guerrilla is a "guiding angel" whose shared "longing of the people for liberation" directs their conversion into an "ascetic" soldier and "social reformer" that fights for a revolutionary new humanity.[6] Regardless of the origin of power, whether from conserving life or liberating it, the theory puts forth the guerrilla as the effect of discipline. The theory further proposes that it is discipline alone that separates the guerrilla from the mere criminal. The criminal selfishly preys on oppressors and the oppressed alike, with the only goal being their own profit. In contrast, the guerrilla lives simply and expropriates resources from the rich and powerful in order to build up the forces that distract, demoralize, and drive away the enemy.⁷ The guerrilla thus shares the fruits of expropriation with allies, teaching those not directly engaged in the struggle to enjoy it nonetheless.

Yet in a world now awash with cheap, ephemeral pleasures, it is difficult to maintain the hardness necessary to remain a guerrilla. "The city is a cemetery," the revolutionary declares, because its inhabitants lose sight of the struggle, as they must live as consumers and inevitably let slip "the vital importance of a square yard of nylon cloth, a can of gun grease, a pound of salt or sugar, a pair of boots," a disregard driven not by malevolent indifference, but by an irreducible difference in the conditions of thought, action, and ultimately life itself.⁸ Diminishing hardness is an effect of biopower, which develops softness through a power that produces more than it represses. The cybernetic disaggregation of the social casts the guerrilla into a sea of difference where the hardness of discipline becomes a burden; for, the shattered masses no longer appear as a people, leaving the guerrilla to make wooden ideological appeals for a humanity no longer there.

Abraham Guillén, veteran of the Spanish Civil War, recognizes the need for innovation. "Strategy," he writes, "is not created by geniuses or by generals, but by the development of the productive forces, the logic of events and the weight of history," which now point almost exclusively to one place: the city.⁹ The most promising avenue for success is thus not the lightening victory, but "the strategy of the artichoke:" "to eat at the enemy bit by bit, and through brief and surprise encounters of encirclement and annihilation to live off the enemy's arms, munitions, and paramilitary effects."¹⁰ Furthermore, in place of the disciplined ascetics of the rural guerrilla, the urban fighter must possess initiative, mobility, flexibility, versatility, and command of any situation.¹¹ These characteristics are responsive to the subjective life of the metropole, which is experienced by subjects as an unending stream of accidents and coincidences. Such accidents and coincidences are merely the expression of the river of contingency that flows through the intersections of modern power, the vital force of renewal that is only barely kept in check by the careful watch of the spectacle and the immense management of cybernetic capitalism.

The urban guerrilla is the embodiment of contingency made into a revolutionary force, as the guerrilla does not try to foresee everything or wait for orders, but instead embraces the duty of initiative: a duty "to act, to find adequate solutions for each problem they face, and to retreat."[12] Thus with every rise in unemployment, social outrage, and cultural discontent, the urban guerrilla does not respond by "encouraging them to demonstrate in the streets just to be trampled by the horses of the police" or "temporarily stopping thousands of them with a barricade," but to "strike unexpectedly here and there with superiority of arms and numbers."[13] And it is with the power of the unexpected that the guerrilla wages armed propaganda, for the goal is to mire the enemy in confusion, much like the disabling power of insinuation. The urban guerrilla is caught in the same fog and can choke while navigating between the hardness that granted victory to their rural counterparts and the softness required to operate in the atomized world of cybernetic capitalism. It is here that most have faltered. Yet, when the guerrilla is considered a progressive force that liberates rather than conserves, then a different route can be plotted, this time between living and struggling, leading neither to the softness of control nor to the hardness of the guerrilla. And this new form of life does not seek to unify the people, but to unleash a deluge of contingency. And to do so, it must shape the force of escape into a weapon of liberation that, like the guerrilla, moves with the fluidity of water and the ease of the blowing wind, but whose movements become as automatic as the daily humiliations they face.

The Decisiveness of Terrain

The guerrilla is mobile and avoids direct conflict. This is because the guerrilla cannot afford the narcissism of political activists who fight only for moral victories. So accustomed to losing, some activists invented a way of winning that parades their weaknesses in front of a higher authority to secure their pity—a ritual of liberalism that Nietzsche ridicules as morality. The theory of guerrilla, in contrast, pinpoints a weakness that can be made into a decisive advantage and compensates for the rest. For the guerrilla, the weakness is the avoidance of direct conflict, an exceptional case in regular combat, which is made orthodox and governed by a strategic principle: the guerrilla should engage the enemy only at a time and place of their own choosing, and only if success is guaranteed. The tactic of the minuet "dance" is an elaboration of this principle: the guerrilla force encircles an advancing column from the four points of a compass but far enough away to avoid encirclement or suffering casualties; the couple begins their dance when one of the guerrilla points attacks and draws out the enemy, after which the guerrilla then falls back to attack from a new safe point, and thus the guerrilla leads by escape.[14] It is with the knowledge of the terrain that the guerrilla dances the movements of life; imaginatively creating new combinations of dispersion, concentration, and the constant change of position. The guerrilla dances to the cadence of organic life's interaction with its environment. Guerrilla logic suggests that power grows by learning new rhythms of advancement and withdrawal, awakening strength by drawing one's partner away from the source of their power one step at a time. It is the choreography of escape that then distinguishes guerrilla warfare from "armed self-defense," which immobilizes life rather than setting it free, and thus suffers from "a profusion of admirable sacrifices, . . . of wasted heroism leading nowhere, . . . leading anywhere except to the conquest of political power."[15] Instead, the guerrilla force is offensive, as it strikes at difficult-to-defend positions but is exclusively clandestine and not equipped to defend or occupy space. Moreover, the environment is the guerrilla's most powerful offensive weapon, for the guerrilla uses it to exact a military cost from any occupying force: "If the enemy is concentrated, it loses ground; if it is scattered, it loses strength."[16] At its absolute limit, the guerrilla force becomes fully realized when all territory is indefensible and the emergence of a new people or a new power is thus inevitable.

Our new cybernetic landscape demands strategic innovation, as it is not like the countryside, yet new maneuvers can still be a variation on the standard movement of dispersion, concentration, and change of position. The Latin American theorists developed one such variation that was necessary because of the difference between their own material conditions and those in other regions practicing guerrilla techniques. Latin America was characterized by the thinness of populations in their own mountain regions, while Vietnam and China had densely populated cities and villages. Moreover, Latin American theorists found themselves confronted by tightly knit Indigenous populations skeptical of all outsiders, imperialists and revolutionaries alike.[17] These innovations are instructive, in that the city poses a problem similar to that developing in the Latin America's mountains: the spider web of modern roads, electrification, cellphones, and globally positioned satellites makes surveillance of the suspicious mountain locals as intense as it is in the Asian cities. Even the rural, once an autonomous outside that was the perfect staging ground for the guerrilla, is now networked and controlled. The prototypical new terrain is the slum, which shares many characteristics with the countryside. In particular, slums are a site of underdevelopment created by management through abandonment. And it is from that abandonment that a new, crueler form of autonomy arises bearing the potential to disrupt. Contemporary military theorists have noticed this risk:

> Because of their warren-like alleys and unpaved roads, the slums have become as impregnable to the security forces as a rural insurgent's jungle or forest base. The police are unable to enter these areas, much less control them. The insurgents thus seek to sever the government's authority over its cities and thereby to weaken both its resolve to govern and its support from the people, the aim being to eventually take power, first in the cities and then in the rest of the country.[18]

The most relevant characteristic of slums is their density. As the Latin American theorists note, it is the density of Asian villages that allowed the guerrilla there to "swim like fish" among the people, something that their own mountains were unable to provide.

In density, guerrillas have been able to employ tactics similar to those used in the countryside. Brazilian students, for instance, have used a street tactic much like the minuet, whereby coordinated teams of protestors would alternately attack and withdraw against advancing lines of police, as well as "the net within the net," which draws police squads designated to snatch an individual into a crowd far enough for them to be surrounded, looted, and immobilized.[19] In spite of the difference of terrain, urban guerrillas ultimately navigate density in the same way as their rural predecessors: the urban guerrilla becomes a friend of density in order to maintain the same advantages of mobility and flexibility, and becomes a scholar of density to realize the same strategic principles, knowing where and when to strike so success is the only conceivable outcome and is certain to fulfill the twin goals of neutralizing the enemy's repressive forces and expropriating resources to expand the forces of liberation.

Escape remains the greatest challenge to politics. As every theory of guerrilla warfare maintains, escape is fundamental because it establishes how direct conflict is replaced by the nonbattle. Rural warfare needs only a crude concept of escape, as combat occurs in an "open field" that radiates outward from nearly any point in the advancing enemy's column. Now, however, capitalism casts a spectacular gaze that touches nearly everything, at least in part, even what is abandoned by the nourishing power of biopower. Therefore, the urban guerrilla cannot depend on density to prevent encirclement, as the open field does, but only on situations porous enough to provide escape routes unknown to the authorities. In fact, these escape routes are so important that the guerrilla must not operate when there is no escape plan, "since to do so will prevent them from breaking through the net which the enemy will surely try to thrown around them."[20] If escape routes are established, then politics can develop by way of the guerrilla, which identifies terrains of struggle that afford the mobility and flexibility necessary for the movement of dispersion, concentration, and escape. Such a terrain can be found where there is density, which is often located in zones of abandonment. Even as the goals of this politics may parallel those of the urban guerrilla, which are the neutralization of repressive forces and the expropriation of force for the powers of liberation, it must develop a new form of escape to avoid their fate: the history of urban action shows that most guerrillas rose like lions only to be hunted, killed, or caged.

The Necessity of Camouflage

The guerrilla demonstrates the importance of selective engagement, which affirms the strategic elements of visibility, anonymity, and escape. In contrast to the enemy, who strains to defend occupied territory, guerrilla logic is born in the shadows and grows under the cover of secrecy.[21] While relying in part on the enemy for arms and ammunition, the guerrilla does not draw political force from the same coherent identity, but instead produces a temporary consistency: the flash of an image that swiftly appears with an explosive force only to immediately recede. The guerrilla thus affirms the potential of difference, whose singular acts must be produced only once, in contrast to reproduction, which is how the state expands its coherent identity over and again.[22]

Controlling terrain in the city is difficult for the guerrilla. In the city as much as in the countryside, the night is a greater friend to the guerrilla than to its enemy. Therefore, "if at night the city belongs to the guerrilla and, in part, to the police by day," then it becomes a battle of endurance rather than a show of strength.[23] There are many parts of the new cybernetic landscape that appear as dark as a moonless night even when the sun is shining its brightest, for anonymity is to our contemporary metropolis as the cover of nighttime is to the city. Within its density, abandoned zones shield activity from prying eyes. It is in these zones that underworlds emerge to address the daily needs of residents whose precarious lives benefit from fewer legal interactions. Yet some of the best hiding spots are in the heart of the beast. Clutter, for instance, temporarily creates cover for movement. Furthermore, the theory of the guerrilla illustrates the importance of time. If mobile, one can move through clutter fast enough to avoid being singled out by the watchful eye of the spectacle or the calculating management of biopower.[24] As the guerrilla shows, subversion does not occur by occupying its space, but by embodying the time of politics. In the face of the perpetual present, the guerrilla controls time, and thus frees space from the enemy. And with no need to reproduce actions, not being tied to defending or extending any particular space or time, the guerrilla has a greater degree of freedom. The guerrilla thus turns byproducts such as zones of abandonment and clutter into camouflage for offensive strikes.

The offensive use of camouflage orients politics away from the spectacle, which limits politics to the space of appearance, and toward the underground movement of forces not descendent from the state. The guerrilla initiates this shift by establishing an indistinguishability between themselves and everyone else. Once the guerrilla becomes imperceptible, actions are no longer viewed as the actions of a crank, madman, or criminal against the public, but as the concrete expression of sentiments held by many: every act "signs itself," claiming responsibility for itself "through its particular *how*" and "through its specific meaning in situation," rendering it immediately discernible.[25] This underground force thus exposes itself to political scrutiny even when hiding its source. The guerrilla therefore lives as the expression of others or dies as a solitary individual, which is to say that the guerrilla renounces the notion of the revolutionary subject and instead gives force to the nonsubject as it is becoming-revolutionary.[26] Imperceptibility is difficult to maintain, however, as the enemy of the guerrilla realizes the power and retaliates by personalizing whatever it faces, which confines problems to isolated subjects and represents their actions as individual dysfunctions.

Although guerrillas are imperceptible, so are so many other operations of power. To the extent that cybernetic capitalism does appear, it is only through management and circulation, whose temporary consistencies are only the effects of its existence. But the imperceptibility of the guerrilla and cybernetic capitalism differ in appearance. While cybernetics maintains the appearance of neutrality, the guerrilla invites an enemy to "attack wildly" and paints them "as utterly black and without a single virtue."[27] The reason is that such a bald characterization of the guerrilla draws a clear line between the guerrilla and the enemy and substantiates that the guerrilla has won "spectacular successes."[28] This desire to be caricatured demonstrates how the guerrilla uses the strength of an enemy, its near-monopoly on the mass communication, as its greatest weakness, showing the enemy's strength to be mere bluster.[29] When imperceptible attacks lead to grand overreaction by the enemy, the image of an unassailable enemy vanishes. While the enemy had previously fostered fear and humility in a deference produced less by sober supporters than by pessimistic critics, guerrillas shatters this unassailability, propagandizing their strength while turning habits of respect for the enemy into belittling mockery. To strip away unassailability, radical politics does not need to follow the militarized path of the guerrilla, however; it needs only to evince the consistency of its intensity. And in that way, there are alternative means to spread the assailability that avoid liquidation.

In summary, guerrilla theory outlines the strategic principles for a politics built around the concept of the underground. The sober, strategic character of guerrilla theory also distinguishes its clandestine potential from both spontaneous protests, such as punks and runaways simply "going it alone" to refuse assimilation, and the politics of compromise, as practiced by power brokers and activists who articulate their demands in the already-existing halls of power. Moreover, for guerrilla theory, the underground is not an abstract ideal, but rather a practical force—a distinction with enough difference to goad Guy Debord to insist, "I am not a philosopher, I am a strategist!"[30] In turn, guerrilla theory establishes the underground as a strategic principle for inclusion in any planning, process, and procedure: "the underground must be guaranteed" means determining how the underground ensures victory, what are the available tactics for growing the underground, and which escape routes will be taken.

To be clear: the present book does not advise anyone to take up arms in guerrilla warfare. Everywhere that control spreads, it makes all previous forms of guerrilla warfare obsolete. New forms of subversion may be clandestine, but the most decisive victories will not be through military means, only through a battle of intensities. The most likely outcome of armed propaganda is death. As the history of guerrilla warfare demonstrates, the underground, when it raises anonymity to a strategic principle, can bring success to forces inferior in numbers, arms, and training. To share in the history of success, struggles must adapt tactics to fit new terrains, outlined here through the abstract principles of contingency, density, and clutter. This struggle can derive advantages from the same elements of guerrilla warfare by transforming the products of power into the means for its destruction: a way of life, knowledge of terrain, and camouflaged operations. And with these strategic advantages, the struggle throws off the nightmare of cynical politics and begins revolutionary dreaming once again.

Chapter 2
Propaganda of the Deed

Radicalism's tame but dignified existence in the early nineteenth century in America was a triumph for well-reasoned order. Immigrant intellectuals spread the heady ideals of socialism across the newly-opened frontier, founding mutualist or collectivist factory towns across Pennsylvania, Ohio, and Indiana and establishing revolutionary societies and educational clubs in New York City, Baltimore, Philadelphia, and Chicago. Allergic to lawbreaking and violence, the communalists set out to foster the best-ordered and most moral dimensions of utopian society. But as corruption and industry grew inseparable, a new radical energy gathered in the darker corners of society. While the socialists kept outrunning the company mines and industrial looms, a growing underclass either unwilling or unable to escape the greed of indecent men toiled away.

Only a short decade after the Civil War, the polite pretensions of American radicalism fell away. This shift was due to two things: first, the Panic of 1873, which threw hundreds of thousands of workers into destitution and unleashed their fury, and second, the arrival of anarchists. It took the entrance of a protagonist, Johann Most, a fiery German anarchist, to give shape to the turbulence. Inspired by Most, a persuasive orator with scorching rhetoric, anarchists and other radicals brought "propaganda by the deed" to America. "Propaganda by the deed," an idea on the lips of the European radicals of the time, is derived from the earlier Italian socialist Carlo Pisacane, who argues that "ideas spring from deeds and not the other way around," so that "conspiracies, plots, and attempted uprisings" are more effective propaganda "than a thousand volumes penned by doctrinarians who are the real blight upon our country and the entire world."[1]

A determined Most found propaganda by the deed straightforward and published fiery celebrations of the growing practice of anarchist regicide, and these writings often landed in him jail. After a stay of a year and a half in an English jail for praising the assassination of Alexander II of Russia, Most immigrated to the United States and soon published a pamphlet entitled *The Science of Revolutionary Warfare: A Manual of Instructions for the Use and Manufacture of Nitroglycerine, Dynamite, Gun-Cotton, Fulminating Mercury, Bombs, Arson, Poisons, etc., etc.*[2] Among these tools of destruction, he had a clear weapon of choice: dynamite. His fervency was matched by Gerhard Lizius, who wrote a letter published by Albert and Lucy Parsons in their paper, *The Alarm*. The words growing only more scandalous after the Haymarket Massacre, the letter was repeated by the prosecution at the trial of five anarchists who were subsequently hung:

> Dynamite! Of all the good stuff, that is the stuff. Stuff several pounds of this sublime stuff into an inch pipe (gas or water pipe), plug up both ends, insert a cap with a fuse attached, place this in the immediate vicinity of a lot of rich loafers who live by the sweat of other people's brows, and light the fuse. A most cheerful and gratifying result will follow. In giving dynamite to the downtrodden millions of the globe science has done its best work. The dear stuff can be carried in the pocket without danger, while it is a formidable weapon against any force of militia, police, or detectives that may want to stifle the cry for justice that goes forth from the plundered slaves. . . . A pound of this good stuff beats a bushel of ballots all hollow, and don't you forget it. . . . It takes more justice and right than is contained in laws to quiet the spirit of unrest.[3]

So, with the arrival of Most, his dynamite, and propaganda by the deed, the anarchist siege against robber barons and the forces of the state commenced.[4]

Striking fear in hearts of the three enemies of classical anarchism—church, state, and capital—radicals committed a remarkable number of regicides and other assassinations from the late 1870s through the early twentieth century. Yet the practice was not universally accepted in radical circles: pacifists, social democrats, and pragmatists hotly debated the principles and effectiveness of attacks on power. Paul Rousse, French socialist and the first to coin the phrase "propaganda by the deed," plays down violence when describing the concept's realization. "Propaganda by the deed is a mighty means of rousing the popular consciousness," he writes, because it serves as the pragmatism of the possible: given that the masses are naturally skeptical of any idea that remains purely abstract, one must actually start a commune or a factory and "let the instruments of production be placed in the hands of the workers, let the workers and their families move into salubrious accommodation and the idlers be tossed into the streets," after which the idea will "spring to life" and "march, in flesh and blood, at the head of the people."[5] Echoing Rousse's possibilism, Gustav Landauer argues that "no language can be loud and decisive enough for the uplifting of our compatriots, so that they may be incited out of their engrained daily drudgery," and thus the seeds of a new society must be prefigured in actual reality to entice others to join.[6] Propaganda by the deed thus has two intentionally distinct valences, as either creative violence or persuasive prefiguration, either the illegalist who masks anonymous force to avoid capture or the possibilist who loudly boasts of achievements.

Our contemporary times are replete with radicals who have found their own boastful propaganda. Anarchists such as David Graeber speak about a new generation of activists that came of age during the antiglobalization movement and practiced a propaganda by prefiguration that "builds a new society in the shell of the old" (as the popular phrase goes used by the Industrial Workers of the World union cofounded by Lucy Parsons). These "new anarchists," as they are called, practice social justice and deep democracy although they cannot hum even a bar of *The Internationale*. Tragically missing from Graeber's description are the many radical tendencies that draw on the first valence of propaganda by the deed, such as civilization-hating anarcho-primitivists, destruction-loving anarcho-queers, democracy-averse nihilists, and anti-organizational insurrectionists. There are many reasons why those elements are often disavowed or even denied by their radical relatives, but one is obvious: these dissident tendencies draw their power from a dangerous source that resists legibility. Rather than constructing their propagandistic appeals on images of a well-ordered society constituted by a moral majority, these hidden elements draw on deeper and darker desires of nonexistence and disappearance. However, this opposition between the reasonable proposals of social anarchists and the excesses of their darker offspring is stale, and so perhaps there is a way to break through.

Is there a power of truth that is not just the truth of power? asks Gilles Deleuze.[7] Written otherwise in the language of anarchism: what is the propaganda by the deed if it is not just the deed of propaganda? The answer is found in a mode of communication in which propaganda and deeds converge, eclipsing the subject. It can be found anywhere that expressions are action and actions are expression: actions that "speak for themselves," not needing to be owned, named, or explained; expressions that speak reason without having to prefigure; passions so common that they cannot be traced back to the head of any particular persons; events that continue to reverberate after their agents have disappeared into the night. In short: the force of anonymity. That is today's dark propaganda by the deed.

Chapter 3
The Voice of Bullets and Bombs

In their first major text, *The Urban Guerilla Concept,* the Red Army Faction (RAF) impugned the German government and press. They wrote that "some people want to use these lies to prove that we're stupid, unreliable, careless, or crazy," and therefore "encourage people to oppose us," which causes them difficulties because "it's not easy to clear things up with denials, even when they're true."[1] But instead of waging their own war of propaganda by denouncing those who spread rumors, they claimed that, "in reality, they are irrelevant to us," because "they are only consumers," and that "we want nothing to do with these gossipmongers, for whom the anti-imperialist struggle is a coffee klatch."[2]

"The notion of the nation state has become a hollow fiction," argued Ulrike Meinhof in a text read at her trial (alongside Hans-Jürgen Bäcker and Horst Mahler).[3] The globalization of capital, new media, economic development policies, and Euro-hegemony have provoked a subjective crisis, she continued. The only name deserving for such a landscape is "the metropole."[4] As "the offspring of metropolitan annihilation and destruction," the RAF and other urban guerrillas were forming a "proletarian international" with fighters in Asia, Latin America, and Africa, such as in Vietnam, Chile, Uruguay, Argentina, and Palestine, as a counter to the "the transnational organization of capital and the military alliances with which U.S. imperialism encircles the world."[5]

Against the authoritarian structure of the party, Meinhof asserts that the guerrilla must operate as a collective in which all sections express themselves with an autonomous orientation toward all other militants. "We don't talk about democratic centralism," she says to explain its distributed geometry of organization, "because the urban guerrilla in the metropole of the Federal Republic [of Germany] can't have a centralizing apparatus."[6]

What the RAF provided in the struggle was their own anonymous communication: operating clandestinely, the group stole cars, robbed banks, broke prisoners out of jail, assassinated former Nazi officials, and bombed the military, the police, and the press. In that way, the RAF approached expression as crude materialists of the metropole whose voices were bullets and bombs, even if they later provided communiqués to endow their expressions with a little more meaning.

To most, the RAF's gestures must appear futile, as they were not strong enough to overthrow the whole of the imperial metropole and did not present a public organization to build mass membership. The novelty of the RAF was that its members fashioned their way of life into liberation struggles even without a colonial power to expel. In particular, they adopted the perspective of military strategists whose life-and-death scenarios had little room for self-abnegation or ineffective action. Moreover, they developed a form of action that broke with the state's politics of compromise and its monopoly on the use of violence. Other "nondogmatic" sections of the German left extended their solidarity to the RAF while criticizing its ludicrous Leninism. The nonhierarchical Revolutionary Cells (RZ) and armed feminist Red Zora (also RZ, in sarcastic appropriation) in fact undertook far more actions than the RAF, but received less popular attention. And the bomb-happy 2 June Movement invented the concept of the "fun guerrilla" to poke fun at both dour militants and the Nazi generation still in control of the political establishment.

The other great victory of the RAF was how it provoked an autoimmunity response by the West Germany state. Horst Herold, the new head of Germany's BKA (*Bundeskriminalamt*, or Federal Criminal Police Office) became infatuated with RAF's Andreas Baader, as is clear in statements like "Baader was the only man who ever really understood me, and I'm the only man who ever really understood him."[7] The infatuation was fed by his other obsession, computers, which he used to create a cybernetic system for collecting millions of names, biometric data like fingerprints, handwriting samples, and photographs, and a terrorism section listing over 135 thousand people.⁸ While effective at surveillance, its chilling paranoia drove many deeper into the arms of the longhaired radicals with guns. Relishing the fact, the RAF continually antagonized him in communiqués by boasting about the popular support they enjoyed.

The urban guerrillas of the RAF are a poor model for us, however. Although they gained substantial popular support, especially among German youth, most were quickly liquidated because of the intensity with which they approached the struggle; similar situations played out in Europe, North America, and elsewhere. The RZs and their undogmatic peers fared slightly better because they encouraged their members to maintain aboveground identities, which allowed many to dissolve back into the fabric of everyday life when conditions changed. To what all of the armed groups point, however, is the conceptual innovation possible when insinuation is taken beyond mere idle talk—most notably, struggle against the metropolitan situation demands a politics of clandestinity that borrows principles from guerrilla war but chooses a different path from the militant hardening into an army.

Chapter 4
Messages without a Sender

A curious internet trend began in the mid 2000s, with a few dozen blogs dedicated to politically tinged criminal activities. Most reposted news journalism from local newspapers, though sometimes mixed with direct action reports or communiques. The news stories chronicled cars being vandalized with anticop slogans, school computers destroyed by thrown rocks, construction equipment being burned to a crisp, big box stores being robbed, trailers at extraction sites being smashed, banks with their keypads and terminals glued, fiber lines delivering the internet to hundreds of thousands cut with a backhoe. Each site had its own focus, one publicizing global events (*Amor y Resistancia*), while another was exclusive to Francophone Europe (*Suie & Cendres*). Though entered by hand, the pages and pages of posts imitated the "feed," a recent digital reimagination of the newswire, that would soon become ubiquitous when incorporated into social media.

Anarchist media is nothing new. Although print culture generally serves the state, it seems to have always found a way to stir up protest and dissent. Early labor newspapers like *The Bee-hive* used their pages to build working-class power and were rightfully accused of manufacturing strikes. Perhaps more remarkable is how even the subtle law-and-order message of mainstream crime reporting can be turned on its head. "My mother," the hobo orator Utah Phillips once said in a story, "made sure that we had appropriate heroes, flesh-and-blood people."[1] Continuing, he recalled that "she would clip columns out of the Cleveland *Plain Dealer*," with the resulting scrapbooks "mainly full of clippings about bank-robbers—she seemed to favor bank robbers, called them 'class heroes.'" Rather than sustaining the crime blotter's subtext looking to shame criminals and enroll the dutiful public in their capture, Phillips's mom demonstrated what Michel Foucault called the strategic reversibility of power relations, resignifying robbery as an act of class warfare against the rich.

Consciousness provided the hinge for a crucial nineteenth-century political debate over these criminals' importance. Willing to pin at least part of the failure of the 1848 revolutions on "vagabonds, discharged soldiers, discharged jailbirds, escaped galley slaves, rogues, mountebanks, *lazzaroni*, pickpockets, tricksters, gamblers, *maquereaus*, brothel keepers, porters, literati, organ-grinders, ragpickers, knife grinders, tinkers, beggars," Karl Marx denounced the "lumpenproletariat" as the failed aspirant bourgeoisie.[2] On these very grounds, he got anarchist Mikhail Bakunin kicked out of the International Working Men's Association during the Hague Congress of 1872. Firing back, Bakunin praised the "riffraff" and the "rabble" as the "flower of proletariat" who already contained "all the seeds of the social future."[3] He went on to denounce the post-Hegelian notion of consciousness that Marxists transform into ideology as the basis for political mobilization (a thread that can be pulled through *The German Ideology,* György Lukács, and Slavoj Žižek, among many others). Political change cannot spring from the head of a unified party, Bakunin contended, no matter how "ambitious, erudite," because a politics of the head is not capable "of embracing the thousand needs of a proletariat no matter how brainy it may be."[4] Political consciousness is something manufactured "for the masses of the people" by rival exploiting classes, good only in the struggle over who rules over the exploitation of labor.[5] What is needed is not the raising of consciousness, but propaganda, which aims to awaken the passions and spread the spark of revolt.

In the age of networks, most encounter propaganda like an alien intruder—arriving as an external force that can be captured but never fully tamed. What if language is a virus from outer space? A semiotic infection, spreading through fragments from passing conversations on the bus, garbled text messages leaping off the screen, billboards mostly ignored, and webpages only skimmed. The infected shed it both before and after symptoms are visible, passing on the virus without even stopping to understand how or why.

"Your wife looked at you with a funny expression. And this morning the mailman handed you a letter from the IRS and crossed his fingers. Then you stepped in a pile of dog shit. You saw two sticks on the sidewalk positioned like the hands of a watch. They were whispering behind your back when you arrived at the office. It doesn't matter what it means, it's still signifying."[6] If so, then expression contains a simple imperative: self-replicate.

Among the most furtive modes of communication is *insinuation,* which provides a dangerous hint without giving away the whole conspiracy. Its conspirators are rumor, allusion, and innuendo, all pushing hot reptilian buttons deep inside the body without offering up a subject to address in turn. Messages without a sender, these ignoble forms of expression mutate and deform expression, treating each receiver as just one hop in a longer chain.[7] This is why anthropologist Michael Taussig looked for social realities in a social "nervous system," finding the spread of nervous delirium a more reliable way to study the terror campaign of the Colombian dirty war than trying to uncover silenced discourses.[8] While providing poor material for fact, insinuations travel quickly and build a heightened need for action as they transform. Their use in propaganda's war of words is as catastrophic as the introduction of biological or chemical weapons to the conventional battlefield.

Insinuation emerges in contrast to authoritarian persuasion and the liberal presentation of facts. Authoritarians call whole peoples into existence through persuasion, using the constitutive power of rhetoric to invent subject positions in which individuals misrecognize themselves.[9] It speaks in the master signifiers of identification, tying subjects to nations, peoples, blood, and soil: "Identity will be achieved when communities attempt to legitimate their right to possession of a territory through myth or the revealed word."[10] At best, it offers the poison of national liberation, always threatening to descend into fascism.[11] Alternatively, liberals stubbornly insist on the facts, motivated by the naïve belief that "the truth sets you free." It is evident that the politics informed by the worn motto "speak truth to power" no longer works (if it ever did):

Truth isn't outside power or lacking in power; . . . truth isn't the reward of free spirits, the child of protracted solitude, nor the privilege of those who have succeeded in liberating themselves. Truth is a thing of this world: it is produced only by virtue of multiple forms of constraint. And it induces regular forms of power. . . . It is produced and transmitted under the control, dominant if not exclusive, of a few great political and economic apparatuses (university, army, writing, media).[12]

Insinuation inverts the question from "what truth works?" to "why is illusion so effective?"

The propagandistic force of insinuation starts with "the transmission of the word as order-word, not the communication of a sign as information."[13] It is made up of those signs that "are never univocal packets of information but rather affective charges" and appropriates them "through free and indirect discourse—properly 'free' and 'indirect' to the degree that emitting singularities are respected as capable of new expressions and connections."[14] Consider a day in the life of the blog *Social Rupture*. On a day back in 2009, it featured a number of news items including "Teens Attack New Cars at Dealership to 'Release Frustration,'" "Incendiary Sabotage on Railways Systems," promotion for an upcoming anarchist action in Montreal, and a report covering the militant Chilean student revolts. Its voice, purely curatorial, is found in the pairing of news clips with cheeky headline images (a film still sporting the subtitle "you'll always have to make your own fun"), design decisions (rather minimal), and what other sites were included on its blogroll. All of these words are spoken in a language that does not seek comprehension, but to be experienced on an impersonal level, like graffiti that "just appears" after a riot.[15] Without an obvious author or even message, it simply announces the incompleteness of control and provokes others to take sides in the spectacle's war of appearances.

At most, the deed–propaganda–insinuation triad builds what the French experiment Tiqqun calls an "Imaginary Party," spreading a partisan doctrine that springs forth outside organization structures and refuses to constitute a recognizable political faction, which is what ultimately distinguishes it from its liberal and authoritarian cousins. Intentionally paradoxical, the Imaginary Party's members are purely imaginary and its party form is nonexistent. Membership is particular, with no subjects allowed. It enrolls only expressions and deeds, further restricted still only to those that subvert all other parties' programs of governance. This partiality means it neither speaks in universal truth nor acts on behalf of a whole. Devoid of the traditional disciplinary purpose of the party to subjugate its parts to the whole, the only thing left for it to become is a pure abstraction of partisanship, the partisanship of negativity that renounces any positive form and whose conspirators communicate only through insinuation.

The object of the Imaginary Party is thus not to build a united front. In fact, its senseless, seemingly nonpolitical gestures (burning a police station, vandalizing ATMs, or ditching school) would appear to the spectacular point of view as a "mere confused ensemble of gratuitous, isolated criminal acts, the meaning of which their authors don't grasp; just the periodic eruption into visibility."[16] But this is the result of a choice, of rejecting the politics of recognition and casting its lot with the underground. It reserves recognition for its enemies, or more precisely: "Its enemies are precisely all those that people *recognize*."[17]

The only point of even uttering the name of the Imaginary Party is to have something to call the unspoken solidarity of all who seek to make society pay for all of the crime it spawns, a sort of revenge on behalf of those who have been deprived and excluded from visibility and recognition. Even then, it does not appear as a concentrated force. So when its actions are attributed to someone or something, they are usually blamed on "a lone individual suffering from mental illness," "without any links or ties to known organizations or ideologies," "not previously known to authorities," and fed up with society. This is how the insinuations of the Imaginary Party have been able to hide in the shadow of every recent political rebellion, from Puerto Rico to Hong Kong, for they do not help in a swift seizure of the state but blaze paths that mimic the strange drift of aesthetic revolutions, which are sometimes sudden and at other times slow.

There are those who try to contain the propaganda of the deed by endlessly speculating about inner motivations or a rational kernel. This is possible because the prevailing paradigms of control are informatic, making whatever they can into transparent conductors of information. News reporters, pundits, and other talking heads of all kinds are the worst perpetrators. Their job is to reduce insinuation's system of charges to the amputated consistency of clear speech. Hence the endless debates over "is it okay to punch a Nazi?" after white supremacist Richard Spencer took a shot to the face during Trump's inauguration. But the real propagandist for the Imaginary Party that day was Connor, the fourteen-year-old son of a famous actor who lit a fire in the street while the cameras watched. Asked by a reporter why he did it, he said: "My name's Connor and I actually kinda started this fire. I felt like it and screw our president." His retort became more imaginary with each shrug, refusing idle chatter and instead letting the act stand on its own.

Insinuation's effects are anything but clear, but that is how it ruptures the perpetual present. To gain the upper hand against the spectacle, insinuation cannot have truck with most forms of thought, particularly political projects premised on clear demands, "best practices," and rational rules of government. As Foucault outlines in his genealogy of the state, liberalism's temporality is pure presentism.[18] It throws off the weight of history in which the sovereign state draped itself, burdened so heavily with the need to constantly pay tribute to its own mythic past. The case for liberalism is built on the spryness of those who live only for the present. But this is where the propagandists have even liberalism beat. Without a specified organization, location, or even membership, the Imaginary Party need not even maintain a hold on the present. Its power is ambient, a sort of background noise that ebbs and flows, sometimes offering a convenient alibi for padding the police budgets or bullshit antiterrorism efforts, but equally capable of inserting itself at the most inconvenient time. Its novelty is not in organizing itself like a state-in-waiting, as political parties do, but as the neglected spark about to catch fire.

Chapter 5

The Sprawl

Degenerate hacker Case is down and out. This protagonist of the definitive book on cyberspace, William Gibson's *Neuromancer*, was unable to jack in after getting his hand caught in the till and now wanders the Japanese underworld as an addict in the search of a cure to get back into the matrix. Although he is outside Tokyo, it is not the outskirts: everything is connected, just some parts have older streets and some areas have no official names. In this world, cities are not distinct dots on the maps, but dissolve into their own regions. The Sprawl, for instance, covers all of the eastern United States from Boston to Atlanta. There is no day or night, but a permanent grey that emanates from an artificial sky cast over each artificial environment. It is a place where "the actors change but the play remains the same." As Case laments, it is like "a deranged experiment" with a bored researcher "who kept one thumb permanently on the fast-forward button" and whose cruel rules are: "Stop hustling and you sank without a trace, but move a little too swiftly and you'd break the fragile surface tension of the black market; either way, you were gone."[1] Moreover, cybernetics has taken over much of people's lives: "Cyberspace: A consensual hallucination experienced daily by billions of legitimate operators, in every nation, by children being taught mathematical concepts, . . . a graphical representation of data abstracted from the banks of every computer in the human system. Unthinkable complexity. Lines of light ranged in the nonspace of the mind, clusters and constellations of data. Like city lights, receding."[2]

Our world is rendered most vividly in these cyberpunk underworlds, places where giant corporations control the world, ubiquitous technology drastically changes the face of humankind, and lowlifes commit actions that cascade into monumental change. These fictional places serve as dramatizations of our own stolen time, and thus update noir's savage depiction of doomed characters languishing in the wastelands of digital culture. "The future is already here, it's just not evenly distributed," Gibson is fond of saying.[3] And perhaps the Sprawl is even more evenly distributed than Gibson lets on. A crucial starting point is the whites-only suburbia of Levittown. But it exploded globally as the utopian vision of malls were turned outward, digested and spit out by capitalism as low-rent strip malls and big box stores. Digital networks now span the globe, connecting billions despite a range of local conditions.

Unique to cyberpunk is how it draws on computers as engines of difference. By installing the computer as the core literary device, the genre offers a dystopian contrast to liberal existentialism. Instead of celebrating difference as an iron-clad vehicle for pluralist harmony, these worlds draw startlingly dark depictions of cultures digitally saturated by difference but plunged deeper into futuristic miseries. Moreover, because The Sprawl mirrors our own cybernetic Metropolis, it points to the transformation of escape: gone is the extensive form of escape to communes in the woods, and immediately relevant are all its intensive forms.[4]

How did our world slowly transform into the fantastical nightmare conjured up by fringe sci-fi authors? Toys first dreamed up by special effects wizards, like the multitouch interfaces that PreCrime captain John Anderton conducts like an orchestra in *Minority Report*, became commonplace in hardly a decade—and so have real-life algorithms meant to "stop crime before it starts." No doubt, Hollywood's fever dreams have merged with today's corporate realism.

To find the Sprawl in our current world, then, perhaps we should take seriously the promotional images put out by military war contractors looking to hawk a new product, talking heads of opinion news media whipping their audiences into a froth, and Hollywood films peddling in futurology. One artist to do this is Ian Alan Paul, in his video essay "Climate, Capitalism, Control." In it, the future (which is to say our present) arrives not at a particular moment, but through its staging. On center stage is a picture within a picture. From the left to right, the scene moves from past to present to future.

The past: A series of books chronicling past struggles and theories. The books include Donna Haraway's *Simians, Cyborgs, and Humans,* in which her famous cyborg manifesto was first republished, Guy Debord's *Society of the Spectacle,* hinting at the artificiality of the images being broadcast, and Jackie Wang's *Carceral Capitalism,* which includes an incisive critique of today's cybernetic approach to policing. Their totem is a Zapatista doll from the 1994 uprising against the Mexican government and NAFTA. The past's mode of expression is the narration on a digital speaker voiced by Google's WaveNet deep neural network, its orality oddly appropriate, as its pre-literate mode has roared back with the postalpha digital generation.

The present: An iPad on which the video plays. The visual essay, a "montage of YouTube videos including data visualizations, drone recordings, defense industry promotions, corporate advertisements, news reports, Silicon Valley product demonstrations, protest documentary, and machine learning research is swiped through in order to visually survey the technical, political, and aesthetic dimensions that compose our disastrous present."[5] In a nod to how the present is still gripped firmly by the past, a phone to the left (in the "past") mirrors the essay on its screen as an object-recognition program paints colored boxes on faces, bodies, and other subjects, adding them to its already-immense dataset for configuring the future. Its avatar is a disembodied human arm that emerges from offscreen to swipe the video between sections, acknowledging the role that human actions play behind the seemingly automatic mechanical process.

The future: Three stratified objects symbolizing nature, insurrection, and recuperation. Each seemingly reiterates a future corresponding to a portion of the essay's title: climate, capitalism, and control. At the top, flowers sit in a jar, though they are already snipped and will die if their fate is tied to the dissolving glacier that opens the piece. Underneath them, a book promises to leave or "destitute" the world, through both an image of graffiti scrolled in French and an essay in Spanish. Sitting on top of it, a moleskin notebook lays open with an abstract technical diagram. The feedback circuit of sensors and control form its central nervous system. Crisscrossing it are barely visible red blocks: on one side, "multiply noise"; the other, blocks like "become indiscernible" and "disable, sabotage, destroy." The weapon available to all three strata is a pair of clear eyeglasses, speculative lenses for seeing past the screens, images, and fantasies of the Sprawl and toward its eventual undoing.

Chapter 6

The Politics of Asymmetry

Network culture reconfigures politics. It does not reach into the sky like the giant mechanical tower of Babel in Fritz Lang's *Metropolis* or spider out in the hub-and-spoke terror network of Stephen Gaghan's *Syriana*.[1] The former depends on a centralized form, like the body of the sovereign; the latter, decentralized but still hierarchical form, like an archipelago of prisons.[2] Now, the prevailing form of control is a distributed network that grows laterally like bamboo or bunchgrass, typified in the overlapping and interconnected neighborhoods of a city whose center long disappeared. Some might foolishly celebrate it for its openness, but it is just as controlled as before, only through different means. As Michael Hardt and Antonio Negri name it, "the Metropolis" is to us today as "the factory was to the industrial working class."[3] These shifts call for a corresponding transformation in strategy.

Gone are Luddite dreams of sabotaging or crippling infrastructure on a mass scale, as well as the type of cyberterrorism that makes nation-states anxious.[4] A prevailing trend is for digital politics to seek cultural expression through a tactical use of media that "signifies the intervention and disruption of a dominant semiotic regime, the temporary creation of a situation in which signs, messages, and narratives are set into play and critical thinking becomes possible."[5] But to think only in terms of the semiotic risks "confusing tactics and strategy."[6] Cultural trends are easily drowned out after being "overwhelmed by the open network ecology" of oceanic difference or get marooned on "a self-contained and self-referential archipelago of the like-minded."[7] This is especially true as digital communication is suited well to persuasion or the presentation of facts. The internet has long served more as a breeding ground for conspiracy and insinuation, as the sheer volume of participants and incredible speed of information accumulation means that, in the time it takes to put one conspiratorial theory to bed, the raw material for many more will have already begun circulating.[8] To keep with the times, radical politics should follow a well-trod move of media studies: to take earnestly the notion that "the content of any medium is always another medium."[9] Trading signs for signals and semiotics for physics, it becomes clear that the Metropolis functions as a media object.

The Metropolis is the materialization of the concept of connectivity, a cybernetic solution to the problem of communication. Its composition follows the cybernetic "environmental architecture" of Nicholas Negroponte's architecture machine and Kevin Lynch's environmental image. The latter explicitly abandons urbanism's utopian aspirations, replacing them with questions of an *imageability* that transforms designers into translators whose job is to make things intelligible through visibility (and change a matter of mere perception).[10] Lynch approaches urban space like music whose intervals and rhythms are meant to compose a "harmonious relationship" between urban dwellers "and the outside world."[11] As such, it speaks to the topology of cybernetics, which does not flatten, make subservient, or impose anything common to its many constituent parts. It performs the rather shallow task of "putting-into-communication" so as to create a "discordant harmony."[12] What the Metropolis concretizes in its expansive network of connections is not information, but relation.[13] It is the lived existence of the many technical diagrams drawn up to use communication by way of control to span the distance between heterogeneous elements. It does not wash away the cosmos of heterogeneous elements that came before it, from nation-states to sedimented social codes; it syncretizes them into a single unitary cosmology, annexing them as if knitting them as parts into a giant patchwork quilt.[14] To put these otherwise foreign elements into communication with one another, the Metropolis connects through inclusive disjunction: the mutual connection and contagion of unrelated elements (as opposed to the simple gathering of the selected).[15] The process of inclusion follows a neoliberal path that does not require pieces to operate through a shared logic, but unfolds their interiors through exposure. This harsh opening-up process makes the Metropolis a hostile expanse that is subjectively experienced as deepening alienation.

How does this connectivity reconfigure antagonism? This question is important, as many political theorists place antagonism, dissensus, or even agonism at the heart of political life.[16] The Metropolis's reconfiguration of antagonism comes from its architecture of connection, a common space that simultaneously differentiates and diverges. A familiar media object with the same architecture is the internet, which connects divergent elements while also sustaining walled gardens and hostile media. The basic function of this architecture is communicative: the overcoming of incompatibilities to enable cooperation, which can be extracted for profit, collaboratively shared, or tied to conflict.[17]

Abstractly, connectivity operates through inclusive disjunction, a process that puts otherwise foreign elements into communication with one another through an encounter that does not require those pieces to operate according to a shared logic.[18] Rather than in-folding some common term, such as the introjection of an imperial dictate, the Metropolis unfolds. It exposes interiors through a mutual opening up (to name a few: the privatization of economic risk through increased debt obligation, the removal of tariffs that protect national industries, or the exemption of citizenship rights against government assassination).[19] In this sense, those who condemn capitalism as a homogenizing force are incorrect—inclusion can spread through divergence. The Metropolis retains differential relations of parts by selecting "a particular zone that varies with each" that will make possible its integration of the "sum of infinitely tiny things."[20] Furthermore, by being more than inclusion based on a common term (the law, a nation, a people), disjunction is pure relation, a movement of "reciprocal asymmetric implication" that expresses only difference itself (not imposing equivalence, resolving into a general category, or synthesizing into a superior identity).[21] The Metropolis hence shares Gilles Deleuze's "most profound insight" that "difference is just as much communication, contagion of heterogeneities," which means, "to connect is always to communicate on either side of a distance, by the very heterogeneity of terms."[22] This contagion does not result in a unity, combination, or fusion; inclusive disjunction maintains its own "politeness" in the art of distances."[23]

Inclusive disjunction gives the Metropolis a categorically different relationship to difference. It spatializes difference, which allows the Metropolis to outmaneuver the traditional politics of difference, such as liberal freedom or multiculturalism. This is why many metropolitan spaces expand without what appears to be pregiven patterns or rules, such as the neocapitalist darlings of The Third Italy or Australia's Gold Coast. The primary strategy of the Metropolis is thus to diffuse differences through inclusion rather than confront them through antagonism. Within this system of inclusion, difference is not a threat, but the means by which contemporary power maintains a hold on the perpetual present.

Such a system of power cannot be escaped by simply celebrating the differences that grow out of life in the Metropolis, for inclusive disjunction allows the Metropolis to connect otherwise incommensurate subjects, flows, temporalities, and visibilities without suppressing their differences. In assembling them, the Metropolis does not leave those incommensurate things unperturbed. Rather, connectivity follows a database logic of positivity unexpectedly prefigured in the metaphysics of Deleuze's *Difference and Repetition* and *The Logic of Sense*. Here, things are introduced into the Metropolis through a plane of positivities that unfolds secured elements, exposes them to risk, and eliminates their futurity. Unlike the human elements of Guy Debord's society of the spectacle, in which the management of society is still dominated by the human eye, we have entered the machine-readable era where informational flows circulate outside the reach of human perception. We are thus given the impression that "the more things change, the more they stay the same." The inclusion and proliferation of difference is thus a motor not for change, but stasis. The political potentials made available through inclusive disjunction are the familiar channels of liberal capitalism, such as public influence, legal privilege, and market power. All of these work through a principle of capture often described as "communicative capitalism," which expands through circuits of exploitation and submission.[24]

Central to the Metropolis is the process of polarization, the motor of capitalist urban development.[25] This polarization drives the politics of digital culture, what Alexander R. Galloway and Eugene Thacker call the "politics of asymmetry," which appears when conflict becomes a struggle between formally distinct diagrams of power and their effects.[26] The politics of asymmetry is in contrast to conflicts between symmetrical forces, such as policy conflicts between two political parties. In symmetry, powers appear as mirror images of each other as they enact comparable strategies. The forces of asymmetric conflict are usually "grassroots networks posed against entrenched power centers."[27] Throughout the twentieth century, asymmetric strategies rose with the influence of guerrilla war in decolonial struggles and expanded into other spheres of life with the new social movements of the 1960s, the computational revolution in industrial production of the 1980s, and networked societies of the 1990s to today. The difference in formal organizing principles is not just an effect, but also the cause: the diagram is the tactic. Mao's insight is that guerrilla war succeeds not on the open field of battle but by wearing down its enemy through protracted war, which eventually makes warfare so costly that occupiers have no choice but to eventually withdraw their own forces. A formal consideration of asymmetric conflicts reveals that, while the sides are opposed, they do not meet on equal footing: "It is not simply that feminism is opposed to patriarchy, but that they are asymmetrically opposed."[28] The strategic question for politics of difference, then, is how to identify something formally asymmetric to the Metropolis and its process of polarization.

Asymmetry names the divergence between the two forms of politics, in polar opposition. Those liberals who naively preach reconciliation merely reiterate the old practice of *Pax Romana*, in which peace is merely the product of imperial capture. It is also at odds with most Marxist theorists (even Hardt and Negri), who retain a dialectical ambivalence toward the products of capitalism in the hopes that they will serve the proletariat after being wrested from the hands of the bourgeoisie. Worse still are the cosmopolitans who would rather diversify the ranks of the metropole than stand with the colonies. In sum, the underground struggle against the Metropolis understands that the strategic terrain begins from a position of difference but chooses exclusion rather than inclusion.

This is why the asymmetric contrast to inclusive disjunction is exclusive disjunction: the forced choice between two options. What exclusive disjunction offers is a path for evading the capture as "just another difference." The first obstacle to exclusive disjunction is liberal pluralism, which is so deeply intertwined with the politics of difference that the very notion of exclusivity may be a tough pill for some to swallow. Forced choice is not the enemy of difference, however, as it does not reduce the world to a simple binary. There are certainly moments of exclusive disjunction that should remain the cause of intense political suspicion, such as the trans-phobic claim that masculinity and femininity are exclusive. Exclusive disjunction does not force a choice between two homogeneous forms; rather, it intensifies whatever incommensurability exists between worlds of difference on each side of a network, on each side of a multiplicity. This is how Deleuze and Félix Guattari can simultaneously affirm "a thousand tiny sexes" and that all radical gender politics begins through "becoming-woman."[29] In fact, the illusion that there is only one possible world is a lie perpetuated in the Metropolis to maintain a perpetual present. Exclusion's difference-making potential appears paradoxical only from the perspective of pluralistic liberalism. If one begins instead from the perspective that the difference of the Metropolis is a repetition of the same, then exclusivity simply clarifies the difference between reform and revolution. To put it suggestively but crudely: instead of promoting a convergence culture that puts everything into communication, exclusive disjunction seeks a divergence culture that spins things off to pursue their own paths. There are already instances of this divergence, as seen in various subcultures of glitch and noise, but they do not politicize incompatibility. It is thus postcolonialism that should be our guide, as it has already politicized the incommensurable, in that its blueprint for global delinking may provide clues for how separation can be won in the cybernetic web of the Metropolis.[30]

Contingency

The strategic principles of guerrilla theory can thus be resurrected to guide anonymous forces in the struggle against the digital culture of the Metropolis even if guerrilla warfare cannot. In the Metropolis, anonymity is not just a force of subversion. In fact, cybernetic capitalism realizes itself as an anonymous force, for it won the Cold War not with an arms race but by precipitously melting into a distributive network. As the Red Army Faction (RAF) notes, it is this anonymity that is the target, as "neither Marx nor Lenin nor Rosa Luxemburg nor Mao had to deal with *Bild* readers, television viewers, car drivers, the psychological conditioning of young students, high school reforms, advertising, the radio, mail order sales, loan contracts, 'quality of life,' etc.," which disperses the state into a diffuse Empire that cannot be combatted as "an openly fascist" enemy, but as a "system in the metropole" that "reproduces itself through an ongoing offensive against the people's psyche."[31] It would be wrong to imagine cybernetic capitalism's offensive as dehumanizing. Rather, it is nonhuman. From the algorithms governing Wall Street financial transactions to the Obama campaign's voter prediction models, material objects are interpreted like information on the internet: inhuman movements "recorded in a myriad of different locations (log files, server statistics, email boxes)" treated as "the clustering of descriptive information around a specific user" and devoid of a real identity.[32] Once fully rendered within this new strategic environment, cultural politics then becomes a struggle over information theory's concept of communication as the accurate reproduction of an encoded signal across a media channel (telephony, radio, computing), which reintroduces the question of materiality. It was with respect to materiality that the guerrilla first found its strategic advantage, and so it is here that the guerrilla's three advantages reappear in terms of media effects: the accidents and coincidences of contingency plague the digital as bugs and glitches, which easily turn into errors and exploits; density creates mobility and flexibility within digital oversaturation, where spam and "big data" make overload possible; and the clutter of the Metropolis that provides the cover of camouflage is found in the opposition of signal and noise of information theory, which both covers up and disrupts through distortion and loss.

Just as the guerrilla makes use of contingency, the glitch introduces accidents into the Metropolis. The glitch is an unexpected moment where a passing fault disrupts a system but fails to crash it. These transitory events are irritating nuisances but common enough that they are routinely ignored, for glitches are still a deviation from the predetermined outcome—in short, an error. And although not immediately catastrophic, these errors indicate the possibility of a deeper problem beneath, whether it be incorrect software, invalid inputs, or hardware malfunction. Thus there are those who choose not to ignore glitches. For developers, chasing glitches is motivated by the desire to clear the bugs out of the system. But for others, the glitch signals the potential for an exploit. In general, an exploit replicates the guerrilla strategy of turning something to one's advantage, such as when a player can exploit a glitch in a video game to gain powers not intended by the developers. When culture takes on characteristics of the digital, then social or economic glitches can hint at exploits that exist as "a resonant flaw designed to resist, threaten, and ultimately desert the dominant political diagram."[33] While culture has a different architecture from that of a computer, exploits are holes generated by the hypercomplexity of any technical system that makes such systems vulnerable to penetration and change. Given that the oceanic difference of the Metropolis expands through complexity, exploits must exist throughout it. And most importantly, as the exploit hijacks an already existing system, it turns the already existing power differentials in that system to its advantage so it does not have to introduce its own.[34] The search for new antagonisms in the digital life of the Metropolis must then begin with tracking down glitches and other traces of exploits.

Density

The struggle continues with the hunt for a new terrain of struggle. If it is density that allows the guerrilla to maintain the dance of concentration and dispersion, oversaturation serves a similar function in the Metropolis. Through the twin forces of biopower and the spectacle, Empire has collected an enormous amount of data about the behaviors, habits, and preferences of the Metropolis. The residents of the Metropolis thus live in an environment with a high degree of exposure. But every data-gathering process suffers from overaccumulation at the point when the cost of transforming the raw data into useful information is more than its predicted payout. Furthermore, if the speed by which Empire poses the limits of the Metropolis is matched only by the swiftness in which it overcomes them, then its accelerating integration of information is both its greatest strength and a potential weakness.[35] This vulnerability

> is not the result of society's inability to integrate its marginal phenomena; on the contrary, it stems from an overcapacity for integration and standardization. When this happens, societies which seem all-powerful are destabilized from within, with serious consequences, for the more efforts the system makes to organize itself in order to get rid of its anomalies, the further it will take its logic of over-organization, and the more it will nourish the outgrowth of those anomalies.[36]

The terrain of the Metropolis is therefore caught in the tension between exposure and overaccumulation that sometimes gives way to overload. The Metropolis is thus most exposed to choreography crafted to manipulate its openness and speed to create temporary escape routes. In contrast to the guerrilla, the overloaded Metropolis leaks time more than space. Just as cyberpunk's adrenaline-fueled hacking scenes illustrate, the terrain of the Metropolis makes space subservient to time—depicted most vividly in the dramatic ticking down of a clock. Adapting the minuet to digital culture, it is conceivable that temporary misapprehension and incomprehensibility could be used for the same strategic purposes as in its guerrilla form: lessening the reactionary forces of the enemy and expropriating their resources.

Clutter

The unavoidable noise of digital culture provides the camouflage for operation. Noise is quite ambivalent even if it sometimes disrupts communication. The rising decibels of a loud dinner party, for example, create a feedback loop that drowns out certain intimacies but initiates others that would be impossible without it. Noise should not then be understood as always detrimental to a system, for even if it "destroys and horrifies," it is also true that "order and flat repetition are in the vicinity of death;" rather, noise holds any system open to its outside and "nourishes a new order."[37] This is because background noise forms "the ground of our perception," whose constant concealments are an unstoppable force of "perennial sustenance" and "the element of the software of all our logic."[38] In fact, a certain degree of noise may even aid transmission, for it may allow signal compression that increases the efficiency of the channel and its system, requiring an asymmetric approach to compression to draw out its potential for encryption, obliteration, unilateral determination, irreversibility, and the generic.[39] Even if the introduction of noise improves signal compression, it does so by sacrificing fidelity for mobility and flexibility. And it is here that the strategic role of noise emerges, as it engenders an indiscernibility like that of the urban guerrilla and the people, but a more fundamental one, for noise is the very material through which information travels. On the one hand, this is why cultural forms of resistance like "culture jamming" focus on signal distortion and other methods for introducing noise to disrupt the easy flow of communication. On a deeper level, however, strategic manipulation of noise allows for the creation of "vacuoles of non-communication," opening up tiny breaches that allow one to evade control, at least temporarily.[40] Noise also marks a destabilizing moment in a system that has a chance to widen the space of noncommunication by invading a channel with the desubjectified force of the outside.

The oversaturated streets of the Metropolis seem to announce that "we do not lack communication," but "on the contrary, we have too much of it," and in fact what we lack is creation, or really, "resistance to the present."[41] If that is the case, then neither the politics of persuasion nor the presentation of facts will do, for the Metropolis will remain unfazed as long as tactical media leans on the force of truth. Rather, in the struggle against it, the only mode of communication appropriate to the task is one that disrupts proper communication, a mode whose signal is one of ungovernability: insinuation. Though its effects are not clear, it is obvious that insinuation unlocks an underground force through an invisibility and anonymity that subverts identification and legibility while distorting signals and overloading the system. Insinuation has barely converged with the dangerous politics of those who desire nonexistence and disappearance—those who have no demands, refuse political representation, and rebuke negotiation with the present.[42] In the battles of appearances that consumes the Metropolis, the two promise to make a potent combination. Perhaps they will be the fusion of force and truth that will defeat cybernetic capitalism, injecting insinuations while fighting cultural politics in digital code, releasing a cascade of affect charges while turning glitches into exploits and overaccumulation into overload, and flooding the Metropolis with the noisy force of the outside.

Part II
Criminality

Straight society is held together by lines. Sovereign among them are the straight lines of filiation harkening back to monarchic blood lines.[1] They are mixed now with the molecular lines of the nuclear bio-family. These are joined by legal lines of the nationalist state, which treat citizens like an extended family. And with the advent of a digital reticular society, the lines do not disappear; they simply proliferate as relations are flattened to connections drawing everyone and everything together into a single network. The history of queerness is the chronicle of being incompatible with these lines, and this antihistory is passed down through gossip or bawdy tales of the lives of those "social enemies" who contribute nothing to society.[2] This is how queerness substitutes linear filiation for an alliance with the underworld. And in turn, it opens up an avenue for queerness not to refute its association with criminality, but instead to refashion it into the threats of other illegalists: the economic illegalism of machine breakers, the social illegalism of forming underground associations, the civil illegalism of rejecting marriage, and the political illegalism of rioters.[3]

The era of the homophile promotion of "the harmless gay" immediately ceased when the state reinforced its reactionary line against queerness in the 1960s. The evasively fluid genders and sexualities caught up in its dragnet were urgently radicalized. Its ranks included Marsha P. Johnson and Sylvia Rivera of the Street Transvestite Action Revolutionaries who fought "pig power" as sex-worker mothers through a new version of queer kinship.[4] They found themselves backed by an intelligentsia typified in Jean Genet; who was "abandoned at birth . . . a vagabond, male prostitute, and thief, who had spent most of his youth in prison" and who called questions about the origins his sexuality "a pointless diversion."[5] These groups flip the last decade of Richard von Krafft-Ebing's pathologizing etiological questions ("how did you end up as a homosexual? Was it dad's fault or mom's?") into political interrogations of how universal desire was forced into the straightjacket of compulsory heterosexuality.[6]

An essential contribution of queerness to the politics of the underground is the aesthetic sensibility of opacity. Most practically, it is a rejection of the liberal pact of the closet, which promises liberation in exchange for confessional declarations of gender or sexual orientation. Conceptually, it is bolstered by the queer refusal of interiority, which dismisses the self (or its past) as some hidden well of truth waiting to be discovered through the "work" of introspection (as the etiological approach has long demanded). "Do not ask who I am and do not ask me to remain the same," Michel Foucault once wrote, "leave it to our bureaucrats and our police to see that our papers are in order."[7]

Echoing Foucault's willfully criminal desire for opacity, queers need not draw lines between good gays and "perverts," the abstinent and "junkies," discrete lesbians from butches, and dysphorics from "gender terrorists."[8] Groups like the Homosexual Revolutionary Action Front (FHAR) revolted against the goal of winning legal protections and social recognition through a well-cultivated identity. They advanced sexuality not as a "revolutionary motor," which is only as far as the straight left was willing to go, but as a model of resistance that called forth the term "expanded homosexuality," which refused to reduce their existence to one more identity living peacefully alongside others ("the homosexual") or to limit their struggle to "sexuality" as one isolatable dimension of the social. Their sexuality is, rather, the disruption of the whole political field through relation ("antisocial").[9]

Going back at least as far as colonialism, the demand for transparency has served as "the bottom of the mirror in which Western humanity reflected the world in its image."[10] Within this framework, the modern criminalization of queers' "every gesture, statement, expression, and opinion" has become a screen upon which straights project their fantasies, from the police officer looking for an excuse to rough someone up to a colleague looking to sink their hooks into you.[11] Opacity may have started as a survival strategy, but it quickly morphed into a masked game of concealment, subtext, and working undercover. As Foucault does by substituting the law with war, opacity's tactics exchange the standpoint-neutral promises of universal transparency for a partisan strategy of disclosure that follows Sun Tzu's maxim that "all warfare is based on deception."[12] The conflict has only accelerated under surveillance, as quantitative researchers knit together sexuality, race, and criminality through cybernetic means.

Two decades after FHAR, Leo Bersani would echo their concerns by writing that "never before have gay men and women been so visible."[13] Its result? "The social project inherent in the nineteenth-century invention of 'the homosexual' can perhaps now be realized: visibility as a precondition of surveillance, disciplinary intervention, and, at the limit, gender-cleansing."[14] Though queers have held a suspicion of identities as found in the distrust of scientific motives, an eye to the exclusionary effects of identity, a mistrust in any internal essence of sexuality, and hyperawareness of the constructed nature of subjects, all of these efforts, "while valuable," have largely had an assimilative rather than subversive effect.[15] Such assimilation can be seen in those who abandon visions of revolution, resigning themselves to the narrow political ambitions of "the micropolitics of local struggles for participatory democracy and social justice."[16] Bersani's proposal is not to "a return to the immobilizing definition of identity," nor even "resistance to normalizing methodologies," but instead to think of homosexuality "as truly disruptive—as a *force*."[17] One force in particular: a "revolutionary inaptitude . . . for sociality."[18] Its mandate is not the liberal pluralist tolerance for diverse lifestyle, but rather "the politically unacceptable and political indispensable choice of an outlaw existence."[19]

Whereas Queer Nation declared in the 1980s that "we are everywhere," the new millennium brought about the criminal queers of Bash Back! who turned their backs on winning respectability through visibility. In response to being queer-bashed, they bashed back through "bar fights, outrunning lynch mobs, glamdalization, attacking the homes of heterosexist murderers, outright chaos, alleged lootings, theory discussions, self-defense tips, social gatherings, beatdowns, the acquisition of large quantities of pepper spray, and attempts at sexual liberation."[20] It is in these gender outlaws that queerness and criminality have always coincided.[21] Their classrooms are found in the walk from the flop pad to the scene of an incident. The first day of their history courses open with "Stonewall was a riot." Their survey textbook, *What Is Gender Nihilism? A Reader*, is made to be encountered "adrift in the world, in coffee shops and libraries, riding on buses and snuck into schools,"[22] And the editors of their flagship journal *Bædan* (*Journal of Queer Nihilism, of Queer Heresy, of Queer Time Travel* . . .) declare that "a non-identitarian, unrepresentable, unintelligible queer revolt will be purely negative, or it won't be at all," as "identity politics, platforms, formal organizations, subcultures, activist campaigns (each being either queer or anarchist) will always arrive at the dead ends of identity and representation."[23]

Chapter 7
Society with Sexual Characteristics

Cybernetic governance would like nothing more than to defang society. One of its most powerful operations it to make its techniques seem neutral, automatic, or at least boring. The appearance it cultivates is a strict system of rules run by technocrats who wield grammar like programmers, laying out laws like a series of subroutines. Artist Zach Blas suggests that there is something much more exciting going on. The seemingly banal corporate representation of bodies (as assessed for risk in airport security theater), images (used to monitor movements indicative of criminal behavior), and information (tracked for regular and anomalous patterns) actually peddles in "sexual stimulation, punishment, and spiritual ecstasy."[1] Airport screeners do not simply scan, he contends; they engage in the pleasure politics of undressing, disciplining, and humiliating. Which raises a question: do all information systems participate in sexual power play?

This is the premise behind Blas's 2018 art installation *SANCTUM*. It can be heard before it is even seen, with throbbing techno music that oozes from a cavernous dungeon. Once inside, a number of large-format digital screens haunt the space. One is caged. A second is hung by a chain from its four corners. Another is balanced over a pair of spanking posts, topped by a tripod. An additional one is bound and hangs upside down, affixed with hoses feeding into something glowing and aqueous. At the center, a tower of screens watches over everything.

Depicted on each screen is a 3D-rendered white figure strikingly similar to a blow-up doll. The figure itself is an odd fabulation of administrative grey media—the invention of L3 (level 3 screening technology, now made by L3Harris Technologies) for their TSA-approved ProVision 2 body scanner, with an accompanying screen in which security threats are represented "image-free" as colors and shapes projected onto a "generic mannequin that resembles a human outline."[2] Relocating them to the sex dungeon, the digital figure's submission to security procedures acquire a new valence as a "reimagining of the power dynamics of BDSM at the heart of contemporary surveillance: an opulent display of desire and capture, exposure and punishment, dominance and submission."[3] As the artist further describes it:

> As prisoners, sex slaves, worshippers, and experimental test subjects, these mannequins experience pleasure, pain, and martyrdom, as they are stretched, scraped, bound, contained, whipped, suspended, dropped, pierced, and mummified. Silent and pliant, the mannequins are also harvested, in order to produce a new line of weapons and sex toys.[4]

One mannequin is stretched across the length of the screen, face down over spanking posts, with the rack's tripod penetrating its hands and anus with such force that the screen cracks at the points of insertion. An array of wire-frame devices sit at the ready on a cart next to it. Another is physically bound and hung upside down, revealing only those parts of the bodies that can be plugged into hoses that create a feedback loop of streaming flows. On a vertical rack, a smaller mannequin is tossed about according to the cruel whims of some invisible force, drawing on the body horror of 3D digital physics simulators.

The largest figure is trapped in a box, hunched over on all fours in pliant surrender. A self-assembling wireframe form blinks to life. It begins like a mesh, a network cradling the body in a web of connections. As quickly as it is formed, an invisible gravity well forms above. Bits begin to fly off. Whole sections are sucked off the body as the swirling vortex travels from head to toe. The largely still body shudders from the rapidity of the stripping. Above, the surging orb lengthens as it whirls, becoming like a tentacle menacing the body. It regathers its force at the rear, disappearing as it enters the body like a projectile. The body's outsides bulge in response. With incredible force, it erupts out the mouth, violently dispersing.

A slightly elevated tower watches over from the center. Its presence is sometimes personal, sometimes structural. Even its personal moments are still anonymized. A faceless mask lords over the room. Its eyes are hollow, part of its ability to repel any visual attempt to locate what lies behind the mask. The power it embodies is so intense that it emits a threatening glow. At other moments, the tower unveils its intricate inner workings. Dark and metallic, it avoids direct apprehension. Yet the structure is so large it cannot be apprehended all at once. The only perspective available glides along its surface, like a motorcycle roaring through a city's streets at night. Even then, what is seen is not the thing itself, but the shine of its edges. Regardless of these limitations, it is clear that its power is architectural in nature.

Black, white, and red light encode the relations of power for the whole scene. Each screen partially hides behind the dark room's large columns. Despite the centralizing influence of the tower, each screen carves out its own space through fractional concealment. Such independence grants each zone a relative autonomy, a partial exclusivity and potential confidentiality. The discreetness is simultaneously amplified and betrayed by harsh neon lights. Some screens are bathed in white light, as if suddenly revealed by a floodlight. Caught in the act. The related sensations heightened by the unforgiving clarity of the bright light. Others catch the glare of red, a color emanating from space of power—the medical gaze of an operating cart with a mix of surgical and torture implements, the spectacle of punishment of various masks worn to shame. Not only does the redness enhance the sense of horror through its association with blood, danger, and carnality; it illuminates the space without casting out the darkness.

The complex matrix of directed light otherwise consumed in darkness allows viewers to select their preferred level of involvement:

fade into the shadows or stand behind a column to see but not be seen; pose in white light, caught in an unrelenting spotlight that makes things appear naked and overexposed; enjoy the operations of the red light, relishing in the power to oversee and control the whole scene.

Chapter 8
Excitement and Exposure

The future is "connectivity," or so say today's tech execs as they outline their plans for a new world order. "Soon everyone on Earth will be connected," they declare, following it with worn promises of increased productivity, health, education, and happiness.[1] On the face of things, they are simply echoing the old trope of the level playing field repeated by empire builders from Niccolò Machiavelli to Thomas Friedman. What then is new? The type of horizontal connections that their connectivity forges between the virtual and physical worlds. In particular, its digital logic of combinatorial difference is now used as a tool of governance to "intensify, accelerate, and exacerbate phenomena in the world so that a difference in degree will become a difference in kind."[2] In sum, connectivity is the new techno-utopian business strategy that braids the physical with the virtual to create a sociopolitical empire of difference.

Google's connectivity thesis is a sign that power is increasingly logistical: its authority resides in roads, cell-phone towers, and data centers, and its legislators are those who keep the flows moving. There are political consequences for this shift; principally, it names a power not usually associated with spaces of appearance like courthouses and presidential palaces.[3] The transformation carries through power's abstract form and material expression. The abstract form of logistical power is not exclusion, but inclusive disjunction (inclusive exclusion, inclusive omission, selective inclusion, etc.).[4] This geographic reconfiguration has also been reflected in an "infrastructural turn" in oppositional politics, as demonstrated in blockades and counterinfrastructure, such as the disruption of Google buses in the San Francisco Bay Area or the development of new computational tools for activists.⁵ Abstractly, such connectivity has made it so "power has become the environment itself."⁶

A curious omission haunts so much talk of biopolitics—sex. Political theorists in particular tend to take for granted Michel Foucault's claim that contemporary power was born with the invention of a science of sex. They quickly generalize biopolitics away from the specific of sexuality to a broader distinction between *zoē* and *bios*, allowing "biopolitics" to mean "the politics of life itself" or the power to "make live and let die."⁷ This is not to say that sexuality is totally absent in such accounts, but that sex is often demoted to an illustrative case study for the broader regulation of the body. In contrast, feminist scholars have used the body as a shared site for a critical analytic, as it serves as a nexus for questions of race science, the violent capitalist reorganization of gender, the medicalization of deviance, spatial programs of urban hygiene, and so on. What if we too take Foucault at his word, that there is something particular about sex at the heart of biopower? If so, then materially, the hardware of infrastructure of the new digital metropolis and the wetware of the subjects who inhabit it are articulated through a whole "pharmaco-pornographic regime," a technosexual mixture of stimulation and exposure embedded in connectivity's liberal dreams of revealing transparency.⁸

"Pornopower" names how contemporary society is fueled by biopower *with sexual characteristics*. Paul B. Preciado elucidates them with a trip through the pornopower of our modern era, with precursors that include two different sets of scientific experiments. On the one hand, the long war on women, witches, alchemists, and mid-wives cleared the way for a chemical biosomatics that would be centralized in the industrial synthesis of pharmaceuticals.⁹ Its exemplary product was the edible panopticon of the pill: a condensed industrialization of the domestic, tested in the colonial brothel and perfect in the lab.¹⁰ With the birth control pill, "the body swallows power," offering a refutation of mass paranoia over the infiltration of a power from the outside, demonstrating instead how biopower can dwell within.¹¹ On the other hand, late capitalist transformations displaced the Fordist factory with a new regime of labor centered on the body as made-available by contract of service.¹² As such, sex work serves as the paradigmatic contract for today's casualized labor, including the reproduction of fantasy, demands for performance, access to bodies, and other somatic mechanisms.¹³ Accompanying such work is the production, circulation, and consumption of audiovisual materials and synthesized molecular products. At the crossroads of the *phármakon* and pornographic are two process: *excitement* and *exposure*.

"Excitement" describes a type of work that seeks not to satisfy, but to frustrate. Advancing a libidinal theory of sexuality echoing electromagnetic conceptions of energy, Sigmund Freud writes about a process of "excitations of the sensory surfaces—the skin and the sense organs."¹⁴ Hence he affords special status to the displacements of the eye, so closely tied to the process of "attraction," for both its remoteness from touching and its tug of war with the veiled body as a whole.¹⁵ Freud theorizes that such excitations can arise simply as a byproduct of a great range of processes innate to any organism, such as emotional distress, so long as they achieve a certain intensity, making life itself fundamentally autoerotic.¹⁶ Peculiar to the generation of sexual excitation is the feeling of tension.¹⁷ Freud's observations include two dimensions: first, that the tension necessarily involves a growing unpleasure; and second, an urgent impulse to resolve the situation.¹⁸ One can imagine an analogy in static electricity that frenetically builds on a surface until the energy discharges, sometimes even being felt, heard, or seen. The discharge makes the tension temporarily subside, bringing about a sense of relief and a feeling of satisfaction.¹⁹

But Freud's theory that frustration is the road to satisfaction does not feel particularly novel today. From advertising to the governing of souls, a sexual logic of productive frustration has come to motivate the social body.²⁰ Moreover, his recourse to a developmental model whose telos ends in genitality and the male achievement of the sexual aim implants a deep misogyny with which feminist, queer, and trans theorists have tarried for over a century. His model of excitation does, however, raise an important question. What happens when satisfaction is no longer the point?

One of the most well-honed excitement devices is the slot machine. Winning is incidental for those repeat gamblers who find themselves hooked into its loops for hour after hour. As one long-time player recounts, "in the beginning, there was excitement about winning," yet now, "*I'm not playing to win,* . . . [but] to keep playing—to stay in that machine zone where nothing else matters."[21] The flow state of the zone is what they seek out, an uninterrupted play-state where time, space, and others seem to disappear—to play, forget, and lose themselves.[22] Winning may even become an irritation because play stops, extra noises and images appear, and others begin paying attention to them. The machine loops can easily be layered on top of a synthetic chemical substrate. One woman describes using her prescription while gambling, "I'd feel the panic if I'd start losing, and also if I'd win—it was like an overload of excitement—and I'd pop two Xanax, or three, and it would calm me right down."[23] The zone is a marvel of design standing at the intersection of ambient architectures, user-centric experience design, and the programming of risk, all coming together to create a subjective shift in the gambler.[24]

Zoning out is a perfection of Karl Marx's basic discovery that "the production of wealth depends on abstract, unqualified, subjective activity irreducible to the domain of either political or linguistic representation."[25] As fundamentally a Skinner box, every zone-machine sets a pace, following a variable schedule of rewards, regulating risk predictably by way of a rhythm. Even psychologists denounce such intermittent reinforcement as having no clinical utility, characterizing the behavior of abusers and serving only as a recipe for addiction. The slot machine's design history is the three-dimensional intensification of "longer, faster, and more" energy extraction common to labor regimes. In sum, machinic excitement becomes the means to replace the highs and lows of satisfaction with a continuous holding pattern. Its purpose is obvious to all involved, a mood-modulating box fueled by an ever-accelerating glut of money. The lesson: with just the right balance of excitement, many will fight for their servitude (to the machine) as stubbornly as though it were their salvation (from their frustrations).

In regards to visual-informational exposure, liberal democracy takes transparency to be an unquestionable virtue. Behind it is the idea that shadowy actors, the foremost being the government itself, can be stopped in their tracks if their secret is revealed. Commonly cited is U.S. Supreme Court justice Louis Brandeis, who wrote that "publicity is justly commended as a remedy for social and industrial diseases. Sunlight is said to be the best of disinfectants; electric light the most efficient policeman."[26] Rooted firmly in an Enlightenment metaphysics of presence, it is aided by new technology and the ideological operations of an information society.[27] While political in its targets, it is emphatically postpolitical in that it espouses values meant to be shared by all across the spectrum of politics. Transparency advocates include prodemocracy movements, who paint their opponents as abusing power through secrecy and corruption. Even the radical left has invested in it as an anticapitalist tool, including the sousveillance tactics of protestors publicizing police actions, doc-dumps by dissidents and groups like WikiLeaks looking to break the "conspiracy" between nation-states and corporate elites, organizations promoting the "transparency circulation" of movement ideas like the World Social Form, and protransparency principles written into the Green New Deal.[28] Transparency's theory of power assumes that the real determinations of politics are hidden from view. Politics becomes locked in a drama of concealment and revelation.[29]

Absent from these accounts is the sexual double meaning of liberal ideas of access, free expression, and transparency, a result of the "god-trick" discussed by Donna Haraway, of "seeing everything from nowhere."[30] Its key mechanism is the elimination of the body of knowledge from which the information is derived. What comes into view when we return the body? Whole economies of visibility that use bodies as narrative commodities that have been used to feed the last century's proliferation of cinema, television, and video.[31] For Judith Butler, as a Lacanian invested in the dialectic of recognition, this is the essence of the political. Not only must the body appear for politics to occur, she argues, but the exposure of the flesh to the gaze, touch, possession, and violence of others: "It is through the body that gender and sexuality become exposed to others, implicated in social processes, inscribed by cultural norms, and apprehended in their social meanings."[32] Such a formulation remains trapped in a paradox of exposure in which making something visible renders it a potential object of harm.³³ Its latest iteration is found in popular feminism, whose politics of visibility for its own sake has been structurally matched by popular misogyny.³⁴ On one side, there is liberal feminism's full-spectrum courting of the dialectic of recognition, and on the other, the libertarianism of #gamergaters, incels, and PUAs ("pickup artists") who all loudly demand greater transparency ("in video game journalism"). With the latter comes a howling insistence on access to certain bodies, the entitled expectation that any sexual expression is available for the right pay, and an ardent defense of the right for ever-more-penetrating forms of exposure.

How does radical feminism fit in this context? Haraway poses the problematic this way: what is more powerful, the ecogoddess or the cyborg feminist? The ecofeminist response is obvious: it would amplify the already existing "natural resistances" of the body. Anxiety, panic, and exhaustion all seem like natural responses to unparalleled levels of exposure and states of constant excitation.³⁵ Moreover, sleep wages a passive war against digital capitalism's attempts to turn every second into a productive moment.³⁶ In sleep, the body finds temporary disengagement from various excitation-frustration cycles induced by technologies of the body (biotechnologies, surgery, pharmaceuticals) and representation (film, television, digital media). It even contains a feminist dimension as a moment when we abandon ourselves to the care of others.

Explaining another natural resistance to the pornographic gaze, porn actress Nina Roberts explains that some of her colleagues "fatten up to a high degree when they stop making films, to avoid being recognized and to desexualize themselves, so they can go out and do their shopping without being taken for sluts in heat looking for hard cocks."³⁷ Considering a way to use "secrecy as a weapon rather than a retreat," Preciado advances an alternative.³⁸ Would it be easier for them to take chemically synthesized testosterone to transition genders? "That way, they could transform themselves into courteous and anonymous customers, with hairy arms and low voices."³⁹ This follows from Preciado's own high-speed study as a "feminist hooked on testosterone," *Testo-Junkie*, self-documenting nonmedical experiments with hormone gel meant to operate as "a manual of gender bioterrorism undertaken on a molecular level."[40] It leans into the cyberfeminist argument that gendered bodies have long been central to technology, whether as typists, telephone operators, the first coders, or other laboring subjects.[41] Forcing them to choose between themselves and technology would then be asking them take away a part of their history. Instead of finding shelter from the most destructive tendencies of medicalized capitalism, technological militarism, and other social processes, the cyborg expands them to the point of revolutionary transformation.

There is nothing more punk rock than the politics of fucking the system. No doubt it took a queer like Lee Edelman to make good on the punk rallying cry "No Future!" Its nose-thumbing politics is not found in the drug-fueled excesses of sellout musicians, but the punk of those who make their lives through squatting, petty theft, dumpster diving, paid medical experiments, and donating plasma. With it comes a strong dose of pugilistic refusal and a mantra to not care about living past twenty-five. Yet, for all its bluster, a punk lifestyle does not evade cycles of frustration-excitation and demands for exposure. Rather, punk engages in an art of distances and involves a hyper-self-exploitative submission to a certain sliver of extreme indignities in exchange for freedom from the rest. The spirit is crystallized in the first written lines in Bernadette Corporation's all-too-cool film *Get Rid of Yourself*:

> They say, "another world is possible." But I am another world. Am I possible? I am here, living, stealing, doing cocaine, subtracting myself from the bad movie of urban love stories, inventing weapons, elaborating the complex constellation of my relations, building the Party. They say "another world is possible." But we do not want another world, another order, another justice: another logical nightmare. We do not want any global governance be it fair, be it ecological, be it certified by Porto Allegre. We want THIS world. We want this world as chaos. We want the chaos of our lives, the chaos of our perceptions, the chaos of our desires and repulsions. The chaos that happens when management collapses. Capitalism defeated traditional societies because it was more exciting than they were,

but now there is something more exciting than Capitalism, itself: its destruction."[42]

For Preciado, this means a deep commitment to queer pornographic self-exposure and the presumed license to fuck with everyone else. Sexuality seems to offer the perfect lever for upsetting all of the other biopolitical dimensions of contemporary control. Yet it is easy to take it too far, especially for someone with as much swagger as Preciado.

Being "careless in wielding the self to describe more serious plights" is a potential pitfall for the autotheory of Preciado and others, notes Crispin Long.[43] Long locates a number of episodes in Preciado's self-centered writing, though the critique also smacks of liberal self-flagellation about how much worse others have it. For instance, Long is concerned with Preciado using his own border crossings (such as physical inspections by agents of the law) as an occasion to theorize about the challenges for migrants and refugees, especially trans and gender-nonconforming ones.[44] There is much to unpack in a second instance in which Preciado experiments with the name "Marcos" as a new masculine first name by "de-privatizing" the nom de guerre of the Zapatista spokesperson, calling him "actually a drag-king" in the process.[45] Latin American activists immediately denounced this as a colonial land-grab (Preciado is a white Spaniard) and an inappropriate comparison to the struggles of Indigenous people against the settler state—something Preciado cops to in his introduction yet still saw fit to include the essay (although he chose not to adopt the name).[46] And a third occasion occurs when Preciado briefly wanders the streets of New York in search of his soul through the technological landscape of always-on digital devices and drone surveillance. Without it, he declares himself "half dead and half alive, . . . an unlikely cross between Freddie Gray and Caitlyn Jenner."[47] The latter comparison is apt, as Preciado condemns how one of Jenner's televised interviews demonstrated how any TV studio, living room, computer, or smart phone can become an "operating theater where a sex reassignment process is taking place." For all of its incisive reflection on others, Preciado's "half dead" embodiment of Freddie Gray is never examined. Gray is tossed away like a loose cigarette, a single disposable thing separated from its pack and thoughtlessly used up in a rush of excitement, then rubbed into the pavement without a another thought.

None of this dismisses the importance of Preciado's essential diagnosis of today's pornopower. Rather, his failure comes from his inability to heed Foucault's gesture of refusal: "to get free of oneself."[48] Nowhere is this more evident than Preciado's political porno-punk tactic of self-exploitation, or in the words of *Testo-Junkie*, the "auto-guinea pig" tradition of scientists first testing chemicals and treatments on themselves.[49] To be clear, this is not some demand for Preciado to ritualistically repeat one of liberalism's many hand-wringing apologies. Those prewritten performatives always fail because they ensnare the "privileged" in endless self-analysis at the expense of the risky politics of taking sides in a struggle (also note how self-reflexivity loops back to the cybernetic anthropology of Margaret Mead).[50] Instead, it means preventing the self from being installed at the center of the universe (or even a planet like *Uranus*), else it will but suck everything into its gravitational pull.[51] Does this not explain Preciado's confinement to digital devices, absolutely transfixed by the pornographic exposure of the camera, logging chemical-sexual encounters in incredible detail from preparation to execution, the prisoner's time-table at the beginning of *Discipline and Punish*? As Gilles Deleuze warns, there is nothing worse than finding yourself trapped in the other's electrifying gaze.[52] As a T junkie, what Preciado adds is the self-absorbed chemical jolt of testosterone gel with a fixation on the resulting subjective shift. In the end, the self-indulgence of *Testo-junkie* remains too singular, which is to say, not abstract enough to generalize to the underground. So, yes, let's fuck the system, but in a way that builds opacity for others to operate, rather than self-ish notoriety.

Chapter 9

A Heart That Burns and Burns

"I don't want these things to happen, they just do," murmurs Rita, a character in Joyce Carol Oates's *Foxfire*.[1] A tragic girl, Rita could not help that terrible things always seemed to happen to her. Her brothers and other boys exploited her. The abuse would begin with teasing and sometimes ended in worse. To speak of a milder incident: one time when she was seven, her brothers yanked off her panties and hoisted them in a high tree for the cruel satisfaction of the neighborhood boys. Every time she apologized in a detached and matter of fact way, as if each injustice happened around but not to her, like the weather, totally absent of anything about her—her body, her status as a female.

One day it all changes. Rita and three other high school girls cram in a small room on New Year's Eve Day 1953. Led by Legs ("First-in-command"), they form a blood-sisterhood. A girl gang. (FOXFIRE IS YOUR HEART!) Foxfire quickly develops a taste for revenge. They feast on the joy and pleasure that follows from breaking through the shame and disdain of long submitting to absent and alcoholic fathers, lecherous teachers and uncles, and ruthless boys and brothers. Separately, the girls felt suffocated. But together, they are delirious with life.

Foxfire's bond is underwritten by love even if it is fueled by vengeance. When others would feel regret or remorse, or guilt and sin, they simply scream FOXFIRE BURNS & BURNS and FOXFIRE NEVER SAYS SORRY! And the way they tell it, there is no reason for you to feel sorry either. As Maddy writes of their notebooks, Foxfire's actions are no doubt crimes, yet "most of these went not only unpunished but unacknowledged—our victims, all male, were too ashamed, or too cowardly, to come forward to complain."[2]

It is not the crime that defines them, however; it just adds to their strength. Simply being together, even before undertaking their campaign of justice, the girls began their migration from forgettable girls to figures of history. Foxfire was already on everyone's lips. Their mere presence bred curiosity and suspicion. But they truly command respect once they begin striking against the men who left them hurt, alone, or vulnerable, and it is this respect that allows the girls to finally embrace the distrust for adults and boys they had long privately nursed.

There is much to say about the history of Foxfire. Tales of youthful exuberance or irresponsibility that lead them astray. Explanations of how FOXFIRE HOMESTEAD and FOXFIRE FINANCES seal their sad fate. But these distract from Foxfire's agonizing truth: the path of liberation and escape winds through negative affects and not around them. For, revenge can serve as the greatest act of love.

Chapter 10
We Are Bad, but We Could Be Worse

Perhaps there is a secret solidarity between all the girls who weather the daily assault of patriarchy like a bad storm. Their innermost feelings well up, some given expression through grief or outrage, but more often, they are nursed in seclusion. Can this shared secret turn bad feelings into outright conspiracy? Or even more importantly, turn revenge into collective liberation? Perhaps it means indulging a bit, as expressed in the slogan circulating around South America in lesbian, sex worker, and trans circles, "we are bad, be we could be worse."

Most sober-minded critics find "ugly feelings" unfit for something as noble as shared liberation. Confirming critic's skepticism, few political projects outwardly declare that they draw their strength from envy, irritation, paranoia, and anxiety. Furthermore, most actions taken on behalf of these emotions are quickly marked within public discourse as hostile, destructive, and uncontrolled. Yet Sianne Ngai argues that, although these negative affects are weaker than "grander passions like anger and fear" and thus lack an orientation powerful enough to form clear political motivations, the unsuitability of weakly intentional feelings "amplifies their power to diagnose situations, and situations marked by blocked or thwarted actions in particular."[1] From this perspective, ugly feelings are blockages, cruel replacements that inspire only enough optimism to discourage the search for a better alternative. Diagnosing such feelings should avoid what Eve Kosofsky Sedgwick calls a paranoid reading, which takes pleasure in the suspicious search for sources of discontent and its subsequent exposure; it must find instead a reparative and transformative reading driven by hope and surprise.[2] The embodiment of reparation, she suggests, echoing Melanie Klein, is a depressive attitude that drains the shock and anxiety of surprise. This approach proposes that, once the world appears as fundamentally ambivalent, with the good always hopelessly tied up in the bad, one sheds paranoid anticipation and becomes open to surprise stripped of the dread that comes with always waiting only for bad news. The key is to prevent the clinical tool of a depressive attitude from blossoming into the clinical blockage of depression.

Depression is a real danger, however, serving as the major cause for concern for the feminist project Public Feelings. After decades of queer activism, the AIDS crisis, antiracist advocacy, electoral campaigns, and antiwar mobilizations, these feminists undertook a program of diagnosis and self-care. The positive valence of a depressive attitude seemed lost as all that seemed possible was full-blown depression. Recognizing collective burnout, they questioned dominant diagnostic paradigms that look for causes in neurochemical imbalances or damaged psyches. Hardly convinced by solely clinical explanations for their shared anxiety, exhaustion, incredulity, split focus, and numbness, they began investigating how the already-alienated life was compounded by the trauma of national crises, beginning with 9/11 and continuing with the war in Iraq, the reelection of George W. Bush, and Hurricane Katrina.[3] This is not to say that they have found psychiatry or psychoanalysis wrong or counterproductive, but these feminists were determined to turn feelings into a collective forces; and from that struggle, Feel Tank Chicago was born.

Feel Tank Chicago sought access to political life through the affective register. The project named their malaise "political depression," which they defined as "the sense that customary forms of political response, including direct action and critical analysis, are no longer working either to change the world or to make us feel better."[4] To further their investigation, Feel Tank has held conferences, exhibitions, and International Days of the Depressed. As a camp celebration of depression, they dress in bathrobes and protest with banners, signs, stickers, and chants emblazoned with slogans diagnosing the environment of hostility produced by Empire:

"Depressed? It Might Be Political"; "Exhausted? It Might Be Politics"; or just "I Feel Lost."[5] Contrary to cynical ideology's denunciation of those who are apathetic as complicit with the status quo, political depression does not blame selfishness or individual illness as the cause of apathy. Causes for this suffering are numerous and easy to identify—the racism of white supremacy, the exploitation of global capitalism, the sexism of patriarchy, the degradation of the environment, and the violence of heteronormativity, to name a few—while the course for their abolition is not readily apparent. Political depression thus demonstrates how Empire spreads depression like a fog, cloaking adequately political alternatives in everyday life. One such blockage is the traditional politics of think tanks who manage technical flows by drawing on "whiz kid" computer models, policy expertise, and insider connections to craft politically relevant briefs. The effect of reducing politics to this form of government is cataclysmic: it reduces time to a perpetual present wherein politics is nothing but the art of compromise. In such a world, the status quo is all that is visible, and thus it reigns supreme. The group has found a less restricted route as a "feel" tank, which works to turn private feelings into a public resource for political action. And to this end, Feel Tank has operated in the nexus of activism, academia, and art. Such an approach reveals different paths to politics, animated by perspectives that still imagine real alternatives.

By making depression political, Feel Tank also challenged a deeper and more pervasive blockage: the interiority of the subject. With its attention to the affective dimension of politics, Feel Tank upset the dark room of the self that is cynically manipulated by policy analysts and liberal political theorists. Affects point to a circuit of power whereby external forces impress themselves on the biological imperatives of bodies and make emotion an emergent quality of politics even if a necessary biological component exists in the body. And although a certain body may be predisposed to depression, its affective cause emerges as a political event. Identifying such a cause may be difficult, as depression often arises due to something as diffuse as bad weather or accumulative time spent in an adverse environment, but it is in this sense that patriarchy appears as a storm. It can therefore be said that affect not only demands that the emotions of subjects count as politics; it also demands a political account of emotion exterior to subjects. As Ann Cvetkovich writes, politicizing feelings requires "the same historicization that is central to Foucauldian and other social constructionist approaches to sexuality" because "Foucault's critique of the repressive hypothesis applies as much to affect as sexuality, warranting a skeptical approach to claims for interiority or emotional expression as the truth of the self."[6]

When this notion is expanded, its political conclusion is decisive: affects do not reveal the truth of a subject's private life and are often merely a habituated response to power. This point may confuse those who imagine affect only as a tool of liberation. But only those who mistake today's power for authoritarianism would think that the state grows only through crippling paralysis. This is not to say fear is no longer used, especially since the general environment it creates is no doubt to blame for political depression. But the difficult truth is that any state form that incorporates the liberal pole of governance also expands its oppressive control through the inspirational force of positive affects. Although social movements may draw on affect as a form of power, so does the social state. Positive affects swirl through both the vortex of Zuccotti Park and the highrises of Goldman Sachs. Negative affects are caught at work at temp jobs but also at feminist conference panels. Like the ambivalence of any other form of power, affect is not a virtue but a diagnostic.

Treating affect as a point of disagreement is one way to maintain its ambivalence, and a crucial aspect of that disagreement is the struggle over happiness. Sara Ahmed contends that, because happiness has been historically given as an emotional reward to women for submission to gendered demands, especially those of the family, the struggle over happiness "forms the political horizon in which feminist claims are made."[7] The complication of happiness enhances the contemporary utilization of Baruch Spinoza's account of affect whereby affective connections with a body are either joyous or sad, with joyous affects being those that increase the capacity of the body and sad affects being those that are destructive to the body. Whereas such a Spinozism intends joyous connections to be virtuous regardless of context, his account of affect theorizes the capacity of objects to evoke feelings of pleasure or disgust in subjects. Furthermore, in our alienated world, the ability for objects and bodies to evoke pleasure in subjects is not always beneficial, as most of its residents are consumed by dark appetites they know to be against their best interest. The ability that objects of desire have to bruise subjects by the uncanny talent to wound while also teaching enjoyment of the wound does not reveal the true nature of the soul; it merely confirms the indelible power of connection.

The world is not at a loss for connections, as today is not the age of sad passions but of the masochistic contract that is sealed by fusing the cruel thrill of exploiting others with the self-destructive delights of being oppressed, bossed around, hopelessly addicted, and completely dependent, creating a split subject that desires happiness but experiences only pleasure. Power now speaks less with the prohibitive "no" and more with the compulsory happiness of "you must enjoy" (whether you like it or not). Feminism's project is to end the tireless pursuit of pleasure, which Ahmed argues begins through becoming a killjoy.

Killjoys initiate a revolt against the promise of happiness through "acts of revolution" and "protests against the costs of agreement."[8] Feminist killjoys complete their revolutionary conversion when they abandon happiness and embrace the affects of troublemakers. The face of their struggles may appear surprisingly common, such as queer novels that end on a sad note or spoilsports who ruin the atmosphere of a room, but their aim is transformative: to deny satisfaction of already-existing tastes and establish new ones. This requires dismantling the current architecture of the soul and the construction of a new one. Killjoys thus open escape routes that "open a life" and "make room for possibility, for chance" by not only wanting "the wrong things" we are asked us to give up but also "create[ing] life worlds around these wants."[9] Yet such openings are only visible to those who have given up on the illusion that positive affects draw out the best in people.

What ultimately characterizes a troublemaker is how they live life. For the troublemaker, life is not about survival, but escape—escape from the causes of suffering, escape to a better world, and most importantly, escape as a form of struggle. The troublemaker dreams of freedom by imaging politics as a utopian space where "we could possibly go somewhere that exists only in our imagination."[10] This freedom is without shape, as it is only the notion that things must change. Such belief is founded on the revolutionary demand to live a life without compromise, and so it demands a world that has made a revolutionary break from anything that collaborates with the reactionary forces of the present. And it is this veiled desire for something better that motivates the dreamer to gamble the transient pleasures of the present for the ecstasy of permanent revolution.

Audre Lorde powerfully distinguishes her own dreams of liberation from her mother's focus on happy survival in her autobiographical biomythography *Zami: A New Spelling of My Name*. As a young child, she was often caught in the tension of a racially mixed neighborhood of Harlem. While walking with her mother, the tension literally spilled over onto the streets and she was spit on by racist whites. She grew to hate the throaty sound of men clearing their throats because she knew it would most likely end in a disgusting mark on her coat or shoe. But her mother, quick to explain the randomness of the event, would deflect the importance of race by complaining about the "lowclass people who had no better sense nor manners than to spit into the wind no matter where they went."[11]

Although she was convinced by her mother, the memory of the event always nagged her. Years later, noticing a decline in the pervasive but seemingly random behavior, she asked her mother, "Have you noticed people don't spit into the wind so much the way they used to?"[12] She immediately realized her mistake after seeing the pain in her mother's face. Rather than admitting that she was helpless to prevent her young daughter from being spit on, her mother used the only protection she knew: to change reality, or at least her daughter's perception of reality. Despite the complicated relationship she has with her mother's classism, Lorde does not seem to begrudge her mother's quietism. What the event ultimately demonstrates is a deeper distinction: the difference between escapism as a compromise with the present and political escape as the struggle for freedom.

Negative affects should thus be seen as weapons. Anger, frustration, disdain, and envy are reasonable reactions to a hostile environment. But when subjects soberly manage those negative affects, they are privately treating symptoms and not publicly addressing their external cause. As Feel Tank shows, those affects can become a resource for political action when the private space of the subject is emptied and feelings are made public. But these affects are also revolutionary, as they imply their own escape: by signaling a bad reaction to a toxic environment, negative affects speak to a cause outside the interiority of the subject as the source of general discontent, a cause that can be changed. Yet ugly feelings are not enough if they are employed only to battle the oppressive conditions of everyday life just to live to fight another day. To become truly antagonistic, then, troublemakers must combine negative affect's motivational force with a refusal of interiority and utopian struggle. For, negatives affects may serve as motivation for a better world (FOXFIRE BURNS AND BURNS), but they generate black holes of misery unless subjects refuse to blame themselves for negative affects (FOXFIRE NEVER SAYS SORRY!) and maintain a revolutionary trajectory without compromise with the present (FOXFIRE NEVER LOOKS BACK!).

Chapter 11
We Don't

"Everybody talks about the weather. . . . We don't," read an advertisement launched in 1966 that depicted a train from the German national rail service plowing through the snow. The message is: regardless of bad weather's obstructions, Deutsche Bahn always powers through. Today's slow-moving climate catastrophe gives the phrase new significance. Such stalwart insistence that the operations of national infrastructure will remain unfazed offers an image into how postpolitics looks to manage the crisis.

But in spite of its clever reworking of Mark Twain's quip that "everybody talks about the weather, but nobody does anything about it," Deutsche Bahn was soon plagued by weather delays, which led to a chilly German reaction and gave rise to a new joke: "Have year heard this one? German rail has four enemies: spring, summer, fall and winter." No doubt a sign of the future that awaits those hoping for a techno fix to our current crisis.

Within a couple years, the slogan reemerged with an explicitly political valence. A new spate of posters arrived bearing the same slogan, "Alle reden vom Wetter. . . . Wir nicht." But this time, the phrase appeared on a bright red background above the faces of Marx, Engels, and Lenin. Made by the German Sozialistische Deutsche Studentenbund (SDS; the Socialist German Student Union), it elevated the original poster to world-historical proportions: regardless of capitalist obstructions to revolution, Marxist socialism will power through.

Ironically, the German SDS would suffer just as Deutsche Bahn did. Peaking a few months after the posters were designed in 1968, the group met extreme government resistance and was unable to mount an effective opposition to the German Emergency Acts, which led to its ultimate collapse in 1970.

As the black clouds of repression gathered, other groups emerged. Waging a New Left revolt against the so-called Auschwitz Generation, post-1968 militants had one goal: agitation. Among them, one of the most innovative forms of agitation came from the Socialists Patients' Collective (Sozialistisches Patientenkollektiv [SPK]), a radical mental-health group at the University of Heidelberg. Convinced that illness is a necessary byproduct of capitalism, they developed a radical form of therapy—agitation therapy—whose therapeutic effects were found in pitting one's mental illness against centers of capitalism. In that way, SPK was determined to "turn illness into a weapon."

By externalizing the cause of one's condition, SPK's agitation therapy echoes an important question: If the subject no longer has the truth of an interior to confess, about what does the subject speak? Moreover, if the subject refuses the idle chatter of the waiting room that Twain so despises, is there a form of talk that is itself a form of action?

Chapter 12
Making Illness into a Weapon

A history of the subject without an interior might be constructed backward. Such a discussion could start with queer history, which seems to lend itself to this backwardness, as its twentieth-century stories are full of personal loss, social detachment, and fragmented community.[1] Such backwardness has ample company, as Walter Benjamin wrote that the angel of history has his open wings caught in "a storm blowing from Paradise" that propels him into the future facing backward, so that all he can see are the horrors of what has already occurred.[2] A similarly backward-focused subject would also feel the full force of the catastrophe, which is pregnant with "shyness, ambivalence, melancholia, loneliness, regression, victimhood, heartbreak, antimodernism, immaturity, self-hatred, despair, [and] shame" that lead more often to failure than satisfaction.[3] Failure is the point of such an orientation. In contrast to work that focuses on transforming negative affects (understood as blockages, traumas, and the cessation of movement) into positive affects (empowerment, capacity, power), a backward history identifies negativity as an antagonism generated within the social. And when this antagonism reemerges, feelings that were previously wished away or ignored reappear, and the gag order on negativity is lifted. When telling the history of failure, however, one speaks of projects that fail to complete their aims. And because most politics is built on positive projects, especially those premised on pride and achievement, the spark of pure revolt rarely burns bright—but it can still be found.

A good place to search for the politics of fire that will engulf the soul is in the home. For, if "the soul is the prison of the body," then John Locke's dark room is not the prison only of the soul; it has served as a private place of torment particularly for women.[4]

As Claire Fontaine maintains, when Virginia Woolf illuminated the dark rooms of the social, all she found society to be was a conspiracy of men:

> conspiracies that sink the private brother, whom many of us have reason to respect, and inflate in his stead a monstrous male, loud of voice, hard of fist, childishly intent upon scoring the floor of the earth with chalk marks, within whose mystic boundaries human beings are penned, rigidly, separately, artificially; where, daubed red and gold, decorated like a savage with feathers he goes through mystic rites and enjoys the dubious pleasures of power and dominion while we, "his" women, are locked in the private house without share in the many societies of which his society is composed.[5]

So, even as the social is unfolded into the sprawling exteriority of cybernetic capitalism and scatters the markings, our home still serves, wherever it appears, as a private place of torment kept separate from the space of politics. Its violence remains unique because, unlike the worker whose spaces of production are public, and who thus has a social infrastructure widely written about by scholars of politics and labor, the housewife at home is marked by isolation and enforced privacy. And the symptoms of such incarceration are severe. As Adrienne Rich explains, "the worker can unionize, go out on strike; mothers are divided from each other in homes, tied to their children by compassionate bonds; our wildcat strikes have often taken the form of physical or mental breakdown."[6] Locked in such a lonely place, many captive souls can hardly imagine rebelling against anything or anyone except themselves.

It is precisely rebellion against oneself that may offer escape. And perhaps that liberation arrives through the failure and incompleteness generated by negative affects. The power of negative affects does not seem to draw from interiority, even if it appears so. Rather, the negative circulates through a radically exterior path. By way of Alfred Hitchcock's *The Birds*, recent queer theories suggest an escape from the violence of the home, especially after the forces of the negative takes flight. The advertising slogan Hitchcock devised, "The Birds is coming," gives the film a sexual dimension.[7] Taking the license to perform a sexualized reading, one must then consider how the birds enter the scene: as an excessive, interrupting force that upsets the heterosexual aim of the film.[8] In particular, not only are the film's lovebirds, Mitch and Melanie, distracted, but their attempts to consummate their love are prematurely disrupted by birds that keep coming without meaning or explanation; as Leo Bersani would note, the birds are not an enjoinment to come together.[9]

The queer birds do not operate at the level of identities that can be imitated, but rather as avatars of the otherwise-imperceptible unconscious, whose flight captures the frenetic power of the libido that circulates outside oneself, something so potent that it empties the home and threatens all imaginable futures (or at least those of the domestic couple). To be clear on how the antisocial force does not emerge from the pleasure of any particular identity, it is both impersonal, neither found in the dark recesses of the home nor patiently received while queuing in the waiting rooms of power. Its movement is found in the swarming birds that feed on the same destructive power that surges through us as the remains of the social are unfolded to be feasted on by capitalism. Such queerness is not possessed by some one group of people, no matter how deviant or transgressive, but is the undoing of any and all identities. Dependent on the antinormative power of unfolding, however, our cybernetic present is also opened to attack from the damaged, failed, or abandoned subjects that litter its crumbling streets.

Looking backward, the Sozialistische Patientenkollektiv (SPK; Socialist Patients' Collective), a militant group in Germany from the 1970s, provides an interesting example of the power of failure. According to the SPK, illness itself is resistance. Recounting a passage from antipsychiatrist D. G. Cooper, SPK found the potential for alienated life to make its mark on history:

> There is the story relayed by Bruno Bettelheim in *The Informed Letter* (1961) about a girl who, in an extreme moment of insight, recognized and broke out of one of the most formidable pieces of alienation in all human history. This girl was one of a group

of Jews queuing naked to enter the gas chamber. The SS officer supervising proceedings heard that she had been a ballet dancer and ordered her to dance. She danced, but gradually approached the officer and suddenly seized his revolver and shot him. Her fate was obvious and it was equally obvious that nothing she could do would alter the physical facts of the situation, namely the extermination of the group. But what she did was to invest her death with an intense personal meaning that at the same time expressed an historic opportunity that was tragically lost in the massified process of the extermination camps.[10]

Knowing that their own illnesses enabled them to make a similar intervention, SPK began "multi-focal expansion" based on the theory that every mentally ill person is a compact point of focus of society, and that the effects of illness can be released back into society through agitation.[11] Acutely aware that society was just as afraid of illness as violence, SPK undertook an exploration of how illness is "a contradiction within life, as the in-itself broken life."[12] They were confident that *"objectively,* illness, as defective (=not exploitable) labor power, is the gravedigger of capitalism," which can be stated geometrically in the formula that "illness = internal limitation of capitalism," suggesting that, if everyone falls acutely ill at once, it would collectively exhaust humanity's potential to take part in capitalist production.[13] Although they saw many different reactions to capitalist alienation, SPK imagined alienation to be fully generalized as a shared condition that makes every subject feel at least some illness of a sort and thus establishes a common strand for collective revolt.[14] Knowing that illness was not oriented exclusively toward revolt, they sought a dialectical explanation for its reactionary and progressive moments. In its reactionary moment, they argue that illness as a destroyed labor force is repaired in order to continue its exploitation by means of a healing process that only performs simple repairs in order to return the ability to work.[15] But in its progressive moment, the SPK cites Spinoza to note a process through which illness expands from the affects of ill people who realize their own suffering, using it to liberate their energies to transform from sufferers to activists, set free like "explosives activated that will smash the controlling system of permanent murder."[16] For SPK, agitation thus unlocks the progressive moment of illness as collective organization focused in protest.[17] SPK thus shows how numerous antagonisms populate this world. The concept of illness produced by SPK is still threatening, not in terms of a mass organization or even focalized expansion, but as an antagonism that spreads through the fabric of power.

In short, the positive task of the SPK is much like that of Feel Tank, which is to turn the inside out by reconnecting internal feelings to external problems in order to short-circuit their cause. On the level of the self, such a rewired circuitry externalizes negative affects and attenuates the destructive impact of interiority by distributing misery throughout the shared space of politics. But negative affects continue to burn cold when locked away inside the isolated depths of victimized subjects or even shared among accomplices like a million tiny daggers. In contrast, the SPK's externalization process intensifies negativity rather than dissipating it, cultivating the force of incapacity that channels power through refusal. In particular, it refuses to make the subject receptive to negative affects. And in refusing to bear even a single negative affect, this politics of fire turns the dark interiority into a weapon against its own very existence, consuming the pain of affliction as its cause recedes. Yet repressive powers lie ready to neutralize subjects that grow too intense. This was the downfall of SPK. After a few turbulent months in 1971, an SPK member committed suicide, dozens of SPK members were jailed, and SPK was evicted from the University of Heidelberg, which lead to the SPK dissolving to protect its patients.

As an organization, SPK unfortunately ended in failure, yet failure need not spell defeat. As the blistering storm beats down on subjects, it is destroying the interiority of subjects. Yet subjects willing to weather the storm have already given up the refuge of the soul and are undertaking a refusal of the interiorities imposed on them. Though they do not abandon interiorities completely, refusal allows these subjects to refashion their dark appetites of this world into weapons for its dissolution. The black clouds of patriarchy often transform their appetites into negative affects and the subsequent pain of isolation, paranoia, or depression, even when the subjects know the true cause of their suffering. It is those negative affects that form the basis of revolt. Troublemakers have shown that they can use their detachment to reorient blame, interruption, and destruction and direct the torrent within. Embracing such a struggle is painful, taxing, and promises to end in failure, but surviving in a hostile environment is not enough. The path out of the desert has never been more certain, for "it isn't running away they're afraid of. We wouldn't get far. It's those other escapes, the ones you can open in yourself, given a cutting edge."[18] As the severity of the weather increases, these opportunities for escape spread. With each additional downpour, a new reservoir of emotion collects. With time, the angel of history will look back on the refusal of interior in revolt as just another catastrophe. Let us hope that instead of horror or failure, it finds joy.

Part III
Fugitivity

What the world says to Blacks is "turn white or disappear."[1] The aesthetic demand was materialized in early American "lantern laws," which required all Blacks to illuminate themselves at night (noncompliance punishable by the spectacle of public torture) in an effort to supervise their movements to prevent insurrection.[2] The opening injunction can be stated more generally: submission or domination, absolute exposure or complete annihilation, infinity or nothingness. To be clear, the command is not the limited demand of "your land or your life" or "your labor or your life," in which dispossession is temporary and can be reversed through struggles for sovereignty or self-possession.[3]

What makes slavery and its afterlives so gratuitously violent is the unconditionality. Anti-Black violence attempts to make real a metaphysical point of no return: limitless surrender secured through ontological terror, waged against every fiber of Black being until there is nothing left to recover, no land, no body, no self.[4] The architecture behind this transformation is the white slave ship, a machine into which the bodies of humans go but from which only the cargo of flesh leaves.[5] The operations of the ship's hold was not a one-time event, but a still-unfolding disaster of containment grinding away in streets, offices, homes, prisons, and carceral landscapes not yet invented.[6]

By design, the activity of whiteness is the irrevocable severing of a slave from any foundation to a way of life. So what happens when there is no possible redress, as the path to being made whole has been irredeemably lost? This is a "problem" that can never be resolved through ethics (as humanism is premised on those free from bondage, once again using the slave as a conceptual scaffold to support the emancipation of others), culture (its terror is hidden by "cultural seeing"), or politics (a result of more vigorous action or hard work).[7] Rather, this intractable problem—the problem of "X"— is how the world keeps Blackness in a suspended state of captivity.[8]

Fugitivity explores a *"capacity* under captivity" that may not objectively exist but still subsists or insists.[9] Escaped-slave maroon communities offer both a model of association and a method for understanding fugitivity (as *marronage* means flight).[10] As a method, it means first throwing off basic categories, such as "community," leaving behind only furtive instances of "struggle, shared pleasures, transient forms of solidarity, and nomadic, oftentimes illegal, forms of association."[11] The maroon's escape spatially marks the crossroads of two movements. The first, the constant flow away from the plantation, best described as a "constant trickle, like water out of a leaking container."[12] The second, the cultivation of a wilds that creates "a very concrete rupture" that leaves "no place for compromise."[13] Even then, there is a risk of it simply being a "fantasy of flight" that prevents thought from staying "in the hold of the ship."[14] This is doubly true for whites, who project dreams of redemption onto Blackness alongside their fears, as if it were a refuge or invigorating tonic.

History is bursting with examples of whiteness laying claim to Blackness, not satisfied to simply possess the flesh of Blacks but feeling a need to collect their bodies of work as well. Hence it is worth mentioning my own position. I do not see myself as a maroon whose captivity implies slavery.

In a word, the trajectory I follow is the trajectory of "self-abolition."[15] As Kieran Aarons notes, that Black and white self-abolition does not converge in a point of interaction, but separates out into parallel lines, a separation that prevents "any model of solidarity premised on reciprocal recognition, on empathy, sympathy, or charity," or even "common interests."[16] The tenuous commonality between the two is found in an absolute refusal of sovereignty and a hostility toward this world. To maintain the delicate balance of this mutual coincidence, I make no claim on Black life.

But rather, through the principles of guerrilla-without-guerrillas, I reveal and attack the white social infrastructure that confines Blackness.[17] The subsequent guerrilla techniques include the masking of Black faces in images to prevent their apprehension, the construction of an underground network for circulating material away from prosecutorial eyes, attacking the putative neutral evidentiary mode of photography, and striking against the white spectacular economy of exposure.

Chapter 13
Uprising

The 2015 Baltimore Uprising: A Teen Epistolary began as a collation-in-print of tweets from Black Baltimore teens during the aftermath of the police killing of Freddie Gray in the back of a van. Later, it became a thick pocketbook, trading the high contrast Xerox-aesthetic cover for a vibrant full-color one. The front depicts an active scene. Two young Black men mugging for the camera jump out as the subjects of the photograph. Postproduction, a black rectangle has been placed over the eyes of each to partially obscure their faces. But their grins shine through. The man closer to the camera is wearing a black sweatshirt with the hood pulled up, sitting on the rear seat of a moped. His driver has stopped, body twisted behind himself with phone held high, snapping a shot of the scene behind them. Captured in his lens is a white sedan, doors flung open, stopped awkwardly at an angle in the street. A cop car. The other man emerges from it with some objects in hand. He seems to be dancing on the broken glass, crumpled police-line tape, and debris like a stage under his feet. Many other people are around, some in the foreground probing the corners of the jail-on-wheels. A large apartment complex hangs in the background, against which a different series of people are going about their business, some running across the street and others perhaps waiting on buses. At the end of the horizon, large plumes of black smoke rise from the fiery shell of another car.

The rest of the book is tweets rendered in ink and paired with quick photographs, editorially transformed through the additive techniques of arrangement and visual overlay, embodying what Christina Sharpe calls "Black visual/textual annotation and redaction."[1] The first page, a viral tweet from the day of Freddie Gray's death, is followed on the next page by another tweet from the same day, depicting three teens literally and figuratively expressing "fuck the police." All of the elements making up a tweet are present, such as a profile image, timestamp, and retweet and like counts, all visible except one: the @-handle has been blacked out with a rectangle as if redacted. The pictures of Gray are taken from TV news and an online video of his arrest. In the first, he stares into the camera with intensity. The contrast on the other makes it difficult to see anything but the pained grimace on his face as he is being brutalized by three white cops. The teens in the next picture pose resolutely in a selfie, but part of their expression is missing as the identifying characteristics of their eyes are obscured by a large black rectangle.

The tweets quickly build to the four days that take up over a hundred pages, the vast majority of the book, and the Black redactions continue. Display names, profile pictures, tweets, and attached images stream across the pages. Full of humor and punctuated with emojis, the teens spread their anger at the police for being murderers, pride in their peers for standing up for Black people, jabs about their city becoming like *Grand Theft Auto* or *The Purge*, worry for friends getting caught up in the frenzy, frustration over prom disruptions, and shock over the intensity of the events grow in the first two major days of tweets. Black handles and Black faces in attached images remain blacked out. The exception being non-Black people, whose identities the "author" of the book considers unworthy of redaction, images of Freddie Gray that have taken on a different status, and the occasional appearance of a Black face in a black mask. In a selfie toward the beginning, a young man in a balaclava, cap, and hoodie poses on the stoop of a house. Black skin and black mask, he appears at the heart of the impending state of emergency.

The black-out spreads over the next two days as the teens become increasingly fascinated by a couple things: white mainstream media coverage of the events and the crumbling spectacle of commodity culture.[2] A middle-aged Black man in a knit cap leans into the frame of a CNN live broadcast, raising a mix-tape CD in a black case up to the camera, its whiteness paralleling the talking head but offering an alternative soundtrack. Later that day, a masked Black man leans on the shoulder of the same CNN live reporter, his presence so dynamic it steals the scene—his silent performance drowning out the idle chatter of the reporter. Images of consumer goods begin to appear with talk of looting. Once currency begins to loosen its grip as the mediating force, other social relations emerge. Humor arrives as one guy is carrying a couple shopping baskets as if all he wanted was groceries for the week. Interest in soda, liquor, fashion items, and small appliances tie together a feeling that rather minor things are kept from them through collective violence. They do not seem to revel in the goods themselves. Their shared glee springs from their sudden access to the actual things they had previously known only through slick prepackaged images.

The youth's reclamation of the Black mask is doubly important as a strike against the long spectacular economy of "White skin, Black masks." Even before the conventions of blackface minstrelsy solidified, it seems that white men in Europe were fascinated with dressing up as Black women. Natalie Davis recalls events of "festive inversion" in the 1760s and 1770s such as the armed Whiteboys in Ireland who wore dresses and blackened their faces for a decade to forcefully "restore the ancient commons" (in addition to other acts of popular justice), and peasants in Beaujolais who similarly appeared as Black women to attack surveyors sent by a new landlord.[3] These events served as ambivalent displays in that they not only reinforced violent social realities but also offered up imaginary alternatives to them, acting as "safety valves" as well as creative means of cultural criticism.[4] The ritualistic inversion of social values perhaps only lasting a night, but still presenting a moment when women or Blacks are "on top."[5]

The problem with whites using Blackness and femaleness to intervene is that it was only possible by first transforming them into a prop. The obvious thrill for men in donning either came from the assumed exclusion of Blackness and femaleness from meaningful participation in civic life.[6] The disguise allowed men to enjoy the pleasures of transgressive disruption, to roleplay as the suffering while simultaneously avoiding the consequences of their actions. Not only did concealment allow a convenient way to deflect blame rather directly, but the social politics of identity provided an abstract mechanism to dismiss unruliness as precisely the sort of abject behavior to be expected of Black women. Costume served as license for men to adopt the characteristics of unruly women already on display in carnivals and games, expressing the sexual power of the female and its connection to fertility, community, and truth-telling they usually repudiated.[7]

These anxieties over female power that consumed white men carried over into minstrelsy, resulting in a "suspiciously draconian punitiveness" reflected in grotesque sexual depictions of the feminine.[8] There is a queer dimension in that such exaggerated sexuality unfixed gender coordinates, allowing performers to insert homosexual subtext or indulge in a general polymorphous blurring of bodies, but it extended only as far as it served as an opportunity for white men to either coopt the "unruliness" by reasserting misogynist representations or lend credibility to the stability of their own identities by contrast.[9]

Chapter 14
Self-Abolition

How might one draw the lines of lineage behind *The 2015 Baltimore Uprising: A Teen Epistolary*, a zine-become-book ripped straight from the internet? Does it not partake in the same sort of ultra-white social infrastructure that underwrote white conceptualist Kenneth Goldsmith's public reading of Michael Brown's autopsy as poetry? Does it redact documents like the American FBI and CIA did, whitewashing history by erasing people a second time, even after they were targeted and killed? Or does it partake in a different form of racial appropriation, like that of M. NourbeSe Philip's *Zong!* and Claudia Rankine's *Citizen*—the former grappling with the fact that Africans were barred from being named in a legal text (forever trapped below), the latter struggling to dedicate pieces *in memoriam*—with the full knowledge that it will continue to go on and on (dissolving to white)?[1]

Uprising is a strategic intervention in and against Twitter's two modes: *fugitivity* and *prosecution*. Tweets offer an unexpected spin on the radical slogan "circulate the struggle." The phrase expresses the motive force of movement behind an autonomist theory, that there are cycles of struggle. It also gestures toward the importance of struggles in the sphere of circulation: struggles over the exchange of commodities that make life livable, struggles over the streets and other infrastructure through which bodies stretch out and move, and struggles over what can be seen and heard. The code behind Twitter was born from one of these struggles. Its first iteration, a mass SMS service named TXTMob was used by radical protestors to coordinate their movements in the streets of Boston and New York as they sought to evade police containment and disrupt the 2004 Democratic and Republican conventions.[2] Signaling a capture by corporate interests indicative of the whole "web 2.0" revolution, the hacker ethos behind protest tech lost out to the entrepreneurial spirit of start-up culture as TXTMob became "a model to be copied / learned from" to create Twitter (Evan Henshaw-Plath serving as a bridge between the two), a platform that would gain the reputation as "a pressure cooker for the worst of humanity" for how it enabled misogynist trolls.[3] But Twitter would still be used in further protests to coordinate activity, such as a series of upheavals in Moldova, Iran, Tunisia, Egypt, and Ukraine that would be dubbed "Twitter Revolutions."[4]

Police reactions to Twitter have been far from sanguine. Attempts to use it in the United States as anything other than a promotional tool have ended in a series of antiterrorism arrests, including preemptive arrests of the anticonventional comms center before the 2008 Republican Convention and the arrest of a Queens social worker who reposted the movements of police from a public police scanner to Twitter during the 2009 G-20 summit in Pittsburgh. Such an aggressive police response is not unique to Twitter, as similar antagonisms have developed alongside other technology booms. For instance, there were aggressive police responses to "copwatch" actions that began in the 1990s, in which crews armed with newly available videotaping equipment intervened in police encounters. And as smart phones began boasting ever-more-powerful cameras in the early 2010s, police began loudly complaining about a "war on police" after individuals started taking unplanned recordings of police interactions, soon coming together over the Twitter hashtag #BlackLivesMatter.[5] Moreover, the police have eagerly incorporated related technology into their own arsenals. Protesters now have to assume that police are deploying StingRay phone trackers, which capture identifying information and even messages by getting phones to connect to simulated cell towers, and that forms of self-surveillance like body-cams may only empower police to use additional violence.[6]

Considering broader questions about the nature of Twitter as a medium, one might ask whether, perhaps, the genealogy of Twitter from protest tool to corporate platform reveals something significant about its operations. For instance, what happens when a fugitive tool for evading capture is made prosecutorial, replacing movement with the furnishing of evidence? Does the shift in registers contaminate the activist dream of freedom through recourse to the force of law inherent to Twitter? Is this why Twitter has served as such a hospitable environment for harassment, dragging, and call-out? And how do these captive functions echo the anti-Black violence at the heart of the policing?

Even as *Uprising* serves as an abbreviated version of the fugitive dream of freedom, it offers precious little in terms of specifying a program, party, or a people. Perhaps, like TXTMob, its contribution to freedom is tied to its capacity for movement, in the practical sense of evading police capture and in moments of outright rebellion. As I write, similar technologies (both analog and digital) are no doubt playing a role in the streets of Free Kurdistan, Hong Kong, and Ecuador. Over a few days, my feeds were filled with videos of anarcho-feminist Kurdish YPG fighters (Yekîneyên Parastina Gell; "People's Protection Units") blasting Rage Against the Machine as their convoy speeds to meet the Turkish invasion, images of the multitudes of indigenous Ecuadorians who are bringing the austerity government to its knees by flooding its city streets, and story after story of Hong Kong ground to a halt by mass tech-savvy disruptions. Though none are a result of the same anti-Black violence that pervades the United States, together, they make up the current cycle of struggle against this world. Unifying them is not a technical platform but something far more aesthetic: they form a mobile block of sensation that inspires, provokes, and insists on revolution.

Formal aesthetic considerations of *Uprising* expand on its fugitive form. Its author/s, for instance, appears as fugitive. They appear underground, on the margins, or not at all, much like the subject of Devin Allen's famous *Time* magazine cover, a masked man chased by a mass of riot police wielding bludgeons, with the headline, "America, ~~1968~~ 2015: What Has Changed. What Hasn't."[7] Like the event itself, neither the cover nor the contents of *Uprising* reveals a name, only that of the already dead: Freddie Gray. A familiar approach to determining its purpose would be to identify its author, but its cover reveals none. A few details emerge after some strategic searching online, all of which track back to a project titled "Research and Destroy New York City." The project's webpage includes a series of anticop materials bearing the punk-rock anarchist aesthetics that adorn a mixture of creative and research-based publications (from "Cops Hate Cops" to "A Brief History of the 23rd Precinct: For the 45th Anniversary of the East Harlem Riots/Rebellion"). None bear a name. Their inspiration is likely a mix of those mid-century intellectuals who proclaimed that to bear a name is to already be marked for death and practical concerns over the extreme risk of being associated with written work that targets the police. "I am no doubt not the only one who writes in order to have no face," Michel Foucault wrote; "do not ask who I am and do not ask me to remain the same: leave it to our bureaucrats and our police to see that our papers are in order."[8] But there are also hints of the "social death" behind the process of making a person into a slave, which includes the disruption of meaningful kinship, the stripping of social status through generalized dishonor, and gratuitous violence for its own sake.[9]

With *Uprising* failing to bear the signature of a name, some might indulge their prosecutorial impulses. Many might perpetuate the unfair association of its aesthetics with white middle-class tastes, unfair because many of the most significant anarchists and punks in large cities, especially New York, Chicago, and Los Angeles, have been nonwhite and working class. Moreover, if the author/s were remaining consistent with their own editorial decisions, then the redaction of their own identity remains hidden ("barred") like the Black people of the book. Such anonymization allows the editor/s to participate in the same freedom extended to its Black subjects, preventing the reader from fixing authorial intent on a particular individual in a way that might shut down its fugitive movement, thus allowing the criminal actions depicted in the book to spread without the identities being stopped for lengthy interrogation. Even if the author/s are not Black—not inhabiting a structural position of Blackness that renders them criminal as an ontological matter of existence—the willful act of publishing the book contingently marks them as criminal accomplices like John Brown or David Gilbert; and even if they still enjoy access to the benefits of whiteness, by proliferating inflammatory anticop literature, they could have some of them revoked at decisive moments as a consequence of their attacks on white solidarity.

Beyond authorial identity lies a consideration of the central technique of the book, the "screencap" (screen capture as in a computer "screenshot," "screen-grab," or a movie still). Paraphrasing what has been said about cinema, media either has an effect or does nothing at all. This is doubly true for the screencap.[10] Photography always relied on the operations of a camera obscura, an enduring metaphor for how images obscure the underlying social relations, systems of meaning, and presumptions of transparency.[11] The graphic user interface of the modern computer contributes an even greater ideological trick: it conceals complexes of gender, labor, and power even more abstractly as changes in voltage across a silicon chip.[12]

Just as the name "captivity" itself speaks of capture, so captivity's long shadow closely associates the screencap with the prosecutorial mode of media. The screencap's carceral logic does not always feed subjects into the prison-industrial complex, but rather traps them in a public matrix of self-appointed judges, juries, and executioners. Consider the ways that radicals have used screenshots. Antifa doxxers routinely screencap white-supremacist social media; sometimes they just circulate it amongst themselves to know how to keep safe, but just as often they (rightfully) send it to employers or landlords to upend their enemies' lives. A number of friends keep screen "grabs" of stomach-churning comments on their feeds by well-known TERFs (trans-exclusionary radical feminists) or examples of abuse by lefty men (such as harassing or creepy direct messages), making them available to friends and allies so they know which "feminists" cannot be trusted. However, a far more common use of doxxing, denial-of-service attacks, and the circulation of private digital documents emerged in "Gamergate": massive crowd-based harassment of women and people of color.

Public pushback to these actions has gained steam in the criticism of "cancel culture" (though not new, it being just another entry in the a succession of ginned-up culture wars over "trigger warnings," "political correctness," and more). Unique is the role played by section 230 of the U.S. Communications Decency Act that prevents digital platforms from being held liable for the speech of their users. Corporate platforms have slowly started to adopts terms of service that allow them to self-regulate content, though it is largely treated as an issue of public relations and brand management. The two major exceptions to voluntary regulation are telling: copyright and FOSTA-SESTA (the expansive 2018 anti-sex trafficking law broadly opposed by sex workers). The first demonstrates how deeply tied the law is to enforcing capitalism property rights. The second encodes sexual paranoia deep into the legal response to online content, encouraging platforms to prohibit sexual content rather than distinguish exploitive from nonexploitive uses.

Given platforms' general hands-off approach, most prosecutorial media operates outside the law and even the voluntary regulation of platforms. It serves as an alternative path to the relief offered by courts and the mechanically abstracted decision of online content moderators. The prosecution proceeds by way of publicity. It does not render legal judgment, but rather one stands accused of violating norms in a perceived transgression of one's place in society. The accused's actions are made to appear so provocative that it only seems right for others to extrajudicially put them in their place (and restore the social order). Prosecutorial media thus takes part in the conservative pleasure of reasserting norms against those who violate them, even when used toward even progressive ends.

If one wanted to avoid the prosecutorial impulse suggested by the term "screen capture," the more colloquial "screen-grab" is hardly any better. Both the Romantic *captura* and the Proto-Indo-European **ghrebh* mean to reach, take, seize, rob, and possess, allowing the words to retain the same basic sense as they evolved through a variety of languages, casting an associative net over agricultural goods, animals, and human bondage. Finally, the "screen shot" references a technique taken from photography, a field in which the camera has long been treated like a gun. As recorded in *The Oxford English Dictionary*, the "snapshot" originated a few decades before the daguerreotype, from discussions of hunting birds and rabbits so speedily that deliberate aim was not possible. On the material level, early moving-image cameras used a gunstock and a revolving cylinder, such as Étienne-Jules Marey's infamous chronophotographic gun, which piggybacked on the machine-gun technologies of the time. The screenshot further weaponizes the gaze without the assistance of a camera and its trigger, with the virtual gestures of point and click enabling a user to "reach out and touch" a targeted area of digital space. This seizure renders it possessable like an artifact, now a delimited object for use as evidence, a visual representation of the instructions and permissions of a particular device, a flattened carving of the layered graphic interfaces, translated into a shareable format like a jpeg image, preserving an instant for as long as the image remains on a drive somewhere. Evidence-in-waiting.

Are there ways of seeing that shift images out of their default captive mode? The task is especially fraught for whites such as myself, who, as bell hooks argues in "Eating the Other," are prone to desiring Blackness through the structure of either denial or fantasy.[13] The danger takes the form of a consumerist cannibalism that decontextualizes Blackness by reducing it to exchange, a particularly prescient worry in the case of grabbing tweets from Black teens for circulation.[14] Digital platforms only exacerbate the issue, as critics have warned in essays about identity tourism and high tech blackface in virtual worlds.[15] Twitter's corporate architecture is similarly built for appropriation through association, especially in how it awards status as derived from commanding a wide list of "followers" who hungrily consume others' content. Tweets about the Baltimore rebellion, for instance, proved irresistible for the voracious appetites of news junkies, concern trolls, and politicians looking to score points. Some even fell for a series of blackface tweets from members of the self-styled "enforcement branch of GamerGate" that proudly identifies as racist.[16] Grabbing images from the 2011 London riots and blogs about consumer shopping hauls, they posted under the hashtag #BaltimoreLootCrew as part of a campaign to do "anything that will help paint African Americans in a bad light."[17]

A growing number of scholars are asking what it means for abolitionists to engage these images, especially if they are not themselves

Black. Alexandra Juhasz writes that the surfeit of images of Black death that now circulate after police shootings challenges the "politics of visibility" that was previously "an obvious strategy."[18] Viewing practices have a long history of witness, activism, and bearing the weight of trauma for Black America, but also globally as a response to mass disappearances and genocide. But Juhasz also suggests other practices of viewing: don't look, look askance, look at death, and look at death's platforms. Each practice of looking in its own way calls the same thing into question: a libidinal economy of violence fueled by the emotional currency of Black death. Here, Saidiya Hartman's argument that breaking through white indifference with "shocking accounts of whipping, rape, mutilation, and suicide" to win empathetic identification serves only to further extend the economy of chattel slavery.[19] Instead of setting the captive free, such identification possesses the slave's body once again through a "projection of one's feelings upon or into the object of property."[20] Whiteness becomes further secured through feelings of "comfort, consolation, contentment, ease, happiness, pleasure, and satisfaction."[21] The risk is that it is consumed like the "riot porn" of the antiglobalization era, in which the filmed cat-and-mouse game of summit-crashers and police was set to a soundtrack and spread across the internet. Though sometimes breaking the spell of capital, it also functioned as wish-fulfillment for many who never stepped foot in the streets. Looped footage of anti-Black police violence contains the same risks, spectacularized as captive media, making Black flesh a sentimental resource, a property of enjoyment.

Uprising avoids scenes of subjection, choosing not to replay the moments of racial terror that would lead to Gray's death. Especially when taken out of the circulatory system of social media, the book's tweets attest to very different practices of looking. Its pages contain a range of tactics Nicholas Mirzoeff has seen in the Black Lives Matter movement more generally: persistent looking; copresence; hands up, don't shoot; the die-in; redacted spaces of nonappearance; and copresent refusal.[22] But such a description misses something essential about the aesthetic practices of the book, which express something profound about Black sociality. They contain something Huey Copeland finds in Arthur Jafa's 2016 film *Love Is the Message,*

The Message Is Death: Black rhetorical savvy in encounters with the spectacle.[23] In particular, an aesthetic decision that "holds out only fleeting depictions of individual subjects, as if to hedge against the visual capture of Black folks, while throwing light—and shade—on viewers' implication in the digital ecologies through which those images circulate and dis/appear."[24]

With the *LMMD* film, Jafa achieves his result through formal mixing meant to disrupt art-house conventions (public/personal, low-fi/high-res) by interjecting "the poor image."[25] The poor image is a viral object that mutates as it is shared, downloaded, converted, re-encoded, edited, subbed, annotated, collaged, color-corrected, and uploaded over and over again, accumulating layers of "neurosis, paranoia, and fear" as everyone in the crowd makes it their own.[26] It is not a media of expression in the revelatory mode that sees itself as giving voice to some hidden truth of experience that can be found only by cutting through mediation in order to gain an immediate proximity to the real thing.[27] The poorness of these images is just as much a function of thwarting police-like attempts to find evidence in the indiscernible as it is about cheapness as an attack on slick corporate hi-fi kitsch and the virtues of expression, distinction, and representation.[28] In contrast to captive media's giant anthropological machine found in mediums like identification photography, the poor image offers up a "negativity with no use" that sabotages attempts to discern "psychological depth, motives, and personal history," swapping them for frivolous laughter, ecstasy, and luxury.[29]

Similar complexity cannot help but spill out of *Uprising*'s pages, with anger at the city and police . . . accompanied by frustrations over a cancelled prom . . . mixed with an overwhelming sense of confusion . . . juxtaposed with proud support for confrontations with the police . . . knit together with deep expressions of fear . . . followed by threaded debates about strategy . . . beside jokes about a neighbor looting the corner store . . . coupled with insightful cracks about commodity culture . . . compounded by biting condemnations of the day's events . . . succeeded by shrewd critiques of the media spectacle . . . next to fretting over future police repression . . . joined by genuine worry about people's safety . . .

Uprising's form proves to be a part of its fugitivity. What began as a series of tweets became the physical form of a zine and then a book (which has still not been made into an e-book or easily circulated PDF). By removing the tweets from circulation, it withdraws them from the whole circulatory economy of adjudication that fuels the online outrage machine. This attests to a political power that only grows with distance, connecting it to other circuits of struggle. It does not yearn for the transparency or universality that have historically been used to extend captivity, but for freedom. The novelty of *Uprising*, then, is its creative act of moving the conversation offline. The book transmuted the database into the codex, taking the scrolling mosaic of a digital feed and transforming it into the pages of a printed book. This is not to say that the struggle no longer circulates, but its participants can no longer be grabbed one-at-a-time. Each entry seems to make sense only as part of a whole, its form resisting the captive isolation of grabbing a tweet in a single snapshot. The event is enveloped in the synoptic whole of a bound volume.

At its most insistent, *Uprising* transforms from documentary into kindling for sparking the event of revolt—that moment when rules no longer apply, when the problem of "what is allowed?" ceases to be important, and the question of freedom becomes an issue of force. It is a refrain echoed in a text sent to the anarchist journal *Hostis,* "a journal of negation," whose name is a call "to be dangerous in a time when antagonism has dissipated."[30] As editors of its third issue, dedicated to the topic of the slogan "Fuck the Police," we received the following poem that issues threats instead of begging for permission. Which is to say, it insists on unconditional abolition.

It was submitted it with the following note:

What up *Hostis,*

This is a thing I made while watching the facebook live of the first night of rioting in Charlotte, NC (and reading the unfortunate comments). I guess the intention behind it is to create space for anti-cop/afro-pessimist leaning conversation among Black people who aren't necessarily anarchist or afro-pessimist, or whatever. If y'all are into it, don't put a name on it, just use it I guess.

Black Skin, Black Masks

I'm writing to you
Because I love you
And I want you to
Be free

We don't need them
When we try to fit into their
shit
We fill ourselves with passion

It's better to flip the table
Than to Smile
And drink more poison

The first cops in america
were slave catchers
They aren't corrupt
when they kill us
They're just doing their job
Confront them to defeat them, not to change them

Be careful in the street
Have a friend around to watch your back
Tell peeps to watch out, not to chill

Not everyone is trying to protest
Some people on the warpath
They right to be mad
If you won't join them
Stay out their way

"No Justice, No Peace!" is a
threat
Don't say it if you don't mean it

The poison is still hurting you
If you're upset that they call us
Animals
Criminals
Savages

We might have to
Burn this shit to the ground

Chapter 15
Searing Flesh

The branding of criminals was extensive in Western Europe and the colonies well into the eighteenth century. The practice literally wrote crime onto the body, categorizing the body into an archive. As a media theorist, Simone Browne performs a reading of Hank Willis Thomas's B®*anded* series, which is about "how Black bodies were branded as a sign of ownership during slavery, and how their descendants' bodies are branded today through corporate advertising."[1] The series' images jump right off the magazine page, including many famous athletes and musicians, like O. J. Simpson showing his third leg in a pair of cowboy boots, Dennis Rodman beefcaking in nothing but a milk mustache, and Lionel Ritchie seductively offering a line of beauty products wiped of their identifying labels, and Thomas pairs each with a title that reveals their hidden semiotics—"Dingo," "Gotten," "Something to Believe In."[2] In some images, the usual identifying features of the body are completely obscured, stripped of anything but fingers and some under-nail dirt (held in contrast as interlaced with a feminine white one, made distinct through red nail polish: "Jungle Fever"), shirtless upper bodies of two basketball players (but faces concealed as one goes in for a dunk on the hanging goal of a noose: "And One"), a close mesh of a dozen legs bent at the knee to produce a tight chevron ("Your Skin Has the Power to Protect You"), and a large greytone, bust-like head and shoulders cropped vertically at the face, light gleaming off a scarified Nike swoosh running across the side of their bald head ("Branded Head").[3] Browne uses this work to illustrate the concept of "epidermalization" as "literally the inscription of race on the skin" that separates a body from the world through specificity, dissection, fixity, and imprisonment.[4]

Understanding the body as a medium inscribed by punishment, Nietzsche says that "if something is to stay in the memory it must be burned in: only that which never ceases to hurt stays in the memory."[5] Through a "fearful mnemotechnics," the historical record is made through a painful marking on the flesh that is strong enough to overcome forgetting. And it is within this economy of pain and pleasure that consciousness is born, most fundamentally as the awareness of one's responsibilities and a memory of the painful cost of forgetting them.[6]

Thomas's 2013 sculpture *Raise Up* raises questions how the body is further transubstantiated. Ten brass figures reach out of a white pedestal, facing away with their hands held up above their heads. Why are their faces obscured? Perhaps it is a lineup (but none of the hands are flat against the wall). They could be at a prayer service (though that is not reason enough to face them away from us). After Officer Darren Wilson's shooting of Michael Brown in 2014, it would certainly be easy to imagine it paying homage to the activist "Hands Up, Don't Shoot!" A 2016 casting of the sculpture would be installed at The National Memorial for Peace and Justice in Alabama, no longer facing a wall, their faces partially visible, their eyes closed as if searching for calm in a time of terror.

Yet there is an even more layered series of references. The basis for Thomas's sculpture is a famous image by South African photographer Ernest Cole, who snuck a camera into a paper lunch bag to get a shot of Black miners stripped nude and undergoing a medical examination.[7] Over a dozen Black bodies are put on display. Facing the wall, they are made to assume a position of vulnerability, both by exposing their body through nudity and also through the inability to meet the gaze of their observer. Stretching to the ceiling until the muscle on their backs ripple, even in the moment the image was taken, it is apparent that their bodies were posed by command. Through this photo and others, Cole's 1967 photo-essay book *House of Bondage* provided one of the first frank depictions of life under apartheid to readers in the United States and the United Kingdom.

Cole worked for nearly a decade as one of the first Black photojournalists in South Africa, stopped often by the police, especially as he photographed frequent passbook arrests of Blacks skirting official zones meant to contain them.[8] His documentation is an index of the overlapping power of the law, images, survival, and fugitivity. On one occasion he was stopped, the police assuming he was using stolen equipment; he defended his actions by saying he was completing a documentary on juvenile delinquency, and keen to unlock the criminological potential, the police sought to enroll him in their activities.[9] He then realized he needed to flee the country, moving to the United States where he died in exile in 1990, a week before the release of Nelson Mandela.

A comparison of Thomas's sculpture to Cole's photograph affirms something specific about the photography's capacity to capture: photo-graphy, literally the drawing of light onto the body of a photo-sensitive plate or paper, mysteriously transfers the surfaces of a body from one medium to another. Thomas's remediation demonstrates that identification is already incidental to the treatment of their bodies. Having been reduced to laboring flesh, the medical gaze treats them as ultimately substitutable. Only one set of shoulders can be seen. The violence crystalized in the sculpture exceeds the explanatory power of Marxism and its theory of labor exploitation. The bronze, as a metal similar to the gold in the famous mines of South Africa, is a physical embodiment of the violent separation of the bodies from themselves. Each figure is submerged so deeply in the white stone base that their torsos, necks, and mouths are sliced off. Metal and stone mark a fundamental *dehiscence* that makes up Blackness—the medical term for the rupture of a suture that opens up a wound, as Fred Moten has remarked elsewhere.[10]

Chapter 16
Captive Media

The contemporary landscape of *captive media* is obvious to those who experience the effects of "the New Jim Code."[1] "You can't buy a bag of chips in Harlem without being surveilled," matter-of-factly reports hacker Matthew Mitchell, accompanied by the observation that this community never gives him the tired "I have nothing to hide" response.[2] He gives this as the reason for founding CryptoHarlem, a meetup "for Black people in Harlem, who are over-policed and heavily surveilled."[3] He further explores the deep time of captive media in a 2017 presentation at Eyeo, building on Simone Browne's insurgent genealogy of surveillance, its logic buried within popular songs, the slave ship, plantations, runaway advertisements, the census, social etiquette, ledgers, public dances, branding, and more.[4]

Remediating the conventions of Black feminist scholarship for the tech talk, Mitchell challenges the audience with a comparative argument.[5] He notes a whole range of techniques. First, how transatlantic slavery serialized Black bodies, cataloguing them as numbers in a database that sorted them by common demographics including "complexions." Second, the surveillance of overseers, whose detailed journaling of daily activities transformed into the techniques of observation done by closed-circuit television cameras. Additionally, he shows how the forced photography by race scientists to construct anthropological theories based on the Black body created the framework for contemporary biometrics, from fingerprint scanning to facial recognition. And finally, he discusses lantern laws as a form of spatially tracking Black bodies that is now performed in big-data programs used for practices like "predictive policing." His conclusion is that this dizzying assortment of technologies enforces a new a cyber Jim Crow and its false charity of "poor doors," against which he encourages self-education as a means to disconnect from these systems of digital captivity. But perhaps it may be equally important to consider Browne's proposal: if digital spaces tend to privilege white users in facial recognition or other surveillant layers, it may be more subversive to remain undetected rather than fight for visibility.[6]

The complicity of certain mediums goes even deeper. Photography, for instance, has long been a form of captive media.[7] Capture is essential to the formal dimension of the white infrastructure of photography.

There is perhaps no more spectacular example of photography's charged exchange in Black bodies than lynching postcards. Lynching developed alongside photography. The putative democratization of images exploded at the same time as anti-Black violence looked to reinforce the post-Reconstruction color line. Photography's contribution was to extend the single event to an open-ended continual disinterment "of the corpse for indiscriminate viewing."[8] Spectatorship culture at that time included gawking at destruction, typified by "Coney Island realism" exhibits of disaster and death, such as Thomas Edison's filmed execution of Topsy the elephant (named after the disorderly slave girl from *Uncle Tom's Cabin*).[9] Lynching played a hand in similar technological innovations, with prominent lynchings taking place on stage at early movie theaters, the recurring early genre of the "chase film" that ends in a lynching (one of the first synchronizations of sound and image was a screening of a lynching that predated later systems of early cinema).[10]

The circulation of lynching photographs have always followed the media inventions of the day. In contrast to the post-Reconstruction popularity of "coon pictures," lynching photographs were circulated discretely (especially after lynching postcards were banned by the U.S. mail).[11] Yet this partial concealment is only what lends the transgression such an enormous charge and facilitates disavowal.[12] Signaling the contradictions that arise from this, white women in the 1890s were prohibited from boxing films but visible participants in lynchings and the circulation of their photographs.[13] In the time between the daguerreotype and Kodak snapshots, Americans collected photocards. Photographers etched their names in the images to make claim to them as their property, establishing a professional–client relationship and preventing other from taking credit. The invention of the Kodak camera changed the composition, making the images more spontaneous, rapid, or serial. Though harder to read, they were easier to take and circulate. As photography became more personal, so did lynching images.

Photography's formal conventions influenced how lynchings themselves were organized. The infrastructure of anti-Black mob violence shifted to accommodate the new technology, reorganizing the composition to fit photography's visual field. Public desecration was not enough; already-existing and new infrastructure was erected so that the bodies of victims could be made vertical to enhance the spectacle.[14] Lynching photography also grew distinct from other death photography. Not partaking in mourning photography's works to secure empathetic identification for individuals or national tragedies, lynching photographs engage in what Jacqueline Goldsby calls "scopic aggression," which is meant to spread to the viewer.[15] Through the proximity of the body to the camera, scopic aggression either zooms in to fill the frame with the wounds inflicted by whites or zooms out to catch the mass fervor of the white crowd.[16] Whereas the victim is left to occupy dead space, vanishing into the void through abjection, empty of speech, action, or will.[17]

Tina D. Campt's *Listening to Images* begins with previously discarded Ugandan photo-portraits exhibited in a long line around the white box of a grave-like gallery in Chelsea.[18] The faces of the images have been cut out, opening a white void set against saturated red and blue backgrounds, the cuts bearing a violence not unlike that of Lucio Fontana's slashed canvases. What strikes Campt most is that the folded hands, dark blazers, colorful dresses, and oversized shirts in the portraits bear all of the traces of identification photography—a ubiquitous technology of postconflict Uganda in which ID photos are essential for successfully navigating institutions, work, governmental authorities, and financial transactions.[19]

The absence of faces reveals something both practical and conceptual. Practically, the cuts demonstrate how the face usually draws viewers into photographs, and without them, the deliberate staging of the scene is drawn to the forefront.[20] Conceptually, the yawning white void comments on the administrative powers that organize the whole scene. This mode of photography is turned toward judgement, as Ariella Azoulay would argue, in which spectators do not question the responsibility for what is seen in the photograph, instead engaging photographs exclusively through their intended effects.[21] Through light, the photographic apparatus tries to disclose each face as if identification resided on its surface. Such technology is a consequence of the investment in the putative transparency of the body. Its purpose here is to bring the body into the light. The absolute limit of photography is complete exposure. Campt wonders whether fugitivity can also be found in this stillness, leading her to ask whether it is possible to hear the quiet refusal of Black faces as they reject access to their bodies?

The photographic interpretation of Blackness has long had to contend with Roland Barthes's now-canonical example of "form" in *Mythologies*, which is secured through his reading of the photograph on a 1955 cover of *Paris Match*. In it, Barthes reports, an African child in military dress is saluting the French flag.[22] Two crucial details remain absent: first, the flag itself (we have to be told that it is the target of the salute by Barthes, who mentions it simply in passing), and second, the occasion (only the magazine itself explains: a military parade of four thousand in Paris to celebrate France's colonial empire). Barthes is breezily critical of the photograph that he ran across "at the barber's," confident that he could "see very well" that it offered a mythic alibi for colonialism in a visual code of devotion to empire that appropriates the native body.[23] Choosing not to render anything whole, Barthes instead argues that the Black subject of the photograph lives on only by first being amputated of everything but the pure presence of existence.[24] This is further complicated by Barthes's own admission that his own homosexuality is something that "society will not tolerate," rendering him "provisional, revocable, insignificant, inessential, in a word irrelevant," ultimately "nothing."[25]

Anchored by Barthes's canonical reading of the photograph, filmmaker Vincent Meessen sought to give "new life" to the image through a film, *Vita Nova* (2009). Meessen's project began by seeking out Diouf Birane, named as the subject, in Burkina Faso to recover the subjectivity stolen through the photograph. But Birane had died decades ago in Senegal. However, Meessen was able to find a schoolmate who had appeared in other photographs in the issue, Issa Kaboré. The film opens with the demons of colonialism being conjured again, fragmented after years of independence. At the insistence of Meessen, Kaboré struggles to sing the French national anthem, at first able only to hum it. A flash of recognition brings back the opening, "arise, the children of the . . . tyranny." As he stumbles past "Fatherland" directly to a later line, his unintentional slippage reveals a greater truth.

As Meessen's story continues, Barthes quickly appears far less heroic. He finds that Barthes' maternal grandfather was Louis-Gustave Binger. As the film reports, the French state funeral held on his death paid respect to him as "the great explorer, founder of a colony, first governor of Ivory Coast, founding member of the Academy of Colonial Sciences, and the Colonial Party," which T. J. Demos finds "an astonishing historical revelation that has hitherto gone unremarked in the scholarship [on Barthes]."[26] The connection was not completely buried, but instead obliquely exhibited by Barthes in the autobiography *Roland Barthes by Roland Barthes*, with him furnishing a picture of his grandfather that bore a brief notation at the end describing him as an officer, administrator, and explorer.[27]

Meessen digs deeper, tying Barthes's *Paris Match* reading to the whole colonial archive on screen. Disembodied Black hands thumb through photos—marching troops, Africans in uniform, and many other old and tattered images—then an image of Barthes's grandfather suddenly takes over the frame. In *Camera Lucida*, Barthes later reflects on the strangeness of the *pose*. He first sees the pose as reflection of self-awareness, with the photographic subject responding to the photographer in a scene of recognition, almost as if bodily comportment alone could testify to one's self-possession and existence.[28] But he also considers its inverse, that the pose also attests to the "law" of how photography turns one into an "object" through a sort of "surgical operation," transmuted into a thing that can be owned and traded through likeness.[29] The fixity of the rigid pose lends more than the durability of a commodity; it foreshadows the terrifying stillness of death.[30] In the photograph of Barthes's grandfather, two colonists in all-white recline under a well-provisioned jungle tent with a dog at their feet (Binger on the right). Their awkward posture exudes a strange liveliness. Standing at each other's sides, scantily clad Black male attendants pose for the camera like statues etched out of stone. A stark rendering of the two poles of self-possession and deathly stillness in black-and-white. It is a story that continues to play out over and over again with the police and other scenes of encounter, where violence guarantees one party to be terrifyingly still and the other furiously unrestrained.

Barthes raises the issue of the pose a second time after disclosing that the death of his mother haunts his visual expedition. To him, the pose is a reminder that even the most lively subject became suddenly motionless, at least for the instant it took to photograph it. In that way, the photograph certifies even in the most animated body "that the corpse is alive, as *corpse*; it is the living image of a dead thing."[31] Hence an early remark of his that death is the fundamental form (*eidos*) of the photograph.[32]

Perhaps then, as Jonathan Beller contends, the true essence of photography is as a "machine of racialization."[33] *Camera Lucida* is interwoven with images of slaves, nonwhites, and non-normative people, making up the majority of the photographs printed in the book. Yet Barthes strangely argues that they should be consumed aesthetically, not politically. This is all-too revealing for Beller, who sees Barthes as using Black bodies as "stepping stones leading to the essence of technology."[34] But he does not stop there. De-oedipalizing the book, Beller finds that the foundational psychic scene does not reside with Barthes's mother but a photograph of a slave market he cherished as child. As Barthes recounts:

> I remember keeping for a long time a photograph I had cut out of a magazine—lost subsequently, like everything too carefully put away—which showed a slave market: the slavemaster, in a hat, standing; the slaves, in loincloths, sitting. I repeat: a photograph, not a drawing or engraving; for my horror and my fascination as a child came from this: that there was a *certainty*

that such a thing had existed: not a question of exactitude, but of reality: the historian was no longer the mediator, slavery was given without mediation, the fact was established without *method*.[35]

In this passage, Barthes is clearly thrilled by the photograph. He is not disgusted, but drawn to the charge of the image. No doubt, his horror is only heightened by his childish fascination. But his confessional description speaks to the pull it still had on him decades later. The photograph was not an illustration or a narrative account from a history book, but a recording that allowed him direct access to participate in the original. More than just presenting a photograph of a slave market, Barthes reenacted the movements of a market offering captured bodies: first selecting it from the many images held in the collectible medium of the magazine, and then keeping it as a trophy to his initial jolt of excitement.

If we are to recover Barthes at all, perhaps it is through his insistence that the photographer's organ is not the eye but the finger.[36] Of course it points knowingly, gesturing toward the reality of that something existed. But it also points with a jeer, like that directed by the little kid at Frantz Fanon as he walked by. It points with the white-hot precision of the police officer who calls out "you there, stop!" It points with the cold stare of informatics carving bodies into data. It points with the fixed gaze of security cameras fingering potential threats.

And if this is all true, then a question raised by Goldsby in the context of lynching postcards remains even more pressing than ever: how to confront the putative "transparency" of "self-evident" documents of racial murder when they were designed to inscribe violence into sight itself?[37]

Chapter 17
Black Out

The bright white exposure of dash cams, body cameras, closed-circuit television (CCTV), and other surveillance images have unleashed a flood of machine-generated images of police killings of Black people.[1] They share in photography's assumed-neutral work as evidence, said to exist in how it putatively "authenticates the existence of a certain being."[2] But what kind of being? Perhaps, as Calvin L. Warren argues, the world is constituted by a nonrelation between Blackness and being.[3] In the very writing of "being," he masks Black ~~being~~ by striking it through, suspending being by putting it under erasure, using both a subtraction and an addition that makes present what is absent.[4] For him, Black nihilism discloses how the anti-Black world abuses the functionality of Blackness without affording it the privileges of being, incarnating Black ~~being~~ in terrifying vast nothingness.

In between pieces dedicated to Trayvon Martin and James Craig Anderson in her book *Citizen*, Claudia Rankine reproduces a grayscale image of a lynching. But the black body is missing; it has become a void, indistinct from the black night. All that remains in the photograph is a group of boisterous whites. The subjects in the foreground make faces at the camera. The new focal point is a man pointing toward the tree with smug satisfaction. One woman wears a wry grin. A man to the side almost seems to be posing for a portrait. Behind a bashful couple holding hands, an excited girl lets out a yelp. This is how the libidinal economy of whiteness comes into the foreground.

But what about the infrastructure of whiteness? Can something even more inhuman be revealed when all bodies leave the frame? Perhaps it begins with the redaction of three infamous images, expanding on the readings performed by Nicholas Mirzoeff: the first, a still from the suppressed October 2014 video of officer Jason van Dyke shooting teenager Laquan McDonald in Chicago; the second, from the July 2015 dash cam of state trooper Brian Encinia's traffic stop of Sandra Bland in Prairie View, Texas, that would lead to her incarceration and death; the third, a grab from the December 2015 video of a mass of jailhouse officials in Chicago brutalizing Philip Coleman, who later died.

Their offenses— "acting erratic," refusing to put out a cigarette, being "combative," and spitting blood—all result in a similar response: "over-kill."[5] A white-hot violence so excessive as to try to push the Black body beyond death, past asserting inferiority to establishing the fact of nonexistence. The repeated shots of a service weapon, over and over again, sixteen times until the clip is empty. Incessant tasering by over a half dozen officers, who crowd together into a jail cell to overpower a Black man in handcuffs, then drag his limp body around the halls, resulting in over fifty bruises and abrasions. A "rough ride" beating by police in the back of their wagon so vicious as to sever the spinal cord. Circulating depictions of this violence and their effects on Black (non)life risk peddling in the same sensationalization that secures its spectacular power.

What does it mean to circulate these images in an attempt to influence the world? What is the white social infrastructure in which images of Black death are treated as objects to be exchanged? Is the politics of visibility nothing more than a performance of-and-for whiteness? The problem further multiplies when non-Black radicals look for ways to join in the struggle. These questions motivate Alexandra Juhasz to ask as an antiracist white scholar: "how do I not look?"[6] Or in contrast, Black scholar Sherri Williams has asked how she can care for her mental and emotional health as a Black woman and continue to consume images of Black death?[7] What would we see when the spectacle of death is erased from them?

What do we see when the spectacular violence that organizes the scene is cropped? What comes into focus when our eyes are no longer drawn to the void of Black nonexistence? What other forms of power take over the frame when the obvious subjects of violence recede?

The first capture (Chicago in October 2014) is a street at night by dashcam.[8] The sanitizing glare of street and security lights frame the scene. A long stretch of sidewalk cuts across the frame to establish the foreground. The presence of city services is felt: everything is amply lit, a sign seems to indicate parking rules, and a pole advertises a bus stop. The background is obscured by a temporary fence. Close to its center, a large sign advertises a coming real estate development. Pessimistic long grass suggests that the fence has been there for a while, that promised construction may never materialize. The bright geometric shape of a digital artifact floats at the top of the frame, its significance arcane. Summarizing its features: a purely infrastructural space, its horizon to elsewhere literally foreclosed by capitalism, its bleak emptiness signifying abandonment. Nothing visibly alive under the hard glare of security lights.

The second capture (Prairie View in July 2015) is a daylight country highway by dashcam.[9] Its resolution is limited to blotchy colors and large shapes, reminiscent of the artificial-intelligence pattern recognition of machine vision. The street stretches from side to side, appearing almost sick in its washed out yellow. The frame is pierced by a silver sky, tinted by a haze that seems to irradiate everything below. The light catches a few ambiguous grey objects. Power line? Some sort of sign? A short squat fence? A run of bushy trees hems in the street, concealing and containing. A group of them cast a deep shadow over the foreground. Under it, a modest silver car hugs the curb, as if unable to escape its dark clutches. The only interruption is a small patch of rolling green grass. Though there are none, it feels that the type of building that would appear would be a pocked barn or something with weathered vinyl siding, aged enough to be ambiguously unoccupied. Desolate, the scene shows the type of place where anything could happen. Why? Because in these places, the rules are simultaneously weaker and stronger, depending on who claims to exercise them.

The third capture (Chicago in December 2015) is a jail cell by CCTV. A fish-eye lens leers into it from on high. The lens makes the cell's blue bars bow outwards, as if bent from the enormous force of a natural disaster. A perfectly straight white rectangle appears over the bar, blocking what must be identifying information.

Yet the number 13 remains clearly displayed above it. Empty, made generic, with only cryptic numbers remaining, the cell's ability to transform human into mere body waiting for judgment is clear. If furniture is a metaphor for both the interior life of the mind and the interior comforts of home, this is a space of pure hostility. A single short, narrow floating slab juts out from the wall. With its sharp geometry and smooth surface so similar to the cement room surrounding it, the bench's only intent must be to cause pain, inspire only fitful sleep, and encourage distress. The only relief it provides is separation from the floor, where all sorts of agony and misery have collected over time. The dirt from thousands of pacing footsteps, the sour air of tears and sweat, the degradation of living with insects, the foul stench of sewage, and a million other kinds of other intentional neglect. The distorted appearance of the space is made further nauseating by the unevenness of the artificial light illuminating it. The sharp contrast of neon spotlights with deep shadows suggests it is a windowless dungeon, the sort of space where natural indications of time recede. It is under these conditions that time cruelly returns through rules, techniques, and habits that are always being amended. The lights never really turn off, but they brighten at a specific time. Locks release, opening up to other spaces and other people. Meals arrive on a regular schedule. TVs turn on. Except when they don't.

Each of the three images opens onto a "killing zone,"[10] a near endless stream of "non-places"—most often long stretches of poured concrete meant as all journey and no destination. Spaces where one is meant to be only passing through. They bear the characteristics of the older "carceral landscape" of the plantation, which transformed the wilderness through agrocapitalist principles to give tactical advantage to slaveholders and overseers, expanding prairies, fields, and other clearings to establish a hypervisibility trained on Black bodies.[11] This landscape remains, having been paved only to be made into a narrowed sidewalk or an expansive road. Former country highways now indefinitely suburban, the formerly gilded suburbs of white flight transitioning into something else with concrete veins opening up into terrain without clear features marking it distinctively public or private. Its vague features invite occupants to use it as the perfect shortcut. But with a space whose purpose is so hazy, the paranoid pathologies of whiteness and its attendant violence are often left to run wild.

Chapter 18
Trapped between Withdrawal and Hypervisibility

In their study of how the white ethics of social responsibility contributes to the violence of police profiling, Steve Martinot and Jared Sexton argue that "to focus on the spectacular event of police violence is to deploy (and thereby reaffirm) the logic of police profiling itself."[1] Consider then the beginning of *Scenes of Subjection*, where Saidiya Hartman notes her refusal to recount Frederick Douglass's description of the beating of his Aunt Hester, "to call attention to the ease with which such scenes are usually reiterated, the casualness with which they are circulated, and the consequence of this routine display of the slave's ravaged body."[2] She goes on to explain that the empathic identification meant to be elicited by such scenes "cannot be extricated from the economy of chattel slavery" because they treat the slave's fungible, commodified body as an empty vessel "to don, occupy, or possess blackness or the black body as a sentimental resource and/or locus of enjoyment."[3]

Similar aesthetic reiterations persist across a variety of mediums. More recently, as intensified by ubiquitous access to the recording and dissemination technologies of smart phones, scenes of police summary executions of Black people have routinely saturated social media feeds and been played by television news networks. The ostensible aim is to combat such shootings by garnering empathy for the victims, but yet it quickly feeds into the established practice of witnessing the spectacularization of suffering as a commodity to be traded.

What can be developed against the spectacular economy of reportage that justifies trafficking in Blackness through journalistic logic? Can there then be a nonaesthetics of Blackness? Such a line of inquiry might begin with François Laruelle's short work on *The Concept of Non-Photography*. In it, Laruelle argues that too many conceive of photography through a realist mode that makes it into a "distanced, reified, deficient mode of perception."[4] This "realist illusion" treats it as a device of autofactualization.[5] It reduces photography to an act of faith: faith in perception, faith in the spontaneity of photographic knowledge, and faith in capturing various things "inscribed in the World" (the eye, the camera, techniques, objects, scene, or event).[6] One might add that even those who circulate images of Black death to challenge it hold faith in a similar fictitious automatic process by which depicting violence somehow brings about its end. Yet what remains automatic about photography is its fundamentally identificatory role found in the mug shot, state identification cards, visas, and wanted posters.[7] There may be fleeting moments of resistance in this world, as Tina D. Campt has argued, with the fugitive study of the compelled poses of identification photos, but it requires a shift in perspective, as in her suggestion for studying "Black quiet."[8]

Against the photograph's reiteration of the philosopher's belief in the world with every press of the button, Laruelle proposes a nonphotography. It is the photography of a special camera that is not physical-mechanical but theoretical: instead of the empirical camera that indexes slices of the real world, the nonphotograph is an operation of thought and not any material substance.[9] A nonphotograph does not confirm anything by the world; it is a machine for introducing indeterminacy, genericness, and uncertainty into the ties that bind this world.

Through a discussion of Black photo-art, Aria Dean proposes "Black genericness" as a novel orientation for photography to "the same old image problem" (to quote Ulysses Jenkins).[10] On Dean's account, the image problem has long confined Blackness to pursuing either "a new universalism" (as in Edward J. Steichen's *The Family of Man*, first exhibited at MoMA) or a "radical multiplicity" (such as W. E. B. DeBois's 1900 World's Fair *Exhibit of American Negroes*).[11] Genericness, by contrast, can be found in photography that presents the condition Blackness. Examples Dean provides are a naturalist's collection of wigs pinned and mounted like butterflies (Lorna Simpson's *Wigs*), reference portraits to "indifference" "uncivil" and other affective states in which corresponding vowels "I" and "U" obscure the repeating-subject's face like stickers (Simpson's *Easy for Who to Say*), or a series of portraits of a Black subject shrouded in white sheets except for the gestures of a pair of hands expressing a variety of sentiments (Sondra Perry, *White Sheets*).[12] Each reveals the condition of Blackness by erasing the subject to reveal the white ground. White race science, white grammars of suffering, white genres of the human. None dispute Blackness, but instead all aesthetically attest to its fraught ontology as a generic condition.

The current preoccupation with "positive" (uplifting presence) and "negative" (degrading absence) images is further disrupted by Simone Browne's study of the surveillance of Blackness. Perhaps inclusive presence is not always advantageous. Through the term "Black luminosity," she demonstrates how policing techniques are the paradigmatic means for rendering Blackness knowable through visibility, from eighteenth-century lantern laws to contemporary facial-recognition technologies.[13] Defenders of cybernetic systems that use facial recognition or artificial intelligence to direct violence, such as computational predictive-policing systems, will only entertain criticisms about discrimination based on bad data (such as the LAPD using data gathered as part of its racist assault on gangs in the 1980s). Yet feeding in more Black faces and more detailed information about Black life does little to challenge its real purpose, which is to legitimize police violence through math-washing and surveillance bureaucracy. Abolitionists like Browne instead look toward "fugitive acts of escape, resistance, and the productive disruptions that happen when Blackness enters the frame."[14]

Along similar lines, Airban Gupta-Nigam has argued that Richard Dyer's history of cinematic lighting reveals a dominant aesthetic presupposition: whiteness is allied with transparency while Blackness resists illumination through proximate opacity.[15] The conflict between these two perspectives is played out on a formal level whenever the color black is considered through addition or subtraction: for the light artist using additive color, blackness is the absence of color, while for a painter using subtractive color, blackness is the combination of all colors.[16] Photography and film long developed lighting to best depict white skin, as did products made by Kodak, often making darker features appear dull, opaque, or even lifeless.[17] Associated lighting techniques are used in photo media to further seal the bond between white illumination and the honesty of transparency, purity of inner fortitude, angelic divinity, radiant beauty, and moral virtue.[18] On the other hand, one color theorist outlines the "corporeal" quality of the painter's colors, which are combined to synthesize blackness.[19] In his mind, "a white square on a black ground will look larger than a black square on a white ground," which lends whiteness a plentitude that "reaches out and overflows the boundary, whereas the black contracts."[20] The consequence for Gupta-Nigam is that Blackness is *trapped between an ontological state of withdrawal and a hyper-visibility* in marking. These two poles establish an aesthetic economy of Blackness that restates Frantz Fanon's comment that "I came into the world . . . at the crossroads between Nothingness and Infinity" (or for Calvin L. Warren, both nothing *and* infinity).[21]

Gupta-Nigam's conclusion is a warning: aesthetic approaches to Blackness risk becoming a "regulative response to Black priority" that thinks Blackness through the analogy of visuality—light and darkness, visages and shadows—seeing it only in relief, rather than thinking Blackness in and of itself.[22] Instructive here is Patrice Douglass and Frank Wilderson's argument that any metaphysical speculation of Blackness must remain grounded by a theory of violence.[23]

Against the backdrop of a spectacular violence simultaneously withdrawn and hypervisible, the aesthetics of Blackness appears almost impossible. The pornotropic process of rendering the Black body as mere flesh seems to result in at least two polar outcomes. Blackness gets objectified as either an empty vessel or an indomitable vitality, either something inert that gains life only when ventriloquized through possession or traded as fungible commodity or something endowed with an unconquerable vibrancy euphemized as real, bold, deep, funky, raw, vivid, or loud.[24]

In his 1988 "On the Black Universe: In the Human Foundations of Color," Laruelle radicalizes blackness by embracing it as the zero degree of light, color, humanity, the world, and even the universe itself.[25] Discussing it through Robert Fludd's black square from *Ultriusque Cosmi* (1671), Eugene Thacker distinguishes blackness from both theory of color and metaphor for ignorance. He distinguishes between darkness that "always exists in some relation to light, however gradated, tenebrous, and shadowy" and blackness that is "anterior to both light and dark." A black universe, then, is not the cosmic study of a color, but "the withdrawal of every relation between self and the world" that results in a "breach" that "makes itself apparent as such."[26] Blackness here stands against the world, which remains all-too-human. Recognizing the risk of such abstract discussions lapsing into the sort of regulative response Gupta-Nigam diagnoses, Alexander R. Galloway elaborates on the implications for blackness as a "crypto-ontology absolutely foreclosed to being":

> Channel that great saint of radical blackness, Toussaint Louverture, and return to the Haitian Constitution of 1804, which stated that all citizens will be called Black regardless of color. Such blanket totality of black, such cataclysm of human color, renders color invalid and denies the endless dynamics of black-as-white or white-as-black. Black is no longer the limit case, no longer the case of the slave, the poor, the indentured or debt-ridden worker. Black is the foundation of a new uchromia, a new color utopia rooted in the generic black universe. "Our uchromia: to learn to think from the point of view of Black as what determines color in the last instance rather than what limits it."[27]

This passage reveals how closely nonphilosophy converges with Black study, not that it needs to take on yet another white European theorist. Both begin by dismissing the insufficiency of the small victories celebrated by the historical politics of contingency, and each identifies how the color black brings about the death of a world constituted through an incomplete concept of humanity: "A phenomenal blackness entirely fills the essence of man."[28]

Could the two approaches ultimately converge? Laruelle's unique proposal is a uchromia, a noncolor, of blackness. Laruelle argues that epistemology has long relied on light-based metaphors to shuttle between confusion and knowledge, bondage and freedom, wrongness and rightness. It is right there in the name of the Enlightenment. The connection is not incidental but metaphysical. Following a similar thread in Black thought, Wilderson has argued that "how we understand suffering and whether we locate its essence in economic exploitation or in anti-Blackness has a direct impact on how we imagine freedom; and on how we foment revolution."[29] He then criticizes Marxism for remaining invested in socialist emancipation narratives based in "equality, liberation, or redress" translated into aesthetic ideas.[30] At the structural level, "turning Absence into Presence is not the same as turning waged workers into free workers," because "the [Presence] reorganizes the world; [Absence] brings it to an end."[31] Why? Blackness inheres not in labor, gender, or land, but as "the mark of slavery."[32] The consequence is that Black positionality, "because it is without world(ly analogy), cannot articulate its demands in the grammar of the world," or said otherwise: "It cannot employ its demands in a narrative passage from present domination to the possibility of future liberation."[33] The result is that Afropessimism has no truck with the story of liberation so common to the Enlightenment and socialism: that the forces of human freedom are waiting to be unleashed through breaking of the remaining forms of bondage. So even if Galloway does not present a theory of suffering, perhaps he still identifies a point of convergence for the two projects in the aesthetics of light. Said another way, perhaps the abolition of the metaphysics of liberation can be at least partially an aesthetic one.

Unless carefully parsed, however, the conceptual foundations of such a Black universe could slip into either possessive liberalism or vitalism, both of which misconstrue Laruelle.[34] If the French *Declaration of the Rights of Man and of the Citizen* is not so much invalidated as determined otherwise, it would shift only concerning who (ontologically) a citizen is. In its crudest form, such a universe would realize the neoliberal multicultural demand that white civil society be populated differently, with different faces in bigger places. More broadly, citizenship could still bear the same possessive individualism of liberal human rights, though Blackened by defining that citizenship by the condition of all individuals as *not* being proprietors of their own capacities—a sort of nonfreedom of incapacity.[35] Given the precision with which Black study theorizes the fungible Black body, the criticism of possessive liberalism needs less rehearsal. While on the other hand, the vitalist interpretation may be far more likely; in it, Blackness is taken to be the substrate of an *élan vital* that animates all color, life, or the cosmos. Such vitalism treats Blackness as an agency that persists even when held captive, something furtive, ineffable, and richly capacious that always escapes structural conditions.

Conflicting interpretations of the aesthetics of Blackness are nowhere more apparent than in recent writing about abstract art. Art historian Darby English proposes that conventions have formed a "Black representation space" that prevents Black art from being truly seen, being instead considered only from a viewpoint beyond the work of art itself.[36] He concretizes this concern through writing by art critics on David Hammon's 2002 installation *Concerto in Black and Blue*, as they perform a vitalist overdetermining of the meaning of the piece while simultaneously failing to see any of the details that make the piece's singular: "There is a sense . . . in which the entire history of Africans in North America can be told through reference to these two colors," he echoes from one, while another says that "bound up with the contemplation of the colors black and blue" is the "suggestion of the universality of African American Cultural Expression."[37]

In her writing about Adam Pendleton's *Black Sun* (2013–14), Adrienne Edwards is keenly aware of English's criticism.[38] "Blackness in abstraction," she writes, "shifts analysis away from the Black artist as subject and instead emphasizes Blackness as material, method and mode, insisting on Blackness as a multiplicity" so that "we can think of what it does in the world without conflating it . . . with a singular historical narrative or monolithic subjectivity."[39] Yet, at the same time, she also describes the work through references to the cosmic ("a constellation," "Sun Ra"), the religious ("barbed" like a thorn crown), and the violent ("projectiles burst"), leading her to descriptions of vitalist plentitude, saying that Blackness, "in the fullest sense of the word, has a seemingly unlimited usefulness in the history of modern art" and is a "profound capaciousness."[40]

Fred Moten further considers the "movement of artworks" through the double-displacement of artworks as things and Blackness as thingness in "The Case of Blackness."[41] He angles into the first by looking to Fanon's famous passage in *Black Skin, White Masks* on the Black man's lack of ontological resistance to a white world.[42] Rather than taking the reading through the conventional transition of a subject into an object, he instead considers the Heideggerian phenomenological question of the split between object and thing.[43] This results instead in him taking Blackness to be a thing, a being-in-its emptiness like a jug that holds a void.[44] As such, it is neither position nor object, but "a clearing, or a kind of flaw."[45] This is where Moten finds the "fact" of Blackness in Fanon, which is neither fact nor lived experience (as the chapter is often rendered in translation), but "an ontology of disorder, an ontology of dehiscence, a para-ontology."[46] Its figure, the fugitivity of/in the slave that reveals an "incalculable rhythm of the life of things," he finds in music and visual art.[47]

Moten gives substance to these ideas through musician Cecil Taylor and visual artist Piet Mondrian. Taylor, a pianist, arrives through an intervention. Excerpting lengthy moments in a conversation between five artists in 1967, Moten draws on Taylor's comments on Blackness in-and-against abstract painter Ad Reinhardt (with brief cosmic interludes by intermedia artist Aldo Tambellini). In Reinhardt, Moten finds the a *technē*-driven artist who wants to reduce Blackness to a noncolor, the absence of color, rendering it purely aesthetic and stripping it of meaning and unmooring it from any sense of community.[48] Taylor, on the other hand, picks up on the phenomenological distinction Moten wants to make, pointing out that "Reinhardt visualizes blackness as some kind of technical problem. I visualize it as the quality that shapes my life, in terms of the quality of the acceptance that my work gets or does not get based on the fact that it is from the Afro-American community."[49]

Moten then combines the sonic rhythms of Taylor with the vibrant visual blackness of Mondrian's *Victory Boogie Woogie*. Put together like a pair of hands playing complementary rhythms, he substantiates Blackness not as an absence or negation, but "a kind of social color and social music" that corresponds to "the victory of escape."[50] Returning to Fanon through the political project of *Wretched of the Earth,* Moten ties aesthetic blackness to the disavowal of the Black thing. He summarizes these moments of refusal and ontological escape "as a kind of social gathering; as undercommon plainsong and dance; as the fugitive, centrifugal word; as the word's auto-interruptive, auto-illuminative shade/s," in which "black(ness) is, in the dispossessive richness of its colors, beautiful."[51] Blackness is not just the technical thingness of a color but also the incalculable substance of social life.

But what is the significance of treating Blackness as material, which is to say, a substance for theorization, speculation, or creativity? As Franco Barchiesi has argued, those who use new ontologies that look to "the self-constitution of collective political subjects in a continuous state of becoming" fail to grasp the fundamental constitution of Blackness through death, especially through its focus on capacity and relationality.[52] This is the concern of Édouard Glissant, who is troubled by the forced relation of whiteness that desires a single, transparent world against which opacity is necessary to secure a different form of existence.[53] Putting a point on it, in a statement to the Humboldt Forum "Das Milieu Der Toten," Hartman and Christina Sharpe said: "How do we attend to Black Death? A question we must return to again and again, since our suffering to the degree that it is recognized, is [pornotropically] exploited in the service of rehabilitating anti Black and colonial institutions. . . . Don't use our death, our suffering, our lives and our work to regenerate your projects. Don't turn our flesh into gold again. We do not consent to this."[54]

Countless more abstract works appeal to Blackness through the cosmic register, but without ending on a redemptive note. Through concepts introduced by Moten in "The Case of Blackness," Sexton argues that abstraction tends to quarantine blackness from Blacks, separating color from people.[55] Here, contrasting claims over an alleged racist inscription hidden under Kazimir Malevich's painting *Black Square* (1915) are ripe for debate: is there a secret anti-Black message cryptically sealed below the surface of the canonical piece of black abstraction?[56] Take, for example, Vincent Como's essay "The Black Singularity: To Know the Unknowable," precisely because it is an extensive treatment of the abstract blackness that fails to mention Black people. Does it perform the quarantining purification of Blackness identified by Moten? Looking at starting points: Como's opening sentence curiously mirrors Afropessimism's fundamental concept of humanity being constituted out of the exclusion of Blackness, as he begins with the onto-aesthetics of black as "the constant through which humanity became manifest," implicitly referring to the expansion and contraction of a big bang that will "one day resorb all of what can be understood as reality, folding everything back into its dark embrace," while Sexton concludes his opening paragraph by proposing that the slave's cause is a cataclysmic struggle for "another world in and on the ruins of this one, in the end of its ends."[57] The two essays also converge in their conclusions, with Como declaring that "Black is Everything. Everything is Nothing. Nothing is All," while Sexton states, "Black is a color, noncolor, and all colors."[58] So, rather than looking for a representation of people, he looks to how each formal arrangement of materials (monochromatic painting, black soap, and an assemblage of rice paper-mesh-acrylic-twine) forms a "conduit" between blackness as symbol and the concept of Black people, "rather than an obstacle to the concept;" using the concrete, "in its infinite depth," to lead the viewer "toward rather than away from the universal and its infinite breadth."[59] It is those materials that enable Sexton to mention the events of the U.S. civil rights movement (the March on Washington for Jobs and Freedom), instruments of slave torture (the scarifying whip and chain), the conditions of sex work (the topic of P-Funk's "Cosmic Slop"), global slave cultures (including East Asia), flesh (skin and bones), and the history of confinement (steel and rope).[60]

In his closing to "All Black Everything," Sexton states that "Black is generous and generative, inclusive, and encompassing."[61] But this statement need not swerve toward post-Spinozist versions of immanence that retain capacity as an animating force; one could turn to Laruelle, who defines blackness as determining all color yet not being a thing to possess or a force that is irrepressibly plentiful. Galloway's quotation rightfully selects determination in the last instance as a Laruellean alternative to blackness-as-limit, and thus sidesteps the deconstructive *à venir* of French theory that poses things as necessary-impossible horizons for which to strive, even if they never arrive (Derrida's democracy to come, Agamben's coming community). The prefix "non-" uses metaphysics as a raw material to discover the logics of real immanence therein. The generic blackness of uchromia is not a potent force, a generative substance, or a horizon, but an opacity: the pointing out of the insufficiency of the whole philosophical endeavor and the failure of its categories of thought ("history," "the human," "liberation"). In this framework, Blackness escapes the dialectical antagonism of the poisoned gift—a "fundamental dependency" that "paradoxically, initiates and sustains our agency"—because it does not seek refuge in whiteness (representation) or lightness (reason).[62] This is because the point of Blackness is not to reproduce the world, but to abolish it. Or to echo Sexton's own words, "slavery is the threshold of the political world, abolition the interminable radicalization of every radical movement."[63]

Conclusion
Communism at the End of the World

The point is not to understand the world but to destroy it.[1] Today's society of the spectacle packages everything as product, cybernetically feeding it back to us through cynicism, making many forms of critique just another means to spread detachment and fatalist alienation. Even if the pervasive use of cynical reason does not completely damn the future of critique, it does serve as a cautionary tale for those engaged in the politics of truth and warns of the declining efficiency of forces backed by critique alone. It is then the destructive power of critique that should be recovered, its critical function, as it realizes a particular type of force: the guerrilla force of asymmetrical conflict.

When engaging in the imperceptible politics of the underground, conflict remains essential. It is not enough to turn one's back on the world, for it persists regardless of how much one denounces, refutes, or scorns it. And even if the cybernetic infrastructure of the world can withstand critique, its forces can still be opposed. Fortunately, opportunities for struggle are numerous, the most important pointing to the ultimate task: abolition.

Life and Strategy

The guerrilla breaks from the dilemma of spontaneity and organization that has long plagued radical politics. This is because its motivating principle is not hegemony but abolition. Central for Vladimir Lenin, the twentieth century's patriarch of revolution, was the opposition of organization to spontaneity. Those operating in the shadow of Lenin follow in seeing organization not only as the proper path for seizing the reins of power but also as a simple fact of nature.

But as marronage has shown, spontaneous forms of revolt are an even more common reaction to the intolerable circumstances of violence and tyranny—a whole criminal history composed of slave uprisings, peasant revolts, and political exoduses. Frantz Fanon, patron saint of the guerrilla, saw this clearly in *Wretched of the Earth*, arguing that the spontaneous elements found in the countryside and the criminals of the *lumpenproletariat* must be called to fight for the forces of liberation (rather than excluded), else they would be enrolled by the enemy in the end.[2]

This formulation turns Lenin on his head. For Lenin, jealous of the elegant geometry of the modern state, suggested a science of revolution meant to turn natural instincts into an objective force, in turn purging or expelling those not willing to toe the line while denouncing them as criminals and lowlifes not capable of embodying party discipline. Following a similarly scientific model, his comrade Leon Trotsky used the metaphor of a steam engine, explaining that the powerful energy of the mass mobilizations driving the Russian Revolution would have dissipated if not for the piston-box of the party, which compressed the people's energy like steam at the decisive moment.[3]

The underground stands with the criminally queer and all of the other "anti-socials" historically thrown into camps by states and their parties. In turn, it rejects the science of organization and its subsequent iterations, Marxist Leninism, Luxemburgism, and more contemporary resurrections of the party, which are all based on an unfortunate error of thought. Their putative science of society holds substance to be hylomorphic, with matter lacking order (the spontaneous actions of a people) and needing laws imposed on it from the outside to give it form (the organization of the party). The underground makes at least two objections to the hylomorphic model of politics. The first is that the emphasis on unity and coherence gives ways to today's hegemonic sociology of social movements, extending the gaze of the spectacle to all matter, representing it as abstract, unspecified, passive, and *in need of form*. The second is that the model reduces the whole world to a form of latent labor, as a master commanding his slaves, whose activity appears as the result of an effective technical operation but whose success is actually due to "a socialized representation of work."[4]

The concepts of life and strategy help sidestep the false dilemma between spontaneity and organization, though there is a danger of casting both life and strategy in hylomorphic terms in preparation for capture by authoritarian, charismatic, or bureaucratic forms. Existential liberalism reduces life, for instance, to the torturous depths of a subjective interiority that reshapes the winds of change into subjects so desperate for relief they are willing to collaborate with their tormentors. Authoritarian strategy similarly reduces politics to a question of coherence and identity for the sake of easy reproduction within a dialectic of recognition. The abolitionist vision of life understands it as a process of becoming otherwise, a movement of constant undoing that generates a set of felt relations, a set of affects.

Though affects are usually registered as feelings, positive, negative, and everything in-between (joy, anxiety, sadness, exhilaration, anticipation, sympathy, fear), they also live an autonomous existence, embodying spontaneous and passive processes that can be drawn on as a political resource for the underground. The strategy of abolition also isolates forces to be used in political struggle, foremost among them, the power of anonymity. Its conceptual figures are found in the streets of Baltimore, the halls of the University of Heidelberg, and the water in which the guerrilla swims like a fish. Each suggests a way that strategic advantages can be exploited by anonymous forces constituted against this world. This is how fugitivity, criminality, and anonymity reveal a new conceptual terrain beyond spontaneity and organization that is populated by redactions, annotations, abstractions, negative affects, killjoys, political illness, insinuations, glitches, clutter, and noise—all forms of escape essential for surviving the end of the world as we know it.

It Begins with Fugitivity... (Intensive Escape)

This world is inhabited by restless souls that dream of other realities beyond the horizon of their own. The imperceptible politics of those who refuse recognition exists far before the white gaze captures it for its projects, for the first escape began before humanity or even life itself. Rather, it is the event of a difference that makes a difference. The "non-" that breaks with the world.[5] It is an ontological interruption that bursts through fissures in the metaphysical bedrock, opening rifts along the fault lines of "the problem of the Negro as a problem of thought" and other issues others would rather wish away through simple-minded solutionism.[6] In short, fugitivity lends the study of imperceptibility a notion of becoming, the force of change, whose temporality is played in reverse: an "unbecoming."[7]

Unbecoming can be arrested, restricted, or otherwise limited in many ways, among which cultural confinements of escape are particularly potent. Capitalism, for instance, clothes itself in cultural representations of freedom, declaring itself as the enemy of slave labor and state control by being the guarantor of "the right to work," "free markets," and "free trade." As the anarchist spirit of abolition has long shown, these freedoms are not escape routes; the right of the worker to leave an employer does not lead to free existence, for "he is driven to it by the same hunger which forced him to sell himself to the first employer," and thus liberty, "so much exalted by the economists, jurists, and bourgeois republicans, is only a theoretical freedom, lacking any means for its possible realization, and consequently it is only a fictitious liberty, an utter falsehood."[8]

Fugitivity suffers an additional cultural confusion when it is taken to be an odyssey through space. From this perspective, fugitivity is a migration from this place to that, such as leaving the country, running to the hills, finding refuge. But "some journeys take place in the same place, they're journeys in intensity."[9] In the hands of Édouard Glissant, it means resisting the universality that arrives packaged in a salesperson's deceitful cosmopolitanism, such as the forced adoption of English or French as a world language into which everything is translated.[10] Against such universal transparency, he fights to extend the opacity that makes the underground imperceptible. It is not a flight, but an evasive maneuver, because its purpose is to "seek to stay in the same place" and evade the codes.[11] As long as we fail to distinguish between spatial movement and the force of imperceptibility, it remains a confused concept.

When fugitivity is an evasion and not a departure, it is a potent political tool. There is a hidden communist history in need of recovering: the formal exclusion of Blackness from the law and civic life pushing research methods past the threshold of official history.[12] But with contemporary liberalism's perverse combination of formal inclusion with material deprivation comes an additional challenge. The brutally productive system of cybernetic control, for instance, has enclosed global space through distance-demolishing technologies, leaving behind a few isolated spaces as graveyards for the scattered peoples that remain there. Moreover, systems of assimilation, from homonationalism to multicultural capitalism, demonstrate how to further divide the oppressed between the deserving in need of social advancement and bad subjects slated for death.

As such, I refuse to partake in whites' paternalistic history of cultivating others to mirror one's own values, nor will I undertake a theological quest to find redemption in Blackness. Additionally, I find little use in concessionist statements like "racism hurts us all," which Derrick Bell succinctly theorizes as benefitting Blackness only in those cases in which it simultaneously advantages whites.[13] This is why I use neither the Marxist social framework of mutual self-interest nor an intersectional analysis that looks to find ways that different peoples' liberation are bound up with each other. I heed Jean Genet, who argues in his famous May Day speech with the Panthers that: "Whites are afraid of freedom. It's a drink that is too strong for them."[14] Frank B. Wilderson III recalls these same sentiments being repeated by Saidiya Hartman about his dissertation:

> No one who's not Black reading this wants to be as free as this work would make them. They'd be free of their cultures, they'd be free of their families, they'd be free of all the coordinates that ground them. They would find themselves in the abyss of nonexistence that you and I are in. That's not exactly what they want. They want to help us while maintaining their own sovereignty.

There is a challenge to be taken seriously, and the political tendencies to which this book is meant to contribute do not shy away from it. The path I follow, then, is neither a more dynamic "constitutive" power (grassroots power, people power, or other putatively "democratic" figures of the sovereign) nor a line of flight. But instead, as I have written elsewhere: the death of "God," the death of "Man," and the death of this "World" as embodied in the abstract line of abolition.

The communist vision of abolition, beyond landmark works in Black study by Lucy Parsons, Selma James, or Angela Davis, might include the two journal issues of Tiqqun. It would begin with a twist of Michael Hardt and Antonio Negri's argument that the path out of capitalism is "the Common": a land of plentiful immaterial products of biopolitical production, such as communication and cooperation, that cannot be fully captured by Empire.[15] But just as Marx accused social anarchist Pierre-Joseph Proudhon of misunderstanding dialectics, as if capitalism had a good side that could be expanded and a bad side that could be suppressed, Tiqqun does not search for the Common as if it was the good side of capitalism. As the Black Panther Party famously argued, the ultimate threshold of capitalism is not what can be saved from it, but its abolition.[16]

Abolition reminds us that the Common is not a "good" form of biopolitical production that can be wrested from unscrupulous hands, any more than are plantations, prisons, or the police. As Tiqqun can see, the project of abolition is set against those who desire "an incestuous relationship with imperial pacification" that can be identified in those fawning over fantasies of "biopolitics without police, communication without spectacle, peace without having to wage war to get it."[17] But just as importantly, on the level of strategy, abolition also contends that forces of domination will not be defeated through a grand dialectical negation. Rather, abolition offers a different definition of communism whereby the Common is the shared efforts of those who oppose this world. Its coordinates are determined through an "ethic of civil war." Its struggle is not an antagonistic battle against any particular institution, but a diffuse warfare against the biopolitical fabric of subject positions that hold the world in bondage.

The politics of fugitivity carries with it a vision of intensive escape. It is a strategy that emerges from a "movement of separation" that breeds hostility toward the forces of control.[18] Some critics have misunderstood this separation, confusing its intensive movement with the *extensive* escape practiced by back-to-the-landers in search of a new outside. However, *intensive* separation proceeds "through the middle" of living and struggling within it, as seen in the streets of Ferguson, the struggles over land on Turtle Island, and in the queer urban underground.[19] Or even more so through the experience of the Middle Passage, which introduced a tear in the world so dramatic that redemption narratives promising to breathe new life into the world no longer make sense.[20] If we are to build a coincidence between living and struggling, it would be only as such: living would follow from the reappropriation of space, the Common, violence, and other tools for basic survival, and struggling would serve as the effect of imperceptible war machines that destroy the political dialectic of recognition. Alone, each leads to failure, as living alone softens into a narcissistic focus on difference while struggling alone hardens into an army that desires its own annihilation.[21] With living and struggle together, the movement of separation makes its intensive escape. And it is this movement of separation that intensifies the distinction between all of the vain attempts to run away from it and the raucous event of its defeat. Its patron saint is George Jackson, whose revolt against "captive society" is against the communicability of the social life of "neo-slavery": as if in contrast to whiteness's liberal structure as a "property" or "possessive investment," he declares in his prison letters that "when I revolt, slavery dies with me. I refuse to pass it down."[22]

The key insight to be taken from subtractive communism is that abolition will not come through the institutional recognition of subjects, but rather with the forces of the outside. The most powerful forces do not strike like lightning, but gradually tear open the biopolitical fabric of the world and cause it to leak. By liberating a cascading series of flows, the world can be turned against itself. Against the violent machines of subjection, resistance takes the form of a human strike that negates the forced reproduction of identity.[23] Such a human strike liberates the conflictual force of life. At the same time, technical objects can be transformed from tools to weapons, rescuing politics back from its long suffering under the police and policy. When detached from their intended purpose, these weapons operate with newfound speed and intensity. And in defiance of the system of compulsory visibility, the forces of antihumanism, insinuation, and illegalism feed the hidden undercurrent of struggle. Spreading the flames of revolt, they work to make the underworld ungovernable. Unified only by a shared enemy, these subversions illustrate the potential of intensive escape: a new Common, not found in property but forged in struggle. It is difficult to say what will emerge from the ashes. Yet what is certain is that the problems it addresses must cease to be problems at all. Just as Marx and Engels identify communism as the real movement that abolishes the present, sweeping away the state, private property, the exploitation of labor, and the class relation, so the common struggle of abolition will dissolve the perpetual present, escaping the problems of governance, subjective interiority, the stratification of difference, and the fragmented self.

Criminality Precedes Thought... (Sensational Politics)

Illegalism arises out of a politics that can only be sensed. It is not motivated by rule-making, but by those things that perplex the soul by troubling, prodding, and pushing it into movement as though they "were the bearer of a problem."[24] No amount of good will prepares one for its imperceptible interruptions, for these sensations are awakened through a violence that carries faculties "to their own limit," that fries nerves and murders souls.[25] The violence of its passions brings sense and memory into a discordant harmony that can provoke an even more important faculty: thought. That is because thought emerges only under constraint. Thought is painful, and it is easy to rely on the idiocies and falsehoods of "what everybody knows," that is, until the event when one is *forced to think*.

Illegalism's guerrilla operations battle alongside philosophers other than the "philosophers of logos"; these are rather the "philosophers of passion, of pathos," and they do not sing, but scream.[26] The scream embodies the imperceptible force of thought that comes from sensations, from how much they poke and prod, and these sensations defy preconceived modes of identity, recognition, and other staid political grids.²⁷ It is the cackles of screaming queens who hurl their shoes at a cop. Overheard in the riotous howls of a black bloc as they use banners to conceal the damage they wreak on a commercial quarter. Its cacophony, the sound of thousands of cooling fans spinning up in computers blasting traffic at Mastercard and Visa's servers as payback. But it is also painted over the shocked faces of those desperately unable to cram the effects of these many actions back into the confines of party politics.

Unlike the music of the scream, which surrenders it to the sounds of distorted guitars or rhythmic blast beats to make an accord, anonymous politics bargains not through representatives, but through concepts that build a relationship with the forces behind the scream. These concepts thus impart thought with "invisible and insensible forces that scramble every spectacle, and that even lie beyond pain and feeling."²⁸ The guerrilla does not think, then, by calming the body to make it receptive to dispassionate information. Its thought comes only after the body is made to spasm, opening it up as a plexus with the force of the scream to liberate "interior forces that climb through the flesh," ending in "the entire body trying to escape, to flow out of itself."²⁹ Its screams are imperceptible. This is not because they cannot be heard. On the contrary, screams push all languages past their threshold of intelligibility. They protest with a force that cannot be written into any policy or bill.

As a concept, imperceptibility is filled with the screams of millions who are fed up with the legal avenues for addressing the indignities of life. It follows from a refusal to recite the psalms of purely philosophical discourses on politics, which have "always maintained an essential relation to the law, the institution, and the contract, all of which are the sovereign's problem, traversing the ages of sedentary history from despotic formations to democracies."³⁰ Rather, imperceptibility takes leave of "right," "peace," and "law" to find the blood and corpses that cemented the foundation of the state.

Imperceptibility's insurrection against state reason need not avoid discourse, but must incite a movement that carries thought far beyond it. Fragmented, discordant bodies now haunt the world, many of them aching to find a release for their negative affects.

Most often, subjects only consume themselves in a slow gnawing misery or burn up in a single outburst. Yet bands of troublemakers with a taste of illegalism have long shown how to turn these dangerous forces against their source. Furthermore, deep within the codes of digital culture, a new strategy has materialized. Borrowing from the strategies of bomb-throwing anarchists and the urban guerrilla, agents of subversion have found new forms of combat. They exploit, overload circuits, and camouflage within noise, turning the sprawling network of modern power into a battlefield.

There is something even more monumental at stake. Digital culture has triggered an anthropological transformation nourished by underground forces that are hard to trace. This shift is occurring faster than we can theorize, and its effects are irreversible. There are those who resist these changes, but perhaps they should be pushed to their limits. Negative affects fuel a human strike against the soul, whose dim interiority is a prison for the body. Tearing down its walls liberates the body, but only to cast it into a whole new universe of pleasures. Worrying about the particular pains and ecstasies that this new world will bring is not foolish, but it is impractical. Instead, we should dare to dream beyond measure, indulging in hallucinatory fantasies where our bodies have lost their interiors altogether and float like the stars, at one with the universe.

And Then It Vanishes... (Beyond Appearances)

At the height of its power, anonymity speaks to a power that does not appear, but disappears. Because it draws on the same power of unbecoming as does the scream, its forces are also expressed best through relation, rather than direct presentation. Invisibility and absence, disappearance and nonexistence, anonymity and illegibility, indistinguishability and indiscernibility all express its force. This is not to say they always end well. Anyone who has spent time in the streets knows the feelings of loneliness, solitude, exile, and defeat that rise up within when the forces of domination restore control. It is doubly disorienting as others act as if nothing happened. Such symbolic whiplash is not an accident. It is the work of the spectacle, which requires everything to give an account of itself—accounts that are broadcast as public displays of preference that are tracked, sorted, and reprogrammed. They are positivities to be cybernetically managed, reducing politics to order and movement in the space of appearance.

Cybernetic control intensifies its power with the assertion of space. And as a consequence, time is frozen. Stuck in a perpetual present, time slows to a standstill. As the veins of the Metropolis that give cybernetic capitalism its material existence cover the earth, difference flourishes but things remain the same.[31] Never before has so much changed without anything actually happening. Unlike those that preceded them, the prevailing forms of power today do not "exist;" they are so abstract as to give up their material existence to subsist only as incorporeal diagrams whose intensive power insists and persists only in management and circulation. This control is extended through space and the spatializing of power, which internalizes the force of the outside and renders bodies incapable of distantiation.[32] Moreover, such spatialization taps into the foreign or otherwise incommensurate worlds of past and present, with their exotic rituals and eccentric rhythms of life, by relating them through space, which makes them concurrent. The effect of this spatialization is the deadening not of space, however, but of time. And with all of the disjointed times recaptured in this way, cybernetic control accelerates difference under the assurance that they will all result in the same perpetual present.

The power of imperceptibility does not come from occupying space. Rather, evading the politics of recognition requires that one exist but without appearing, like the guerrilla who hides in the jungles of Brazil. In the Metropolis, one does not vanish through isolation, however. To escape, one dissolves and fades away by becoming indistinguishable from everyone else. This was done by members of the Red Army Faction, who resembled all the other citizens disaffected with the Auschwitz generation. And rather than shrinking until one is too worthless to be seen, this form of escape increases potential by amplifying intensity to the point of legality, for the strategy is not to occupy territory, but to *be* the territory.[33] So many movements have formed barely visible tears in the Metropolis with each protest, riot, burned car, occupied police precinct, and trail of graffiti. Finally, formal asymmetry can be elevated to the level of strategy, which uses escape to exploit weaknesses in the Metropolis. It is the cyberpunk hacker who hides in the codes.

The politics of the perpetual present may operate through appearances, but the politics of the future does not. The dislocated times of the present are embodied, if only for a moment, and then captured again. Yet in that short time, they give life to differences that reach beyond the present. For, even in its absence, the persistence of escape powerfully affirms the force of liberation. It is the voice of a silent struggle of abolition already underway, crying out, declaring the ongoing conflict: "A war without a battlefield. A war without an enemy. A war that is everywhere. A thousand civil wars. A war without end."[34] It continues:

> It is hard, now, to remember what life was like back then. . . . I believed them when they told me that I was alone in the world, and that this place and time were invincible . . . Before that day in September, in April, in December, in May, in November, when this city's veins opened, and we lived a hundred years of history in one afternoon. The world has changed and we have changed with it.[35]

This voice speaks for all the forces that evade power's grasp, fueling a clandestine rebellion. They are dramatic stories that flow like water to feed the underground current of revolt. They are incoherent attacks that gather like clouds to cast shadows over the world. And they are strategies for escape that shift with the changes in the weather. The underground does not negotiate. The underground is the legend of FOXFIRE that burns and burns. It does not demand political representation. It is the group agitations of the Socialist Patients' Collective that turns illness into a weapon. It makes no demands. It is the terrifying excess of "the birds" that interrupt normalcy. It does not make a claim to power. It is the deadly dance of the guerrilla's minuet making mobility lethal. It does not want to be. It is the flood of digital noise that destroys and horrifies. While meager, these are the best weapons we can furnish the unseen still trapped in their prison cells.

    in the evenings after supper there's a strange silence we no longer call to one another from our cells you can see the blue rectangles of the spy-holes uniformly lit up by the reflections from the television sets you can only ever hear the same monotonous rise and fall of music mingled with voices the ceiling is patterned with the beams of the yellow floodlights cutting through the huge window grid pinning you to your bed you're inside an enormous tin of sardines squashed pressed together you're inside a sealed tin hermetically soldered shut what is there outside this tin who is there outside what are they doing what are they doing now why do they go on doing things doing all the things they're doing without me where am I what am I which is my face now that all I have left is my face here crushed flattened squashed

    I broke the mirror with a leg of the stool I threw all the pieces down the toilet I flushed it I flushed it five six seven times I kept on flushing it staring at the black hole of the toilet that black circle where the water rushed down I put my hand inside it then deeper down to feel the bottom I put my head in it I pushed my head down but it wouldn't fit it wouldn't go through the hole to come out somewhere else to see out to see where I am where you are when we were a thousand ten thousand a hundred thousand it can't be true that there's no one outside it can't be true that I feel nothing any more that I no longer hear any voice any sound any breath it can't be true that outside there's only a vast cemetery where you are can you hear me I can't hear I can't hear you I can't hear anything any more suddenly the floodlights cut through the darkness they fill the cell with light

    when the opaque morning light slid through the bars and the window grids things in the cell regained their usual banal ordinary appearance we began again to think and imagine how we could see how we could make ourselves seen outside that prison that was becoming a cemetery the place of greatest silence where no message no voice no sound passes in or out any longer we looked at the problem of how to regain communication with the outside world and we decided to launch new protests to break that deadly silence we began by beating the bars during the night we'd agree on the time for this at exercise we had no watches we had no alarm clocks but we could see what time it was on the television sets that were kept on all night[36]

Acknowledgments

The shape of this book mirrors my own itinerant path. It has taken on various aliases, sailed under different flags, and been rebuilt many times over. Its beginnings owe everything to the Department of Comparative Studies at The Ohio State University, the only place I could have written the dissertation that I did. Faculty and colleagues helped it get off the ground, especially Gene Holland, Philip Armstrong, Mat Coleman, Franco Barchiesi, Cricket Keating, Shannon Winnubst, Gabriel Piser, Josh Kurz, Oded Nir, RaShelle Peck, Damon Berry, Jennifer Black, Vidar Thorsteinsen, Perry Miller, Allison Fish, Elo-Hanna Seljamaa, Kate Dean-Haidet, Wamae Muriuki, Ilana Maymind, Tahseen Kazi, Ricky Crano, Brian Murphy, Nick Crane, Chris Hemmig, and Brett Zehner. Essential ideas were hatched while wrenching on bikes in the Third-Hand Bike Co-op, overseen by the shelves of the Sporeprint Infoshop, and in the furtive spaces occupied by the Get Rowdy Crew (you all know who you are). Anarchists, ultras, and post-situationists everywhere have been crucial to the project, especially those in the occupied lands of the Tongva—your anonymity is safe with me.

Critical ideas germinated through intellectual exchanges that often migrated to email with Fulvia Carnevale, Alex Galloway, Achim Szepanski, Philippe Theophanidis, Alejandro de Acosta, Delio Vasquez, Frédéric Neyrat, Bogna Konior, Yvette Granata, Gabriel Salomon, Jason Smith, Zach Blas, Charles Athanasopoulos, Corinne Sugino, Jedidjah DeVries, Adrian Drummond-Cole, Eric Beck, Robert Hurley, Aragorn!, Kai Bosworth, Darien Belemu, and John Parman. I am deeply indebted to collegial feedback and mentorship from Josef Nguyen, Jaafar Aksikas, Michelle Janning, Justin Lincoln, Geert Lovink, Kevin Kuswa, Matt DeTar, Lisa Uddin, Tarik Elseewi, Lauren Osborne, Lydia McDermott, Matt May, Greg Seigworth, Jack

Bratich, Olivia Banner, Lisa Bell, Kim Knight, Sabrina Starnaman, Gavin Mueller, Heath Schultz, Paul Smith, Helen Kapstein, Brian Evenson, Arne DeBoever, Janet Sarbanes, Gabrielle Civil, Amanda Beech, Sara Mameni, Tom Leeser, Dominic Pettman, Daniel Spaulding, and Glenn Griffin. Ideas developed in intensive conversations with Matt Applegate and Hil Malatino and their colleagues at Binghamton University; the editors of the Institute for Experimental Freedom, *Bœdan* journal, No New Idea Press, and other antiauthoritarian publishers; Karyn Ball and the Marxist Literary Group; Mark Purcell, Keith Harris, Cheryl Gilge, and others at the University of Washington; Eric Jenkins and Peter Zhang of the Media Ecology Association; the many comrades of Commie Camp; Nandita Biswas Mellamphy and the theory graduate students of the University of Western Ontario; the brave radicals of Russia, especially Alexander Vileykis, Armen Aramayan, Yoel Regev, Oxana Timofeeva, Andrei Rodin, Artyom Kolganov, Denis Shalaginov, Marina Simakova, and all of the Stasis editorial board; Leo Zausen and McKenzie Wark at the New School; Tamás Nagypál, Scott Birdwise, Reşat Fuat Cam, and the Spiral Film-Philosophy Conference; Maggie Nelson and her students at the University of Southern California; Jessie Beier and the vibrant intellectuals at the University of Alberta; Yair Agmon and Brian Justie at the iSchool at UCLA; Rob Carley and international studies at Texas A&M; everyone at The Public School Los Angeles; and the graduate students of the CalArts Aesthetics and Politics program. I am incredibly grateful to Jamie Warren for his help preparing and indexing the manuscript. And thank you to Danielle Kasprzak, Leah Pennywark, Jason Weidemann, Anne Carter, and everyone at the University of Minnesota Press who helped the book become a reality.

Four people deserve special thanks: Wayne and Camille, for their unwavering support; my long-time collaborator Jose, from whom I learned how to write with fire instead of words; and Eva Della Lana, whose fighting spirit appears on every page.

Notes

Introduction

1. Peter Galison, "The Ontology of the Enemy: Norbert Wiener and the Cybernetic Vision," *Critical Inquiry* 21, no. 1 (1994): 228–66.
2. Seb Franklin, *Control: Digitality as Cultural Logic* (Cambridge, Mass.: MIT Press, 2015); Orit Halpern, *Beautiful Data: A History of Vision and Reason Since 1945* (Durham, N.C.: Duke University Press, 2014).
3. Plan C, "We Are All Very Anxious," *Plan C* (blog), April 4, 2014, weareplanc.org/blog/we-are-all-very-anxious/.
4. Tiqqun, *The Cybernetic Hypothesis*, trans. Robert Hurley (Los Angeles: Semiotext(e), 2020), 28–31.
5. For an extended discussion of cybernetics as a military-capitalist technology, intellectual formation, and philosophy, see my forthcoming entry in the *Bloomsbury Handbook of World Theory*.
6. James R. Beniger, *The Control Revolution: Technological and Economic Origins of the Information Society* (Cambridge, Mass.: Harvard University Press, 1986).
7. Teilhard de Chardin as quoted in Tiqqun, *Cybernetic Hypothesis*, 85.
8. Halpern, *Beautiful Data*, 180–84.
9. Jean-Paul Sartre, *Anti-Semite and Jew*, trans. George Joseph Becker (New York: Schocken, 1948), 13–14.
10. Invisible Committee, *The Coming Insurrection* (Cambridge, Mass.: Semiotext(e), 2009), 25–26.
11. Michael Hardt and Antonio Negri, *Empire* (Cambridge, Mass.: Harvard University Press, 2000), 284–89.
12. Gilles Deleuze, "Postscript on the Societies of Control," *October* 59 (Winter 1992): 3–7.
13. Gilles Châtelet, *To Live and Think Like Pigs: The Incitement of Envy and Boredom in Market Democracies*, trans. Robin Mackay (Falmouth, England: Urbanomic; New York: Sequence, 2014), 55–73.
14. Châtelet, 67–73.
15. Châtelet, 56–64. See also chapter 3 of the present volume.
16. Châtelet, 55–73. See also chapter 6 of the present volume.
17. Châtelet, 55–73. See also chapter 10 of the present volume.

18. Mitchell Dean, *Governmentality: Power and Rule in Modern Society*, 2nd ed. (Los Angeles: SAGE, 2009), 184–185.

19. Michel Foucault, "Omnes et Singulatim: Towards a Criticism of Political Reason," *The Tanner Lectures on Human Values* 2 (1981): 223–54.

20. Gilles Deleuze, *Nietzsche and Philosophy* (New York: Columbia University Press, 1983), 10.

21. Indebted to Hegel, the dialectic of recognition follows a "law of desire" in which the subject is forged through an encounter with an alien other, resulting in an identity, the product of two movements: the internalization of otherness, and the projection of something shared with the other. See Georg Wilhelm Friedrich Hegel, *Phenomenology of Spirit*, trans. Arnold Vincent Miller (Oxford: Oxford University Press, 1977), 111–19 (though Hegel's *Philosophy of Right* arguably serves as the liberal pole of his work).

22. Glen Sean Coulthard, *Red Skin, White Masks : Rejecting the Colonial Politics of Recognition* (Minneapolis: University of Minnesota Press, 2014), 3.

23. Gilles Deleuze and Félix Guattari, *A Thousand Plateaus*, vol. 2 of *Capitalism and Schizophrenia*, trans. Brian Massumi (Minneapolis: University of Minnesota Press, 1987), 3.

24. Deleuze and Guattari, 6.

25. Deleuze and Guattari, 5–7, 17–18, 21, 24–25.

26. Deleuze and Guattari, 6.

27. Gilles Deleuze, *Difference and Repetition*, trans. Paul Patton (New York: Columbia University Press, 1994), 56.

28. Michel Foucault, *Discipline and Punish: The Birth of the Prison* (New York: Vintage, 1977), 200.

29. Peggy Phelan, *Unmarked: The Politics of Performance* (New York: Routledge, 1993), 6.

30. Deleuze and Guattari, *Thousand Plateaus*, 3.

31. Nandita Biswas Mellamphy, "Larval Terror and the Digital Darkside," *E-International Relations*, November 14, 2015, e-ir.info/2015/11/14/larval-terror-and-the-digital-darkside/.

32. Deleuze and Guattari, *Thousand Plateaus*, 3.

33. Deleuze and Guattari, 3.

34. Deleuze and Guattari, 11; 6.

35. Deleuze and Guattari, 24.

36. Deleuze and Guattari, 24.

37. Deleuze and Guattari, 24.

38. Deleuze and Guattari, 24.

39. Deleuze and Guattari, 24.

40. Deleuze and Guattari, 171, 187.

41. Deleuze and Guattari, 199–200, 193–94, 197.

42. Deleuze and Guattari, 200.
43. Deleuze and Guattari, 200.
44. Deleuze and Guattari, 216.
45. Richard Gilman-Opalsky and Ill Will Editions, "The Eternal Return of Revolt: A Conversation with Richard Gilman-Opalsky," *Ill Will Editions* (blog), July 7, 2020, illwilleditions.com/the-eternal-return-of-revolt/.
46. Deleuze and Guattari, *Thousand Plateaus*, 292.
47. Deleuze and Guattari, 292.
48. Deleuze and Guattari, 266–67.
49. Daniel Kalder, "Dictator-Lit: Gaddafi's Surreal Gibberish," *The Guardian*, March 24, 2010, theguardian.com/books/booksblog/2010/mar/24/dictator-lit-gaddafi; Deleuze and Guattari, *Thousand Plateaus*, 248–50.
50. Deleuze and Guattari, *Thousand Plateaus*, 279–80.
51. Deleuze and Guattari, 279–80. Each of the strata roughly overlap with Jacques Lacan's three orders: anorganic/real; organic/symbolic; alloplastic/imaginary.
52. Hito Steyerl, *How Not to Be Seen: A Fucking Didactic Educational .MOV File*, 2013, video, 15:52, artforum.com/video/hito-steyerl-how-not-to-be-seen-a-fucking-didactic-educational-mov-file-2013-51651.
53. Halpern, *Beautiful Data*.
54. Deleuze and Guattari, *Thousand Plateaus*, 280.
55. André Moncourt and J. Smith, *Projectiles for the People*, vol. 1 of *The Red Army Faction: A Documentary History* (Montreal: Kersplebedeb; Oakland, Calif.: PM Press, 2009), 437.
56. Moncourt and Smith, 438.
57. Moncourt and Smith, 438.
58. Deleuze and Guattari, *Thousand Plateaus*, 197, 279.
59. Alexander R. Galloway and Eugene. Thacker, *The Exploit: A Theory of Networks* (Minneapolis: University of Minnesota Press, 2007), 135–38.
60. Finn Brunton and Helen Nissenbaum, *Obfuscation: A User's Guide for Privacy and Protest* (Cambridge, Mass.: MIT Press, 2016), 1 (italics original).
61. Brunton and Nissenbaum, 8–24.
62. Deleuze and Guattari, *Thousand Plateaus*, 280.
63. On the abstraction of grids, see Rosalind Krauss, "Grids," *October* 9 (Summer 1979): 50–64.
64. Deleuze and Guattari, *Thousand Plateaus*, 261–63.
65. Édouard Glissant, *Poetics of Relation*, trans. Betsy Wing (Ann Arbor: University of Michigan Press, 2010), 189.
66. Jean Genet, *Prisoner of Love*, trans. Barbara Bray (New York: New York Review Books, 2003), 50–51, 172.
67. William Haver, "The Ontological Priority of Violence: On Several

Really Smart Things about Violence in Jean Genet's Work," *Polylog*, 2004, nos. 35–36, them.polylog.org/5/fhw-en.htm.

68. Deleuze and Guattari, *Thousand Plateaus*, 286; 285.

69. Deleuze and Guattari, 275–79; Jose Rosales, "The Girl With the Bomb, The Guardian of Dynamite: Notes on the Politics of Becoming-Woman," *The Tragic Community* (blog), November 28, 2017, thetragiccommunity.wordpress.com/2017/11/28/the-girl-with-the-bomb-the-guardian-of-dynamite/; Lucy E. Parsons, "Dynamite: Its Voice the Only Voice That Oppressors of the People Can Understand," *The Labor Enquirer* 5, no. 14 (April 4, 1885).

70. Deleuze and Guattari, *Thousand Plateaus*, 290. They follow this line with a reference to a Noh actor, whose mask ("with which to cover his lack of a face") bears a fixed expression. In essence they are arguing that identity may appear to hide beneath structural positions, but in the last instance, there is only positionality.

71. Deleuze and Guattari, 17. It is important to note the "guerrilla" is the diminuitive form of the Spanish word for war, "guerra," thus implying a minoritarian form of war that is smaller in size, scale, or form.

72. For additional commentary on Deleuze and Guattari's relationship to George Jackson, see: Daniel Colucciello Barber, "The Creation of Non-Being," *Rhizomes*, no. 29 (2016), rhizomes.net/issue29/pdf/barber.pdf; Michelle Koerner, "Line of Escape: Gilles Deleuze's Encounter with George Jackson," *Genre: Forms of Discourse and Culture* 44, no. 2 (2011): 157–80; Taija McDougall, "Left Out: Notes on Absence, Nothingness and the Black Prisoner Theorist," *Anthurium* 15, no. 2 (2019): 8.

73. Martin van Creveld, "Tactics," in *Encyclopædia Britannica*, britannica.com/topic/tactics.

74. U.S. military strategy remains obsessed with lines. The U.S. Army's *Field Manual 3-0: Operations* (Washington, D.C.: Department of the Army, 2017) is a deeply linear approach to engagement through lines and points: one diagram describes combat through a "passage of lines" between the battle handover line, lines of contact, phase lines, passage points, release points, and starting points (figure 6-21).

75. François Dosse, *Gilles Deleuze and Félix Guattari: Intersecting Lives*, trans. Deborah Glassman (New York: Columbia University Press, 2010), 296–301.

76. Dosse, 468–69; George Katsiaficas, *The Subversion of Politics: European Autonomous Social Movements and the Decolonization of Everyday Life* (Oakland, Calif.: AK Press, 2006), 52–54.

77. Curious here is that Lawrence's text ("T.E. Lawrence on Guerrilla Warfare," in *Encyclopædia Britannica*, britannica.com/topic/T-E-Lawrence-on-guerrilla-warfare-1984900) is not the first on irregular tactics, as is evi-

dent in Greek myths, biblical battles, and military texts through the ages. Nor is it the most influential text on guerrilla warfare.

78. Deleuze and Guattari, *Thousand Plateaus*, 416. They also cite Guy Brossollet on the "non-battle"; see also Alexander R. Galloway, "Guy Brossollet's 'Non-Battle,'" *Culture and Communication* (blog), December 1, 2014, cultureandcommunication.org/galloway/guy-brossollets-non-battle.

79. C. A. Fraser, "Unconventional Warfare," *Koers: Bulletin for Christian Scholarship* 36, no. 2 (1968): 137.

80. Lawrence, "T.E. Lawrence on Guerrilla Warfare."

81. This and all proceeding unmarked quotations are from "Lawrence on Guerrilla Warfare."

82. Gilles Deleuze, "The Shame and the Glory: T. E. Lawrence," in *Essays Critical and Clinical*, trans. Daniel W. Smith and Michael A. Greco (New York: Verso, 1998), 120–21.

83. Deleuze, "Postscript," 4.

84. Kimberly Mair, *Guerrilla Aesthetics: Art, Memory, and the West German Guerrilla* (Montreal: McGill-Queen's University Press, 2016), 24.

85. Mair, 24; 7–9.

86. Paul Ryan, "Cybernetic Guerrilla Warfare," *Radical Software* 1, no. 3 (1971): 1–2.

87. Mair, *Guerrilla Aesthetics*, 22–23.

88. Mair, 72–73.

89. Mair, 71. She here further quotes the explanation: "You realize how important it is to not speak when you see how they celebrate every one of your words like a victory—in reality something to ease their conscience, their knowledge that they are torturers and assassins. You help them to carry the burden of their responsibility, you make yourself into their accomplice. You are supposed to show them that you consent to the torture you are being subjected to. They want a total victory—and in this way they will have it."

90. Mair, 24–25.

91. Michel Foucault, *The History of Sexuality*, vol. 1, *An Introduction* (New York: Vintage, 1990), 93.

92. Michel Foucault, *"Society Must Be Defended": Lectures at the Collège de France, 1975–1976*, ed. Mauro Bertani and Alessandro Fontana, trans. David Macey (New York: Palgrave Macmillan, 2003), 16–17.

93. Foucault, 222–25; this coincides with the liberal revolution that paradoxically scales back the state (relative to monarchical absolutism) through the logic of efficiency, in which the state's maximum power is found in a virtuous balance between it and other forces (the market, civil society, etc.).

94. Foucault, 236–37.

95. Foucault, 61–62.

96. U.S. Army, *Field Manual 3-24: Insurgencies and Countering Insurgency* (Washington, D.C.: Department of the Army, 2014), nos. 1–3 and 1–27.

97. U.S. Army, no. 4-57.

98. U.S. Army, *Army Doctrine Publication 3-90: Offense and Defense* (Washington, D.C.: Department of the Army, 2019).

99. U.S. Army, no. 2-10; reference refers to section not page.

100. Stop LAPD Spying Coalition, *Fuck the Police, Trust the People: Surveillance Bureaucracy Expands the Stalker State* (Los Angeles: Stop LAPD Spying Coalition, 2020), 2, stoplapdspying.org/wp-content/uploads/2020/06/TRUST-THE-PPL-not-the-POLICE.pdf.

101. Stop LAPD Spying Coalition, 4.

102. Ann Laura Stoler, *Race and the Education of Desire: Foucault's History of Sexuality and the Colonial Order of Things* (Durham, N.C.: Duke University Press, 1995); Paul Rabinow, *French Modern: Norms and Forms of the Social Environment* (Chicago: University of Chicago Press, 1995). Parenthetically, the colonies were a key site for the invention of modern policing, in both the general and particular, such as violently suppressing slave revolts in the Americas or Robert Peel exporting his experience in colonial Ireland to London to found its first modern police force.

103. Richard H. Thaler and Cass R. Sunstein, *Nudge: Improving Decisions about Health, Wealth, and Happiness* (New Haven, Conn.: Yale University Press, 2008).

104. U.S. Army, *Field Manual 3-24*, nos. 1-30 and 1-29.

105. U.S. Army, nos. 10-25–30.

106. Aaron Morrison and Tim Sullivan, "Minneapolis Overwhelmed Again by Protests over Floyd Death," *Minneapolis Star Tribune*, May 30, 2020, dailyherald.com/article/20200530/news/305309989.

107. Martin Schoots-McAlpine, "Anatomy of a Counter-Insurgency: Efforts to Undermine the George Floyd Uprising," *Monthly Review*, July 3, 2020, mronline.org/2020/07/03/anatomy-of-a-counter-insurgency/.

108. Violet Chrysanthemum and Tancrède Fulconis, "The Spectre of 'Antifa': A Reterritorialisation of the Uprising," *Discursive Constructs* (blog), July 5, 2020, discursiveconstructs.wordpress.com/2020/07/05/the-spectre-of-antifa-a-reterritorialisation-of-the-uprising-1/.

109. U.S. Army, *Field Manual 3-24*, nos. 10-17 and 10-10.

110. Foucault, *"Society Must Be Defended,"* 50.

111. Foucault, *History of Sexuality*, 1:112.

112. Foucault, *"Society Must Be Defended,"* 55–56.

113. Foucault, 50.

114. Foucault, 55–56.

115. Foucault, 57.
116. Foucault, 60.
117. Foucault, 224–25.
118. Foucault, 14–17.
119. Jean Genet, *The Declared Enemy: Texts and Interviews*, ed. Albert Dichy, trans. Jeff Fort (Stanford, Calif.: Stanford University Press, 2004), 244.
120. Emilio Bejel, *Gay Cuban Nation* (Chicago: University of Chicago Press, 2001), 97.
121. Bejel, 100–104.
122. Huey P. Newton, "Huey Talks About Gay and Women's Liberation," *The Black Panther* 5, no. 8 (1970): 5.
123. Tiqqun, *This Is Not a Program*, trans. Joshua David Jordan (Los Angeles: Semiotext(e), 2011), 84.
124. Tiqqun, 84.
125. Tiqqun, 84–85. Tiqqun suggests that such spaces worked best when they were abandoned, when they either stopped emitting lines of becoming or became too costly to maintain.
126. Tiqqun, 85.
127. Max G. Manwaring, *Shadows of Things Past and Images of the Future: Lessons for the Insurgencies in Our Midst* (Carlisle, PA: Strategic Studies Institute, 2004), 7; Tiqqun, *This Is Not a Program*, 85.
128. U.S. Army, *Field Manual 3-24: Insurgencies and Countering Insurgency*, 1–29.
129. Lawrence, "T. E. Lawrence on Guerrilla Warfare."
130. Gilles Deleuze and Martin Joughin, *Negotiations, 1972–1990* (New York: Columbia University Press, 1995), vii.
131. Deleuze and Joughin, vii.
132. Michel Foucault, "Preface," trans. Robert Hurley, Mark Seem, and Helen R. Lane, in Gilles Deleuze and Félix Guattari, *Anti-Oedipus*, vol. 1 of *Capitalism and Schizophrenia* (Minneapolis: University of Minnesota Press, 1977), xiii–iv; Stefano Harney and Fred. Moten, *The Undercommons: Fugitive Planning et Black Study* (Wivenhoe, England: Minor Compositions, 2013); Anonymous, *Call*, bloomo101.org/wp-content/uploads/2015/02/ENGcall2.pdf.
133. Harney and Moten, *Undercommons*, 26.
134. The *Call* text also echoes Foucault in Proposition V ("To any moral preoccupation, to any concern for purity, we substitute the collective working out of a strategy" [Anonymous, 49]), and Moten and Harney in Proposition III ("we serenely envisage the criminal nature of our existence, and of our gestures" [Anonymous, 25]).
135. Anonymous, 61.

136. Jesse Cohn, *Underground Passages: Anarchist Resistance Culture 1848–2011* (Oakland, Calif.: AK Press, 2014), 382.

137. Cohn, 382. A thread Cohn pulls through the book is the relationship between politically active anarchists and aesthetic movements inspired by them, with David Weir's work as the key reference point. While Cohn comes to conclusions very different from those offered here, his list of the five "non-s" concisely describes what the avant-garde took from anarchism.

138. Deleuze and Guattari, *Thousand Plateaus*, 386.

139. Dosse, *Gilles Deleuze and Félix Guattari*, 33–34, 170–79.

140. Gilles Deleuze and Elias Sanbar, "The Indians of Palestine," trans. Timothy S. Murphy, *Discourse* 20, no. 3 (1988): 25–29.

141. Dosse, *Gilles Deleuze and Félix Guattari*, 296–301.

142. Dosse, 289–301.

143. Gilles Deleuze and Félix Guattari, "Europe The Wrong Way," in *Two Regimes of Madness: Texts and Interviews 1975–1995* (Los Angeles: Semiotext(e), 2006); David Macey, *The Lives of Michel Foucault* (New York: Vintage, 1995), 392–96.

144. Franco "Bifo" Berardi, "Anatomy of Autonomy," trans. Jared Becker, Richard Reid, and Andrew Rosenbaum, in *Autonomia: Post-Political Politics*, ed. Sylvère Lotringer and Christian Marazzi (Los Angeles: Semiotext(e), 2007), 148–70. More generally see the other pieces in Lotringer and Marazzi, *Autonomia*.

145. Quoted in Fraser, "Unconventional Warfare," 138.

146. Lawrence, "T. E. Lawrence on Guerrilla Warfare."

147. Kristian Williams, "The Other Side of the COIN: Counterinsurgency and Community Policing," in *Life During Wartime: Resistance Counterinsurgency*, ed. Kristian Williams, Will Munger, and Lara Messersmith-Glavin (Oakland, Calif.: AK Press, 2013), 83–110.

148. Ralph Ellison, *Invisible Man* (New York: Random House, 1952), 6–7.

I. Anonymity

1. Shannon Mattern, "Cloud and Field," *Places Journal*, August 2016, placesjournal.org/article/cloud-and-field/.

2. Geoff Manaugh, *A Burglar's Guide to the City* (Toronto: McClelland and Stewart, 2016), 9.

3. Antonio Senta, *Luigi Galleani: The Most Dangerous Anarchist in America*, trans. Andrea Asali and Sean Sayers (Chico, Calif.: AK Press, 2019), 19.

4. Grégoire Chamayou, *Manhunts: A Philosophical History*, trans. Steven Rendall (Princeton, N.J.: Princeton University Press, 2012).

5. Chamayou, 150.

6. Orit Halpern, *Beautiful Data: A History of Vision and Reason Since 1945* (Durham, N.C.: Duke University Press, 2014), 199–207.
7. On this point, see the films of Harun Farocki.
8. McKenzie Wark, *A Hacker Manifesto* (Cambridge, Mass.: Harvard University Press, 2004), 4–5, 274.
9. Marco Deseriis, *Improper Names: Collective Pseudonyms from the Luddites to Anonymous* (Minneapolis: University of Minnesota Press, 2015), 8–18.
10. Deseriis, 4.
11. McKenzie Wark and Ali Dur, "New New Bablyon," *October*, no. 138 (2011): 43–45.
12. Wark and Dur, 43–47.
13. Wark and Dur, 46.

1. The Force of Liberation

1. James C. Scott, *The Art of Not Being Governed: An Anarchist History of Upland Southeast Asia* (New Haven, Conn.: Yale University Press, 2011), 166; see also xii for an explanation of its significance for non-state peoples.
2. Régis Debray, *Revolution in the Revolution?: Armed Struggle and Political Struggle in Latin America*, trans. Bobbye Ortis (New York: MR Press, 1967), 50–53; Abraham Guillén, *Philosophy of the Urban Guerrilla*, trans. Donald C. Hodges (New York: Morrow, 1973), 284–86.
3. Debray, *Revolution in the Revolution?*, 75–78.
4. Gilles Deleuze and Félix Guattari, *What Is Philosophy?*, trans. Hugh Tomlinson and Graham Burchell III (New York: Columbia University Press, 1996), 279 (trans. modified).
5. Tse-Tung Mao, *Mao Tse-Tung on Guerrilla Warfare* (FMFRP 12-18), trans. Samuel B. Griffith with introduction (Washington, D.C.: U.S. Marine Corps, 1989), 42.
6. Che Guevara, *Guerrilla Warfare*, with revised and updated introduction and case studies (Wilmington, Del.: SR Press, 2001), 72–73.
7. Carlos Marighella, *Mini-Manual of the Urban Guerrilla* (Montreal: Abraham Guillen; Toronto: Arm the Spirit, 2002), 4.
8. Guillén, *Philosophy*, 69, 70–71.
9. Guillén, 240.
10. Guillén, 250–51.
11. Marighella, *Mini-Manual*, 5.
12. Marighella, 5 (trans. modified).
13. Guillén, *Philosophy*, 240 (trans. modified).
14. Guevara, *Guerrilla Warfare*, 58–59.
15. Debray, *Revolution in the Revolution?*, 29. As an emergent response

to its milieu, life's rhythmic expansion and contraction of difference lead to the internalization of its surroundings, encouraging it to leave and explore new environments. Shaping this Darwinian analogy into the movement of life, Deleuze uses this among many other analogies to describe the character of a line of becoming. For more, consult the work of Henri Bergson, Gilles Deleuze, *Difference and Repetition*, trans. Paul Patton (New York: Columbia University Press, 1994); Deleuze, *Bergsonism*, trans. Barbara Habberjam and Hugh Tomlinson (New York: Zone, 1988); and Gilles Deleuze and Félix Guattari, *A Thousand Plateaus*, vol. 2 of *Capitalism and Schizophrenia*, trans. Brian Massumi (Minneapolis: University of Minnesota Press, 1987).

16. Debray, *Revolution in the Revolution?*, 49.

17. Debray, 50–53.

18. Jennifer Morrison Taw and Bruce Hoffman, "The Urbanisation of Insurgency: The Potential Challenge to US Army Operations," *Small Wars & Insurgencies* 6, no. 1 (1995): 74.

19. Marighella, *Mini-Manual*, 24–25.

20. Marighella, 25 (trans. modified).

21. Debray, *Revolution in the Revolution*, 41.

22. Maurizio Lazzarato, "From Capital-Labour to Capital-Life," *Ephemera* 4, no. 3 (2004): 200–205.

23. Guillén, *Philosophy*, 241.

24. Marighella, *Mini-Manual*, 15–17.

25. Tiqqun, *This Is Not a Program*, trans. Joshua David Jordan (Los Angeles: Semiotext(e), 2011), 85.

26. Tiqqun, 85.

27. Red Army Faction, "The Urban Guerilla Concept," in *The Red Army Faction, a Documentary History*, vol. 1, *Projectiles for the People*, ed. J. Smith and André Moncourt (Oakland, Calif.: PM Press, 2009), 83.

28. Red Army Faction, 83.

29. Debray, *Revolution in the Revolution?*, 52.

30. Quoted in Giorgio Agamben, "Metropolis," trans. Arianna Bove, transcribed from Uninomade audio files available on globalproject.info in 2005, *Generation Online*, generation-online.org/p/fpagamben4.htm.

2. Propaganda of the Deed

1. Robert Graham, *From Anarchy to Anarchism (300CE to 1939)*, vol. 1, *Anarchism: A Documentary History of Libertarian Ideas* (Montreal: Black Rose Books, 2005), 68.

2. Johann Most, *Revolutionäre Kriegswissenschaft: Ein Handbüchlein zur Anleitung betreffend Gebrauches und Herstellung von Nitroglycerin, Dynamit,*

Schiessbaumwolle, Knallquecksilber, Bomben, Brandsätzen, Giften u.s.w., u.s.w. (New York: Internationaler Zeitungs-Verein, 1885).

3. Paul Avrich, *The Haymarket Tragedy* (Princeton, N.J.: Princeton University Press, 1984), 170–71.

4. See also Louis Adamic, *Dynamite: The Story of Class Violence in America* (New York: Viking, 1931).

5. Graham, *From Anarchy to Anarchism*, 1:151.

6. Graham, 1:139.

7. Gilles Deleuze, *Foucault*, trans. Seán Hand (Minneapolis: University of Minnesota Press, 1988), 94–95.

3. The Voice of Bullets and Bombs

1. Red Army Faction, "The Urban Guerilla Concept," in *The Red Army Faction, a Documentary History*, vol. 1, *Projectiles for the People*, ed. J. Smith and André Moncourt (Oakland, Calif.: PM Press, 2009), 85.

2. Red Army Faction, 1:85.

3. Red Army Faction, "On the Liberation of Andreas Baader," in Smith and Moncourt, *Red Army Faction, a Documentary History*, 1:361.

4. Red Army Faction, 1:361.

5. Red Army Faction, 1:363 and 1:359.

6. Red Army Faction, 1:365.

7. Tom Vague, *Televisionaries: The Red Army Faction Story, 1963–1993* (San Francisco: AK Press, 1994), 37.

8. Vague, 37.

4. Messages without a Sender

1. Utah Phillips, "Heroes," track 10 on *The Past Didn't Go Anywhere*, with Ani Defranco, Righteous Babe Records, 1996.

2. Karl Marx, "The Eighteenth Brumaire of Louis Bonaparte," in *Marx/Engels Collected Works* (London: Lawrence and Wishart, 2010), 148–50.

3. Mikhail Bakunin, *Bakunin on Anarchy*, trans. Sam Dolgoff (New York: Vintage, 1972), 294.

4. Bakunin, 297–98.

5. Bakunin, 308.

6. Deleuze and Guattari, *A Thousand Plateaus*, vol. 2 of *Capitalism and Schizophrenia*, trans. Brian Massumi (Minneapolis: University of Minnesota Press, 1987), 112.

7. Insinuation thus blurs the distinction between two dominant models of communication, the transmission model and the cultural, because it asks

the materialist question of transmission of a signal through a medium but without focusing on the genesis or reception of that signal, but also asks questions about the cultural effects of common forms and a communication event. For more on the distinction between the two approaches, see James Carey, "A Cultural Approach to Communication," in *Communication as Culture: Essays on Media and Society* (New York: Routledge, 1992), 13–36, and Lawrence Grossberg, Ellen Wartella, D. Charles Whitney, and J. Macgregor Wise, "Media in Context," in *MediaMaking: Mass Media in a Popular Culture* (London: SAGE, 2006), 3–33.

8. Michael Taussig, *The Nervous System* (New York: Routledge, 1991).

9. Maurice Charland, "Constitutive Rhetoric: The Case of the Peuple Québécois," *Quarterly Journal of Speech* 73, no. 2 (1987): 133–50.

10. Édouard Glissant, *Poetics of Relation*, trans. Betsy Wing (Ann Arbor: University of Michigan Press, 2010), 13.

11. Michael Hardt and Antonio Negri, *Empire* (Cambridge, Mass.: Harvard University Press, 2000), 132–34.

12. Michel Foucault, "Truth and Power: Interview by Alessandro Fontana and Pasquale Pasquino," in *Power/Knowledge: Selected Interviews and Other Writings, 1972–1977*, ed. Colin Gordon, trans. Leo Marshall, John Mepham, and Kate Soper (New York: Vintage, 1980), 131–32.

13. Deleuze and Guattari, *A Thousand Plateaus*, 77.

14. Dominic Smith, "Deleuze's Ethics of Reading: Deleuze, Badiou, and Primo Levi," *Angelaki: Journal of Theoretical Humanities* 12, no. 3 (2007): 49.

15. Benjamin Arditi, "Insurgencies Don't Have a Plan—They Are the Plan: Political Performatives and Vanishing Mediators in 2011," *JOMEC Journal*, June 2012, 1–16, at 15.

16. Tiqqun, *Theses on the Imaginary Party* (Ill Will Editions, 2011), 12 (no. 15), forpartisans.noblogs.org/files/2011/09/imaginary-party.pdf.

17. Tiqqun, 12 (no. 16).

18. Michel Foucault, *"Society Must Be Defended": Lectures at the Collège de France, 1975–1976*, ed. Mauro Bertani and Alessandro Fontana, trans. David Macey (New York: Palgrave Macmillan, 2003), 217–23.

5. The Sprawl

1. William Gibson, *Neuromancer* (New York: Ace, 1984), 7.

2. Gibson, 51.

3. Walter Gibson, interview by Brooke Gladstone, "The Science in Science Fiction" (with David Brin and Anne Simon), *National Public Radio*, October 22, 2018, audio, 50:00, at 11:25, npr.org/2018/10/22/1067220/the-science-in-science-fiction.

4. The term "Metropolis" is taken from Italian political thought, such as the Venice School of Architecture. It proliferated during the *Autonomia* period and has been subsequently revisited by Tiqqun, Giorgio Agamben, Michael Hardt and Antonio Negri, and others. I use the concept throughout this book to describe the lived material reality under cybernetic capitalism.

5. Ian Alan Paul, *Climate, Capitalism, Control Artist's Description*, 2019, video, 28:39, ianalanpaul.com/climate-capitalism-control/.

6. The Politics of Asymmetry

1. On Stephen Gaghan's *Syriana* as an aesthetic lament over narrowness and friction in a complex world, making it a conservative elegy written in the pen of the centralized, see Patrick Jagoda, *Network Aesthetics* (Chicago: University of Chicago Press, 2016), 99–102.

2. Alexander R. Galloway, *Protocol: How Control Exists after Decentralization* (Cambridge, Mass.: MIT Press, 2004), 3.

3. Michael Hardt and Antonio Negri, *Commonwealth* (Cambridge, Mass.: Harvard University Press, 2009), 250. See also Manfredo Tafuri, Giorgio Piccinato, and Vieri Quilici, "La Città Territorio: Verso Una Nuova Dimensione," *Casabella Continuà*, no. 270 (December 1962): 16–25.

4. Peter Krapp, *Noise Channels: Glitch and Error in Digital Culture* (Minneapolis: University of Minnesota Press, 2011), 49–51.

5. Rita Raley, *Tactical Media* (Minneapolis: University of Minnesota Press, 2009), 6.

6. Abraham Guillén, *Philosophy of the Urban Guerrilla*, trans. Donald C. Hodges (New York: Morrow, 1973), 257.

7. Tiziana Terranova, *Network Culture: Cultural Politics for the Information Age* (London: Pluto, 2004), 70.

8. See Esther Dyson, "End of the Official Story: You No Longer Control Your Message," *Executive Excellence* 17, no. 5 (2000): 20.

9. Marshall McLuhan, *Understanding Media: The Extensions of Man* (New York: McGraw-Hill, 1964), 8.

10. Orit Halpern, *Beautiful Data: A History of Vision and Reason Since 1945* (Durham, N.C.: Duke University Press, 2014), 113, 115, 117–21.

11. Kevin Lynch, *The Image of the City* (Cambridge, Mass.: MIT Press, 1960), 5.

12. Gilles Deleuze, *Difference and Repetition*, trans. Paul Patton (New York: Columbia University Press, 1994), 180.

13. Giorgio Agamben, "Metropolis," trans. Arianna Bove, transcribed from Uninomade audio files available on globalproject.info in 2005, *Generation Online*, generation-online.org/p/fpagamben4.htm.

14. Gilles Deleuze and Félix Guattari, *A Thousand Plateaus*, vol. 2 of *Capitalism and Schizophrenia*, trans. Brian Massumi (Minneapolis: University of Minnesota Press, 1987), 434; 435.

15. Helen Palmer, *Deleuze and Futurism: A Manifesto for Nonsense* (London: Bloomsbury, 2014), 64.

16. Ernesto Laclau and Chantal Mouffe, *Hegemony and Socialist Strategy: Towards a Radical Democratic Politics* (New York: Verso Trade, 1985); Jacques Rancière, *Disagreement: Politics and Philosophy*, trans. Julie Rose (Minneapolis: University of Minnesota Press, 1999); Michel Foucault, "The Subject and Power," in *Michel Foucault: Beyond Structuralism and Hermeneutics*, ed. Hubert Dreyfus and Paul Rabinow, trans. Leslie Sawyer (Chicago: University of Chicago Press, 1982), 208–26.

17. Tiziana Terranova, "New Economy, Financialization and Social Production in the Web 2.0," in *Crisis in the Global Economy: Financial Markets, Social Struggles, and New Political Scenarios*, ed. Andrea Fumagalli and Sandro Mezzadra, trans. Jason Francis McGimsey (Los Angeles: Semiotext(e), 2010), 153–70.

18. Gilles Deleuze and Félix Guattari, *Anti-Oedipus*, vol. 1 of *Capitalism and Schizophrenia*, trans. Robert Hurley, Mark Seem, and Helen R. Lane (Minneapolis: University of Minnesota, 1977).

19. Gilles Deleuze, *The Fold: Leibniz and the Baroque*, trans. Tom Conley (Minneapolis: University of Minnesota Press, 1993), 136–37.

20. Deleuze, 130–31.

21. François Zourabichvili, *Deleuze: A Philosophy of the Event together with the Vocabulary of Desire*, ed. Gregg Lambert and Daniel W. Smith, trans. Kieran Aarons (Edinburgh: Edinburgh University Press, 2012), 168.

22. Zourabichvili, 121.

23. Zourabichvili, 121.

24. Jodi Dean, *Blog Theory: Feedback and Capture in the Circuits of Drive* (Cambridge: Polity, 2010).

25. Saskia Sassen, *The Global City: New York, London, Tokyo* (Princeton, N.J.: Princeton University Press, 1991); John Friedmann and Goetz Wolff, "World City Formation: An Agenda for Research and Action," *International Journal of Urban and Regional Research* 6, no. 3 (1982): 309–44.

26. Alexander R. Galloway and Eugine Thacker, *The Exploit: A Theory of Networks* (Minneapolis: University of Minnesota Press, 2007), 14 (emphasis added).

27. Galloway and Thatcher, 59.

28. Galloway and Thacker, 14.

29. Deleuze and Guattari, *A Thousand Plateaus*, 213, 275–80.

30. Homi K. Bhabha, "Location, Intervention, Incommensurability: A Conversation with Homi Bhabha," *Emergences* 1, no. 1 (1989): 63–88; Kenneth

Surin, *Freedom Not yet: Liberation and the Next World Order* (Durham, N.C.: Duke University Press, 2009).

31. Red Army Faction, "The Black September Action in Munich: Regarding the Strategy for Anti-Imperialist Struggle," in *The Red Army Faction, a Documentary History*, vol. 1, *Projectiles for the People*, ed. J. Smith and André Moncourt (Oakland, Calif.: PM Press, 2009), 223. Although there are some notable disagreements, there is a general agreement over the use of "Empire" (as with "Metropolis") between militant anti-imperialists and the Autonomist and post-Autonomist tradition. Most notable for this book are Michael Hardt and Antonio Negri, *Empire* (Cambridge, Mass: Harvard University Press, 2000); Hardt and Negri, *Commonwealth*; Tiqqun, *Introduction to Civil War*, trans. Alexander R. Galloway and Jason E. Smith (Los Angeles: Semiotext(e), 2010).

32. Galloway, *Protocol*, 69.

33. Galloway and Thacker, *Exploit*, 21.

34. Galloway and Thacker, 21.

35. Deleuze and Guattari, *Anti-Oedipus*, 230–32; Deleuze and Guattari, *Thousand Plateaus*, 436–37, 472–73.

36. Jean Baudrillard, "A Perverse Logic (Society's Attitude Towards Drugs)," *The Courier*, no. 9 (July 1987): 6.

37. Michel Serres, *The Parasite*, trans. Lawrence R. Schehr (Baltimore, Md.: Johns Hopkins Press, 1982), 127.

38. Michel Serres, *Genesis*, trans. Geneviève James and James Nielson (Ann Arbor: University of Michigan Press, 1995), 7.

39. Greg Hainge, "Of Glitch and Men: The Place of the Human in the Successful Integration of Failure and Noise in the Digital Realm," *Communication Theory* 17, no. 1 (2007): 26–42; Alexander R. Galloway and Jason R. LaRivière, "Compression in Philosophy," *Boundary 2* 44, no. 1 (2017): 125–47.

40. Gilles Deleuze, "Control and Becoming," in *Negotiations, 1972–1990* (New York: Columbia University Press, 1995), 195.

41. Deleuze and Guattari, *What Is Philosophy?*, trans. Hugh Tomlinson and Graham Burchell III (New York: Columbia University Press, 1996), 108.

42. Alexander R. Galloway, "Black Box, Black Bloc," in *Communization and Its Discontents: Contestation, Critique, and Contemporary Struggles*, ed. Benjamin Noys (Wivenhoe; N.Y.: Minor Compositions, 2011), 244.

II. Criminality

1. On Western myths of filiation as constitutive of the-world-as-we-know-it, see "Expanse and Filiation," in Éduoard Glissant, *Poetics of Relation*, trans. Betsy Wing (Ann Arbor: University of Michigan Press, 2010), 47–62.

2. Michel Foucault, *The Punitive Society: Lectures at the Collège de France, 1972–1973*, ed. Bernard E. Harcourt, trans. Graham Burchell III (New York: Palgrave Macmillan, 2015), 32–33.

3. Foucault, 151.

4. Samuel Galen Ng, "Trans Power! Sylvia Lee Rivera's STAR and the Black Panther Party," *Left History* 17, no. 1 (2013): 21–22; Susan Stryker, *Transgender History* (Berkeley, Calif.: Seal, 2008), 79.

5. William Haver, "The Ontological Priority of Violence: On Several Really Smart Things About Violence in Jean Genet's Work," *polylog*, 2004, them.polylog.org/5/fhw-en.htm; Jean Genet, *The Declared Enemy: Texts and Interviews*, ed. Albert Dichy, trans. Jeff Fort (Stanford, Calif.: Stanford University Press, 2004), 148.

6. Paul B. Preciado, "Anal Terror: Notes on the First Days of the Sexual Revolution," *Bæden*, no. 3 (2015): 152; See also the queer Autonomia book by Mario Mieli, *Towards a Gay Communism*, trans. David Fernbach and Evan Calder Williams (London: Pluto, 2018).

7. Michel Foucault, *The Archaeology of Knowledge*, trans. A. M. Sheridan Smith (New York: Pantheon, 1972), 17.

8. Preciado, "Anal Terror," 154.

9. Preciado, 153–54.

10. Glissant, *Poetics of Relation*, 111.

11. See David M. Halperin, *Saint Foucault: Towards a Gay Hagiography* (Oxford: Oxford University Press, 1995), 30, for a Foucauldian reworking of Eve Sedgwick's monumental epistemology of the closet.

12. Nicholas de Villiers, *Opacity and the Closet: Queer Tactics in Foucault, Barthes, and Warhol* (Minneapolis: University of Minnesota Press, 2012), 5–7.

13. Leo Bersani, *Homos* (Cambridge, Mass.: Harvard University Press, 1996), 11.

14. Bersani, 11.

15. Bersani, 1–5.

16. Bersani, 5.

17. Bersani, 76.

18. Bersani, 76.

19. Bersani, 76.

20. Fray Baroque, "Introduction," in *Queer UltraViolence*, ed. Fray Baroque and Tegan Eanelli (Berkeley, Calif.: Ardent, 2011), 10.

21. Reina Gossett, Eric A. Stanley, and Johanna Burton, eds., *Trap Door: Trans Cultural Production and the Politics of Visibility* (Cambridge, Mass.: MIT Press, 2017); Dean Spade, *Normal Life: Administrative Violence, Critical Trans Politics, and the Limits of Law* (Durham, N.C.: Duke University Press, 2015); Zach Blas, "Opacities: An Introduction," *Camera Obscura* 31, no. 2 (92) (September 1, 2016): 149–53.

22. *What Is Gender Nihilism? A Reader* (2016), iii–iv.
23. Editorial, "The Anti-Social Turn," *Baedan: Journal of Queer Nihilism*, no. 1 (2012): 17.

7. Society with Sexual Characteristics

1. Zach Blas, "Artist's Statement: *SANCTUM*," 2018, zachblas.info/works/sanctum/.
2. "ProVision 2" (L3 Harris Security and Detection Systems, n.d.); images for this source can be found on the internet archive (the "wayback machine" at archive.org) for https://www.sds.l3t.com/advancedimaging/provision-2.htm.
3. Blas, "Artist's Statement."
4. Blas.

8. Excitement and Exposure

1. Eric Schmidt and Jared Cohen, *The New Digital Age: Transforming Nations, Businesses, and Our Lives* (New York: Random House, 2013), 13.
2. Schmidt and Cohen, 6.
3. The Invisible Committee, *To Our Friends*, trans. Robert Hurley (Los Angeles: Semiotext(e), 2015), 82.
4. Joshua J. Kurz, "(Dis) Locating Control: Transmigration, Precarity and the Governmentality of Control," *Behemoth: A Journal on Civilisation* 2, no. 1 (2012): 30–51; Sandro Mezzadra and Brett Neilson, *Border as Method, or, the Multiplication of Labor* (Durham, N.C.: Duke University Press, 2013); Adi Ophir, Michal Givoni, and Sārī Ḥanafī, *The Power of Inclusive Exclusion: Anatomy of Israeli Rule in the Occupied Palestinian Territories* (New York: Zone Books, 2009).
5. Michael Hardt and Antonio Negri, *Commonwealth* (Cambridge, Mass.: Harvard University Press, 2009), 99–129; The Invisible Committee, "Fuck Off Google," 2014, anonymous-france.eu/IMG/pdf/the-invisible-committee-fuck-off-google.pdf; Jasper Bernes, "Logistics, Counterlogistics and the Communist Prospect," *Endnotes* 3 (2013): 172–201.
6. Invisible Committee, *To Our Friends*, 87.
7. Giorgio Agamben, *Homo Sacer: Sovereign Power and Bare Life* (Palo Alto, Calif.: Stanford University Press, 1998); Nikolas Rose, *The Politics of Life Itself: Biomedicine, Power and Subjectivity in the Twenty-First Century* (Princeton, N.J.: Princeton University Press, 2006); Michel Foucault, *The History of Sexuality*, vol. 1, *An Introduction* (New York: Vintage, 1990), 136.
8. Paul B. Preciado, "Pharmaco-pornographic Politics: Towards a New Gender Ecology," *Parallax* 14, no. 1 (2008): 105–17.

9. Paul B. Preciado, *Testo Junkie: Sex, Drugs, and Biopolitics in the Pharmacopornographic Era* (New York: The Feminist Press at City University of New York, 2013), 144–235.

10. Preciado, 183–215.

11. Preciado, 207–8.

12. Preciado, 275.

13. Preciado, 273–74.

14. Sigmund Freud, "Three Essays on Sexuality," in *The Standard Edition of the Complete Psychological Works of Sigmund Freud*, trans. James Strachey, vol. 7 (London: Hogarth, 1905), 204.

15. Freud, 156, 209.

16. Freud, 233.

17. Freud, 209.

18. Freud, 209.

19. Freud, 210.

20. Preciado, *Testo Junkie*, 304.

21. Natasha Dow Schüll, *Addiction by Design: Machine Gambling in Las Vegas* (Princeton, N.J.: Princeton University Press, 2014), 2.

22. Schüll, 170–71.

23. Schüll, 252.

24. Schüll, 17–18.

25. Maurizio Lazzarato, *Signs and Machines: Capitalism and the Production of Subjectivity*, trans. Joshua David Jordan (Los Angeles: Semiotext(e), 2014), 23.

26. Louis D. Brandeis, "What Publicity Can Do," in *Other People's Money: And How Bankers Use It* (New York: Frederick A. Stokes, 1914), 92.

27. Clare Birchall, "This Transparency," in *Future Light*, ed. Maria Lind, Vanessa Joan Müller, and Martina Kandeler-Fritsch (Vienna Biennale: Kunsthalle Wien, 2015), 31.

28. Clare Birchall, "Transparency, Interrupted: Secrets of the Left," *Theory, Culture & Society* 28, no. 7–8 (2011): 62.

29. Jodi Dean, *Publicity's Secret: How Technoculture Capitalizes on Democracy* (Ithaca, N.Y.: Cornell University Press, 2002), 9–12.

30. Donna Haraway, "Situated Knowledges: The Science Question in Feminism and the Privilege of Partial Perspective," *Feminist Studies* 14, no. 3 (1988): 581.

31. Robyn Wiegman, *American Anatomies: Theorizing Race and Gender* (Durham, N.C.: Duke University Press, 1995), 8.

32. Judith Butler, *Undoing Gender* (New York: Routledge, 2004), 20–21.

33. Shannon Mattern, Twitter thread, October 17, 2018, twitter.com/shannonmattern/status/1052731087317815296.

34. Sarah Banet-Weiser, *Empowered: Popular Feminism and Popular Misogyny* (Durham, N,C,: Duke University Press, 2018), 184.

35. Geert Lovink, *Networks without a Cause: A Critique of Social Media* (Cambridge: Polity, 2011), 29–31.

36. Jonathan Crary, *24/7: Late Capitalism and the Ends of Sleep* (New York: Verso, 2013).

37. Preciado, *Testo Junkie*, 290.

38. Sven Lütticken, *Secret Publicity. Essays on Contemporary Art* (Rotterdam: NAi Uitgevers, 2005), 32.

39. Preciado, *Testo Junkie*, 290.

40. Preciado, 12.

41. Sadie Plant, *Zeros and Ones: Digital Women and the New Technologies* (New York: Doubleday, 1997).

42. Bernadette Corporation, *Get Rid of Yourself*, 2003, video, 1:03:53, at 6:51, youtube.com/watch?v=Qi7rq7ofD5.

43. Crispin Long, "Boundary Issues," *Bookforum*, July 30, 2020, bookforum.com/culture/in-an-apartment-on-uranus-paul-preciado-undermines-geopolitical-technological-and-gender-binaries-24118.

44. Long locates "Identity in Transition" as a source for Preciado comparing trans experience with migrant border crossings, though I think "In the Arms of Rodina Mat" is as appropriate. See Paul B. Preciado, *An Apartment on Uranus: Chronicles of the Crossing* (Los Angeles: Semiotext(e), 2020), 128–31.

45. Preciado, *Testo Junkie*, 82.

46. Preciado, 35.

47. Preciado, 117.

48. Michel Foucault, *The History of Sexuality*, vol. 2, *The Use of Pleasure*, trans. Robert Hurley (Vintage, 1990), 94–95.

49. Preciado, *Testo Junkie*, 348. It is also worth noting the racial overtones of the word "guinea."

50. For more on this topic in the context of the Oscar Grant rebellion and subsequent uprisings, see Cindy Milstein, ed., *Taking Sides: Revolutionary Solidarity and the Poverty of Liberalism* (Oakland, Calif.: AK Press, 2015).

51. For a critique of chemical-molecular sexualities common to Preciado and New Materialism as complicit in primitivism, settler colonialism, and primitive accumulation, see Jordy Rosenberg, "The Molecularization of Sexuality: On Some Primitivisms of the Present," *Theory & Event* 17, no. 2 (2014).

52. Gilles Deleuze and Félix Guattari, "What Is the Creative Act?," in *Two Regimes of Madness: Texts and Interviews 1975–1995* (Los Angeles: Semiotext(e), 2006), 318.

9. A Heart That Burns and Burns

1. Joyce Carol Oates, *Foxfire: Confessions of a Girl Gang* (New York: Dutton, 1993).
2. Oates, 4.

10. We Are Bad, but We Could Be Worse

1. Ngai Sianne, *Ugly Feelings* (Cambridge, Mass.: Harvard University Press, 2009), 27.
2. Eve Kosofsky Sedgwick, "Paranoid Reading and Reparative Reading, or, You're so Paranoid, You Probably Think This Essay Is about You," in *Touching Feeling: Affect, Pedagogy, Performativity* (Durham, N.C.: Duke University Press, 2003), 123–51.
3. Ann Cvetkovich, "Public Feelings," *South Atlantic Quarterly* 106, no. 3 (2007): 459–68.
4. Cvetkovich, 460.
5. Rebecca Elizabeth Zorach, "Make It Stop," *Journal of Aesthetics & Protest*, no. 6 (2008): 265–70. "Empire" is a term I use throughout the book to give a proper name to the union of exploitative biopower and the spectacle that dominates the present. For more, see Michael Hardt and Antonio Negri, *Empire* (Cambridge, Mass.: Harvard University Press, 2000) and Tiqqun, Introduction to Civil War, trans. Alexander R. Galloway and Jason E. Smith (Los Angeles: Semiotext(e), 2010).
6. Cvetkovich, "Public Feelings," 462.
7. Sara Ahmed, *The Promise of Happiness* (Durham, N.C.: Duke University Press, 2010), 59.
8. Ahmed, 213.
9. Ahmed, 20, 218.
10. Robin D. G. Kelley, *Freedom Dreams: The Black Radical Imagination* (Boston: Beacon, 2002), 2.
11. Audre Lorde, *Zami: A New Spelling of My Name* (New York: Crossing, 1982), 18–19.
12. Lorde, 19.

12. Making Illness into a Weapon

1. Heather Love, *Feeling Backward* (Cambridge, Mass.: Harvard University Press, 2009), 146.
2. Walter Benjamin, "Theses on the Philosophy of History," in *Illuminations*, ed. Hannah Arendt, trans. Harry Zohn (New York: Schocken Books, 1968), 257–58.

3. Love, *Feeling Backward*, 146.
4. Michel Foucault, *Discipline and Punish: The Birth of the Prison* (New York: Vintage, 1977), 30.
5. Claire Fontaine, "Human Strike Within the Field of Libidinal Economy," in *Human Strike Has Already Begun and Other Writings* (London: PML, 2013), 39–40.
6. Adrienne Rich, *Of Woman Born: Motherhood as Experience and Institution* (New York: Norton, 1976), 30.
7. Tony Lee Moral, *The Making of Hitchcock's The Birds* (Harpenden, England.: Kamera, 2013), 184–85.
8. Lee Edelman, *No Future: Queer Theory and the Death Drive* (Durham, N.C.: Duke University Press, 2004), 129–33.
9. Leo Bersani, *Homos* (Cambridge, Mass.: Harvard University Press, 1995), 129.
10. David Cooper, *Psychiatry and Anti-Psychiatry* (London: Tavistock, 1967), 40. The reference to Naziism is not hyperbole, for SPK was agitating against what some in Germany called the "Auschwitz generation," which formed a cultural and political hegemony that had not found much distance from National Socialism and even included many former Nazis.
11. Socialist Patients' Collective, *Turn Illness Into a Weapon: A Polemic and Call to Action*, trans. "K. D." (unauthorized), 2013, 51, indybay.org/uploads/2013/11/14/turn_illness_into_a_weapon.pdf (originally *SPK: Aus Krankheit Eine WaffeMachen* [Munich: TriKont, 1972]). The *foco* theory of guerrilla warfare was conceived by Régis Debray, though he attributed it to Ernesto "Che" Guevara. *Foco* unifies all three of Mao's stages of guerrilla warfare in a single movement whereby the role of the vanguard is not to seize state power but to stoke a popular insurrection through armed struggle. For more on the original concept of the *foco*, see the subsequent chapter and Debray, *The Revolution in the Revolution?*
12. Socialist Patients' Collective, *Turn Illness Into a Weapon*, 54.
13. Socialist Patients' Collective, 59–60.
14. Socialist Patients' Collective, 59–60.
15. Socialist Patients' Collective, 60–62.
16. Socialist Patients' Collective, 44.
17. For a more personal description of SPK's activities, consider former member Magrit Schiller's account: "I immediately put my name down for one-on-one meetings, which were called 'individual agitations' in the SPK. During the meetings, I had a great need to talk first of all about me, my life up to now, my insecurities, my fears and my search for something different. At the beginning, this was the only reason I went to the SPK several times a week. During all of this, it became clear to me that my loneliness and

sadness and the many problems I had with myself were not my personal and inescapable fate. . . . I realized that there were lots of people who felt the same way I did, that there were social and political reasons for many things that made people suffer. . . . After a few weeks, I felt at home in the SPK. I took part in several working groups, put together flyers with others, and printed them on our small machine. I felt good about things and I worked eagerly. We had an old record player on which we repeatedly played the 'Ton Steine Scherben' song *'Macht kaputt, was euch kaputt macht'* [destroy what is destroying you] and sang along with passion to the texts that expressed exactly how we felt about life. There was always something going on. Small or larger groups of people held heated discussions about the latest events, the situation in the world, books or personal questions. We prepared protest actions and demonstrations" (*Remembering the Armed Struggle: Life in Baader-Meinhof* [London: Zidane, 2009], 21–24).

18. Margaret E. Atwood, *The Handmaid's Tale* (Toronto: McClelland and Stewart, 1985), 8.

III. Fugitivity

1. In making this statement, Frank B. Wilderson III notes that it is his paraphrase of Frantz Fanon; see Wilderson and Zamansele Nsele, "Part III: Afropessimism and Rituals of Anti-Black Violence," *Mail & Guardian*, June 2, 2020, mg.co.za/friday/2020-07-02-part-iii-afropessimism-and-rituals-of-anti-black-violence/.

2. Simone Browne, *Dark Matters: On the Surveillance of Blackness* (Durham, N.C.: Duke University Press, 2015), 76–83.

3. Wilderson and Nsele, "Part III: Afropessimism"; Jared Sexton, "The Vel of Slavery: Tracking the Figure of Unsovereign," *Critical Sociology* 42, no. 4-5 (2014): 1–15; Saidiya V. Hartman, *Scenes of Subjection: Terror, Slavery, and Self-Making in Nineteenth-Century America* (Oxford: Oxford University Press, 1997), 66. For the "cruel mockery" of self-possession as seen through freedom papers, see Calvin L. Warren, *Ontological Terror: Blackness, Nihilism, and Emancipation* (Durham, N.C.: Duke University Press, 2018), 99–106.

4. Warren, *Ontological Terror*, 26–37; Sexton, "Vel of Slavery."

5. Hortense Spillers, *Black, White, and In Color: Essays on American Literature and Culture* (Chicago: University of Chicago Press, 2003), 214–15.

6. Christina Sharpe, *In The Wake: On Blackness and Being* (Durham, N.C.: Duke University Press, 2016), 13–17.

7. Frank B. Wilderson III, *Red, White, and Black: Cinema and the Structure of U.S. Antagonisms* (Durham, N.C.: Duke University Press, 2010), 17; Spillers, *Black, White, and In Color*, 207; Warren, *Ontological Terror*, 90.

8. Nahum Dimitri Chandler, *X—The Problem of the Negro as a Problem for Thought* (New York: Fordham University Press, 2014).

9. Marquis Bey, *Them Goon Rules: Fugitive Essays on Radical Black Feminism* (Tucson: University of Arizona Press, 2019), 72 (citing an unspecified work by C. Riley Snorton).

10. Neil Roberts, *Freedom as Marronage* (Chicago: University of Chicago Press, 2015), 6.

11. Hartman, *Scenes*, 61.

12. Alvin O. Thompson, *Flight to Freedom: African Runaways and Maroons in the Americas* (Kingston, Jamaica: University of the West Indies Press, 2006), 65.

13. Sylviane A. Diouf, *Slavery's Exiles: The Story of the American Maroons* (New York: New York University Press, 2016), 309.

14. Wilderson, *Red, White, and Black*, xi.

15. Kieran Aarons, "No Selves to Abolish: Afro-Pessimism, Anti-Politics, and the End of the World," *Hostis* 2 (2016): 103–27.

16. Aarons, 124.

17. The legacy of the white underground's contribution to other struggles is mixed (such as the Weather Underground Organization), largely complicated through Marxological theories of popular sovereignty, nationalism within anti-imperialism and decolonization, and the socialist voluntarism of white-skin privilege. I have omitted a discussion of them here, as it would shift the balance in a self-serving direction.

13. Uprising

1. Christina Sharpe, *In the Wake: On Blackness and Being* (Durham, N.C.: Duke University Press, 2016), 117.

2. See the discussion of looting as a natural reaction to commodity abundance in Situationist International, "The Decline and the Fall of the Spectacular Commodity-Economy [original unsigned tract "Le déclin et la chute de l'économie spectaculaire-marchande," 1965]," trans. Donald Nicholson-Smith, *Internationale Situationniste*, no. 10 (1965; ed. Guy Debord), theanarchistlibrary.org/library/situationist-international-the-decline-and-fall-of-the-spectacle-commodity-economy.

3. Natalie Zemon Davis, *Society and Culture in Early Modern France: Eight Essays* (Stanford, Calif.: Stanford University Press, 1975), 147–49.

4. Davis, 97; Eric Lott, *Love and Theft: Blackface Minstrelsy and the American Working Class* (Oxford: Oxford University Press, 2013), 28.

5. Lott, *Love and Theft*, 30.

6. Lott, 28.

7. Lott, 28.

8. Lott, 26–27.
9. Lott, 27.

14. Self-Abolition

1. M. NourbeSe Philip, *Zong!* (Middleton, Conn.: Wesleyan University Press, 2008), 13; Claudia Rankine, *Citizen: An American Lyric* (Minneapolis, Minn.: Graywolf, 2014), 134; Michael Leong, "Conceptualisms in Crisis: The Fate of Late Conceptual Poetry," *Journal of Modern Literature* 41, no. 3 (2018): 109–31.

2. Micah L. Sifry, "From TXTMob to Twitter: How an Activist Tool Took Over the Conventions," *TechPresident*, August 25, 2012, web.archive.org/web/20120827173926/techpresident.com/news/22775/txtmob-twitter-how-activist-tool-took-over-conventions; Jack Z. Bratich, "Sovereign Networks, Pre-Emptive Transgression, Communications Warfare: Case Studies in Social Movement Media," in *Transgression 2.0: Media, Culture, and the Politics of a Digital Age*, ed. Ted Gournelos and David J. Gunkel (New York: Bloomsbury, 2011).

3. Evan Henshaw-Plath, "Txtmob Gets Subpoenaed—Data Retention in the Surveillance Era," *Anarchogeek* (blog), April 14, 2008, web.archive.org/web/20080727011313/http://anarchogeek.com/2008/3/31/txtmob-gets-subpoenaed-data-retention-in-the-surveillance-era; David Auerbach, "Twitter Is Borken," *Slate*, October 7, 2014, slate.com/technology/2014/10/twitter-is-broken-gamergate-proves-it.html.

4. A most significant entry in this conversation is Zeynep Tufekci, *Twitter and Tear Gas: The Power and Fragility of Networked Protest* (New Haven, Conn.: Yale University Press, 2017).

5. George Hunter, "War on Police? Many Officers Fear Growing Tensions," *The Detroit Times*, August 24, 2017, detroitnews.com/story/news/local/detroit-city/2017/08/23/detroit-police-tensions/104902710/.

6. Linda Lye, *StingRays: The Most Common Surveillance Tool the Government Won't Tell You About: A Guide for Criminal Defense Attorneys* (San Francisco: American Civil Liberties Union of Northern California, 2014), aclunc.org/sites/default/files/StingRays_The_Most_Common_Surveillance_Tool_the_Govt_Won%27t_Tell_You_About_0.pdf. See also Min-Seok Pang and Paul A. Pavlou, "Armed with Technology: The Impact on Fatal Shootings by the Police," research paper for Fox School of Business, Temple University, 2016, bja.ojp.gov/sites/g/files/xyckuh186/files/bwc/pdfs/SSRN-id2808662.pdf.

7. Devin Allen, cover of *Time*, April 30, 2015.

8. Michel Foucault, *The Archaeology of Knowledge*, trans. A. M. Sheridan Smith (New York: Pantheon, 1972), 17.

9. Orlando Patterson, *Slavery and Social Death* (Cambridge, Mass.: Harvard University Press, 1982).

10. Sean Cubitt, *The Cinema Effect* (Cambridge, Mass.: MIT Press, 2004), 1.

11. Sarah Kofman, *Camera Obscura: Of Ideology*, trans. Will Straw (Ithaca, N.Y.: Cornell University Press, 1999).

12. Wendy Hui Kyong Chun, "On Software, or the Persistence of Visual Knowledge," *Grey Room* 18 (2004): 26–51; Alexander R. Galloway, "Language Wants to Be Overlooked: On Software and Ideology," *Journal of Visual Culture* 5, no. 3 (2006): 315–51.

13. bell hooks, "Eating the Other," in *Black Looks: Race and Representation* (Boston, Mass.: South End, 1992), 21–39.

14. hooks, 31.

15. Lisa Nakamura, "Race In/For Cyberspace: Identity Tourism and Racial Passing on the Internet," *Works and Days* 13, no. 1–2 (1995): 181–93; David J. Leonard, "High Tech Blackface: Race, Sports Video Games and Becoming the Other," *Intelligent Agent* 4, no. 4 (2004): 1–5.

16. Ema O'Connor, "A Racist Gamer Group Has Been Posing as Baltimore Looters on Twitter," *BuzzFeed News*, April 30, 2015, buzzfeednews.com/article/emaoconnor/baltimore-loot-crew-is-fake.

17. O'Connor.

18. Alexandra Juhasz, "How Do I (Not) Look? Live Feed Video and Viral Black Death," *JSTOR Daily*, July 20, 2016, daily.jstor.org/daily-author/alexandra-juhasz/.

19. Saidiya V. Hartman, *Scenes of Subjection: Terror, Slavery, and Self-Making in Nineteenth-Century America* (Oxford: Oxford University Press, 1997),18, 21.

20. Hartman, 21.

21. Hartman, 23.

22. Nicholas Mirzoeff, "Tactics of Appearance for Abolition Democracy #BlackLivesMatter," *Critical Inquiry*, March 1, 2018, criticalinquiry.uchicago.edu/tactics_of_appearance/.

23. Huey Copeland, Review of Arthur Jaffa, *Love Is the Message, The Message Is Death* (Black One Shot 1.3), *ASAP Journal*, June 4, 2018, asapjournal.com/love-is-the-message-the-message-is-death-huey-copeland/.

24. Copeland.

25. Copeland; Hito Steyerl, "In Defense of the Poor Image," *E-Flux*, no. 10 (November 2009): 7; Aria Dean, "Poor Meme, Rich Meme," *Real Life*, July 25, 2016, reallifemag.com/poor-meme-rich-meme/.

26. Steyerl, "In Defense of the Poor Image," 6–7.

27. Alexander R. Galloway and Jason R. LaRivière, "Compression in Philosophy," *Boundary 2* 44, no. 1 (2017): 125–47, at 138–43.

28. Galloway and LaRivière, 143.

29. Galloway and LaRivière, 136–38. The authors move through a dense set of references quite quickly, beginning with Giorgio Agamben's marshalling of Georges Bataille against anthropology, followed by Nicholas de Villiers's use of queer opacity as a subversion of the imperatives of paranoid reading revealed by Eve Kosofsky Sedgwick.

30. The journal's full self-description is that *Hostis* is a journal of negation. It emerges devoid of ethics, lacking any sense of democracy, and without a care for prefiguring anything. Fed up with the search for a social solution to the present crisis, it aspires to be attacked wildly and painted as utterly black without a single virtue. In thought, *Hostis* is the construction of incommensurability that figures politics in formal asymmetry to the powers that be. In action, *Hostis* is an exercise in partisanship, speaking in a tongue made only for those that it wants to listen. The journal's partisanship is the work of neither fascists, who look for fights to give their limp lives temporary jolts of excitement, nor martyrs, who take hopeless stands to live the righteousness of loss. *Hostis* is the struggle to be dangerous in a time when antagonism is dissipated. This is all because *Hostis* is the enemy.

15. Searing Flesh

1. Simone Browne, *Dark Matters: On the Surveillance of Blackness* (Durham, N.C.: Duke University Press, 2015), 123–24.

2. Hank Willis Thomas and Sarah Lookofsky, "Branding USA," *dis*, 2013, dismagazine.com/disillusioned/46123/hank-willis-thomas-branding-usa/.

3. Thomas and Lookofsky.

4. Stuart Hall, "The After-Life of Frantz Fanon: Why Fanon? Why Now? Why Black Skin, White Masks?," in *The Fact of Blackness: Frantz Fanon and Visual Representation*, ed. Alan Read (Seattle, Wash.: Bay Press, 1996), 12–37, at 16; Browne, *Dark Matters*, 97–102.

5. Friedrich Wilhelm Nietzsche, *On the Genealogy of Morality*, ed. Keith Ansell-Pearson, trans. Carol Diethe (Cambridge: Cambridge University Press, 2006), bk. II, §3.

6. Nietzsche, bk. II, §3.

7. Liesl Bradner, "'Ernest Cole: Photographer' Opens at Fowler Museum," *Los Angeles Times*, April 7, 2013, latimes.com/entertainment/arts/la-xpm-2013-apr-07-la-et-cm-ernest-cole-apartheid-fowler-museum-20130407-story.html.

8. Allan Sekula, "The Body and the Archive," *October* 39 (Winter 1986): 3–64, at 64.

9. Sekula, 64.

10. Fred Moten, "Black Op," *PMLA* 123, no. 5 (2008): 1743.

16. Captive Media

1. Ruha Benjamin, *Race After Technology: Abolitionist Tools for the New Jim Code* (Cambridge: Polity, 2019), 5–6.
2. Motherboard, *CryptoHarlem Is Teaching Encryption to the Over-Policed and Heavily Surveilled* (feat. Matt Mitchell), March , 2018, video, 4:55, youtube.com/watch?v=yUqGVx-74Do.
3. Motherboard, *CryptoHarlem* (feat. Matt Mitchell).
4. Matt Mitchell, "Cyber JimCrow: Virtual Public Housing and Poor Doors in Digital Security and Surveillance," presentation at Eyeo Festival 20174, video, 34:50, vimeo.com/232659054; Simone Browne, *Dark Matters: On the Surveillance of Blackness* (Durham, N.C.: Duke University Press, 2015).
5. Mitchell, "Cyber JimCrow."
6. Browne, *Dark Matters*, 161–64.
7. See Molly Rogers, *Delia's Tears: Race, Science, and Photography in Nineteenth-Century America* (New Haven, Conn.: Yale University Press, 2010), for a discussion of early photography's coincidence with race science. Moreover, the materials necessary for photography have always been implicated in slavery, for instance the silver salts or other silver compounds made possible by the transatlantic silver trade or today's digital devices, which require heavy metals such as coltan only available through slave labor.
8. Jacqueline Denise Goldsby, *A Spectacular Secret: Lynching in American Life and Literature* (Chicago: University of Chicago Press, 2006), 235.
9. Goldsby, 222–26.
10. Goldsby, 224–28.
11. Goldsby, 247.
12. Goldsby, 248.
13. Goldsby, 248.
14. Goldsby, 230–31.
15. Goldsby, 230–33.
16. Goldsby, 236.
17. Goldsby, 231.
18. Tina Campt, *Listening to Images* (Durham, N.C.: Duke University Press, 2017), 18–23.
19. Campt, 21.
20. Campt, 20.
21. Ariella Azoulay, *The Civil Contract of Photography*, trans. Rela Melazi and Ruvik Danieli (New York: Zone, 2008), 130.
22. Roland Barthes, *Mythologies*, trans. Annette Lavers (New York: Hill and Wang, 1972), 116–17.
23. Barthes, 116, 128.
24. Barthes, 122–23; It is further worth mentioning that Barthes uses the word *nègre* at a time when anticolonial intellectuals instead used *noir*. For

this and other remarks on the essay, see Lydie Moudileno, "Barthes's Black Soldier: The Making of a Mythological Celebrity," *The Yearbook of Comparative Literature* 62 (2016): 57–72.

25. From Barthes's preface to a novel of gay cruising, quoted in Nicholas de Villiers, *Opacity and the Closet: Queer Tactics in Foucault, Barthes, and Warhol* (Minneapolis: University of Minnesota Press, 2012), 3.

26. T. J. Demos, *Return to the Postcolony: Specters of Colonialism in Contemporary Art* (Berlin: Sternberg, 2013), 14.

27. Roland Barthes, *Roland Barthes by Roland Barthes*, trans. Richard Howard (Berkeley and Los Angeles: University of California Press, 1994), 12, 185.

28. Roland. Barthes, *Camera Lucida: Reflections on Photography*, trans. Richard. Howard (New York: Hill and Wang, 1981), 10–13.

29. Barthes, 13.

30. Barthes, 14.

31. Barthes, 78.

32. Barthes, 15.

33. Jonathan Beller, *The Message Is Murder: Substrates of Computational Capitalism* (London: Pluto, 2018), 105.

34. Beller, 106–7.

35. Barthes, *Camera Lucida*, 80.

36. Barthes, *Camera Lucida*, 15.

37. Goldsby, *Spectacular Secret*, 238.

17. Black Out

1. Nicholas Mirzoeff, "Tactics of Appearance for Abolition Democracy #BlackLivesMatter," *Critical Inquiry*, March 1, 2018, criticalinquiry.uchicago.edu/tactics_of_appearance/. The subsequent three readings I undertake in this chapter are mere remediations of Mirzoeff's original work, and all credit should go to him for its direction and insight.

2. Roland Barthes, *Camera Lucida: Reflections on Photography*, trans. Richard Howard (Berkeley and Los Angeles: University of California Press, 1994), 107.

3. Calvin L. Warren, *Ontological Terror: Blackness, Nihilism, and Emancipation* (Durham, N.C.: Duke University Press, 2018), 5.

4. Warren, 179n1.

5. Eric A. Stanley, "Near Life, Queer Death: Overkill and Ontological Capture," *Social Text 107* 29, no. 2 (2011): 107.

6. Alexandra Juhasz, "How Do I (Not) Look? Live Feed Video and Viral Black Death," *JSTOR Daily,* July 20, 2016, daily.jstor.org/daily-author/alexandra-juhasz/; Juhasz, "Nothing Is Unwatchable for All," in *Unwatch-*

able, ed. Nicholas Baer et al. (New Brunswick, N.J.: Rutgers University Press, 2019), 121–25.

7. Sherri Williams, "How Does a Steady Stream of Images of Black Death Affect Us?," *NBC News*, July 12, 2016, nbcnews.com/news/nbcblk/editorial-how-does-steady-stream-images-%20black-death-affect-us-n607221.

8. The address is 4100 South Pulaski Road, Chicago, IL 60632, and can be seen in an October 2014 Google Street view image at goo.gl/maps/ndv7GicjKmsgsWRu6.

9. The address is 703 Sandra Bland Parkway, Hempstead, TX 77445, previously named University Drive, and can be seen in a May 2016 Google Street View image at goo.gl/maps/m5XauuAkbiHaMbrX8.

10. Mirzoeff, "Tactics of Appearance."

11. Walter Johnson, "The Carceral Landscape," in *River of Dark Dreams: Slavery and Empire in the Cotton Kingdom* (Cambridge, Mass.: Harvard University Press, 2013), 217–22.

18. Trapped between Withdrawal and Hypervisibility

1. Steve Martinot and Jared Sexton, "The Avant-Garde of White Supremacy," *Social Identities* 9, no. 2 (2003): 173.

2. Saidiya V. Hartman, *Scenes of Subjection: Terror, Slavery, and Self-Making in Nineteenth-Century America* (Oxford: Oxford University Press, 1997), 3.

3. Hartman, 21.

4. François Laruelle, *The Concept of Non-Photography*, trans. Robin Mackay (Falmouth, England: Urbanomic; New York: Sequence, 2011), 8.

5. Laruelle, 8.

6. Laruelle, 8.

7. Laruelle, 27.

8. Tina Campt, *Listening to Images* (Durham, N.C.: Duke University Press, 2017). See also the work of Kevin Quashie.

9. François Laruelle, "Photo-Fiction: An Exercise in Non-Standard Aesthetics," presentation at Goldsmiths University, May 10, 2012, trans. Robin Mackay, readthis.wtf/translation/francois-laruelle-photo-fiction-an-exercise-in-non-standard-aesthetics/.

10. Aria Dean, "On the Black Generic," *NGV Triennial Voices*, 2017, ngv.vic.gov.au/exhibition_post/on-the-black-generic/.

11. Dean.

12. Dean.

13. Simone Browne, *Dark Matters: On the Surveillance of Blackness* (Durham, N.C.: Duke University Press, 2015), 67–68.

14. Browne, 164.

15. Anirban Gupta-Nigam, "Black Infrastructure: Media and the Trap

of Visibility," *Media Fields Journal,* no. 11 (2016): 1–11. John Gillespie has persuasively argued that it is a hyper-real overrepresentation ("On the Prospect of Weaponized Death," *Propter Nos* 2, no. 1 [2017]: 5–11).

16. Johannes Itten, *The Elements of Color,* trans. Ernst Van Hagen (New York: John Wiley and Sons, 1970), 16.

17. The better presentation of white skin and dulling of black skin could be "fixed" by increasing the exposure, see Henry Louis Gates Jr., "Frederick Douglass's Camera Obscura: Representing the Antislave 'Clothed and in Their Own Form,'" *Critical Inquiry* 42, no. 1 (Autumn 2015): 32–33.

18. Richard Dyer, "The Light of the World," in *White* (New York: Routledge, 1997), 82–144.

19. Itten, *Elements,* 16.

20. Itten, 17.

21. Frantz Fanon, *Black Skin, White Masks,* trans. Richard Philcox (New York: Grove, 2008), 89, 119.

22. Gupta-Nigam, "Black Infrastructure," 8.

23. Patrice Douglass and Frank B. Wilderson III, "The Violence of Presence: Metaphysics in a Blackened World," *The Black Scholar* 43, no. 4 (2013): 117–23.

24. For a critique of Black culture being flattened through the familiar terms of "expressiveness, resistance, colorful, loud, dramatic, doubled," see Kevin Quashie, *The Sovereignty of Quiet: Beyond Resistance in Black Culture* (New Burnswick, N.J.: Rutgers University Press, 2012), 133. Additionally, this is the problem of the harsh "muscular style" of intellectuals who substitute vigor for concepts, outlined in Frantz Fanon, *Wretched of the Earth,* trans. Constance Farrington (New York: Grove, 1968), 219–22.

25. Eugene Thacker, *Starry Speculative Corpse: Horror of Philosophy* (Winchester, England: Zero Books, 2015), 52, 60.

26. Thacker, 51.

27. Alexander R. Galloway, *Laruelle: Against the Digital* (Minneapolis: University of Minnesota Press, 2014), 145 (Galloway takes the final quotation from Laruelle).

28. François Laruelle, "On the Black Universe: In the Human Foundations of Color," in *Dark Nights of the Universe,* ed. Eugene Thacker et al. (Miami: NAME, 2013), 105.

29. Frank B. Wilderson III, "Biko and the Problematic of Presence," in *Biko Lives!,* ed. Andile Mngxitama, Amanda Alexander, and Nigel C. Gibson (New York: Palgrave Macmillan, 2008), 97.

30. Frank B. Wilderson III, "The Black Liberation Army and the Paradox of Political Engagement," in *Postcoloniality, Decoloniality, Black Critique: Joints and Fissures,* ed. Sabine Broeck and Carsten Junker (Frankfurt: Campus Verlag, 2014), 178.

31. Wilderson III, "Biko," 100.
32. Daniel Colucciello Barber, "World-Making and Grammatical Impasse," *Qui Parle: Critical Humanities and Social Sciences* 25, no. 1–2 (2016): 188.
33. Barber, 191.
34. For Laruelle contra Rawls, see Galloway, *Laruelle*, 204–6.
35. Crawford Brough Macpherson, *The Political Theory of Possessive Individualism: Hobbes to Locke* (Oxford: Clarendon, 1962), 3.
36. Darby English, *How to See a Work of Art in Total Darkness* (Cambridge, Mass.: MIT Press, 2007), 3, 6.
37. English, 4.
38. Adrienne Edwards, "Blackness in Abstraction," *Art in America*, January 5, 2015, web.archive.org/web/20161107032917/http://www.artinamericamagazine.com/news-features/magazine/blackness-in-abstraction/.
39. Edwards, n.p.
40. Edwards, n.p.
41. Fred Moten, "The Case of Blackness," *Criticism* 50, no. 2 (2008): 189, 212.
42. Fanon, *Black Skin, White Masks*, 89–90.
43. Moten, "Case of Blackness," 180–86.
44. Moten, 184.
45. Moten, 186.
46. Moten, 187.
47. Moten, 187–202.
48. Moten, 190–93, 197–98.
49. Moten, 198.
50. Moten, 203–4.
51. Moten, 211–12.
52. Franco Barchiesi, "Precarity as Capture: A Conceptual Reconstruction and Critique of the Worker-Slave Analogy," *Ponencia Presentada En El Coloquio Internacional The Politics of Precarious Society* (Johannesburgo: Universidad de Witwatersrand) 5 (2012): n.p.
53. Glissant, *Poetics of Relation*, 121–25, 148, 173, 194.
54. Saidiya V. Hartman and Christina Sharpe, "Statement from Saidiya Hartman and Christina Sharpe at the Humboldt Forum [December 8, 2017]," *Processed Lives*, processedlives.tumblr.com/post/168319118010/last-night-saidiya-hartman-began-with-a-question.
55. Jared Sexton, "All Black Everything," *E-Flux*, no. 79 (February 2017): 5.
56. E.g., see hot takes on the announcement by researchers at Russia's State Tretyakov Gallery, such as Carey Dunne, "Art Historians Find Racist Joke Hidden Under Malevich's Black Square" (November 13, 2015, *Hyperallergic*, hyperallergic.com/253361/art-historian-finds-racist-joke-hidden-under-malevichs-black-square/), and art historians looking to shore up Malevich's

legacy, as in Aleksandra Shatskikh, "Inscribed Vandalism: The Black Square at One Hundred," *E-Flux*, no. 85 (October 2017): 1–10.

57. Vincent Como, "The Black Singularity: To Know the Unknowable," *Drain*, 2015, drainmag.com/the-black-singularity/; Sexton, "All Black Everything," 1.

58. Como, "Black Singularity"; Sexton, "All Black Everything," 10.

59. Sexton, "All Black Everything," 8. A Larueallean approach would characterize the black as universal and *finite*.

60. Sexton, 8–10.

61. Sexton, 10.

62. Judith Butler, quoted in Sexton, 10.

63. Jared Sexton, "The Vel of Slavery: Tracking the Figure of Unsovereign," *Critical Sociology* 42, no. 4–5 (2014): 1–15, at 11.

Conclusion

1. Many of these concepts are further elaborated in Andrew Culp, *Dark Deleuze* (Minneapolis: University of Minnesota Press, 2016).

2. Frantz Fanon, *Wretched of the Earth*, trans. Constance Farrington (New York: Grove, 1968),136–37.

3. Leon Trotsky, *History of the Russian Revolution*, trans. Max Eastman (Chicago: Haymarket, 2008), xvi.

4. Gilbert Simondon, *L'individu et sa genèse physico-biologique* (Grenoble: Jérôme Millon, 1995), 46–49.

5. Daniel Coluccinello Barber, "The Creation of Non-Being," *Rhizomes*, no. 29 (2016), rhizomes.net/issue29/pdf/barber.pdf.

6. Nahum Dimitri Chandler, *X—The Problem of the Negro as a Problem for Thought* (New York: Fordham University Press, 2014), 51–52.

7. Elizabeth Grosz, "Bergson, Deleuze and the Becoming of Unbecoming," *Parallax* 11, no. 2 (2005): 10–11.

8. Mikhail Bakunin, "The Communist System" (excerpt from "The Knouto-Germanic Empire and the Social Revolution," in *The Complete Works of Michael Bakunin* as "Fragment"; parts trans. G. P. Maximoff, missing parts trans. Jeff Stein from Spanish edition, trans. Diego Abad de Santillan, vol. 3 [Buenos Aires 1926] 181–96), theanarchistlibrary.org/library/michail-bakunin-the-capitalist-system.

9. Gilles Deleuze, "Nomadic Thought," in *Desert Islands and Other Texts, 1953–1974*, ed. David Lapoujade, trans. Michael Taormina (Los Angeles: Semiotext(e), 2004), 259–60.

10. Édouard Glissant, *Poetics of Relation*, trans. Betsy Wing (Ann Arbor: University of Michigan Press, 2010), 111–12.

11. Deleuze, "Nomadic Thought," 260.

12. Demonstrative here is Robin D. G. Kelley's innovative research methods that look to infrapolitics, culture, and surrealism not as limit cases but as the degree zero of radical research.

13. Derrick A. Bell Jr., "Brown v. Board of Education and the Interest-Convergence Dilemma," *Harvard Law Review* 93, no. 3 (1980): 518–33.

14. Jean Genet, *The Declared Enemy: Texts and Interviews*, ed. Albert Dichy, trans. Jeff Fort (Stanford, Calif.: Stanford University Press, 2004), 38.

15. Michael Hardt and Antonio Negri, *Empire* (Cambridge, Mass.: Harvard University Press, 2000), 348–49.

16. See, for instance, George Jackson and Huey Newton on the oppressive nature of technology and the antagonism between lumpen and production (unlike productivists such as Negri, Soviets, or Maoists).

17. Tiqqun, *This Is Not a Program*, trans. Joshua David Jordan (Los Angeles: Semiotext(e), 2011), 117.

18. Tiqqun, 55.

19. Deleuze suggests finding revolutionary war machines here, stating that, "just as the despot internalizes the nomadic war-machine, capitalist society never stops internalizing a revolutionary war-machine. It's not on the periphery that the new nomads are being born (because there is no more periphery)" ("Nomadic Thought," 261). Such a path would presumably proceed by "going through the middle," thus avoiding the dangers that lie in trying to succeed "from above" or "from below," which would establish "golden ghettos" of the hyper-bourgeoisie or "no-go-area" of the hyper-exploited (Tiqqun, *This Is Not a Program*, 68).

20. Jared Sexton, "Unbearable Blackness," *Cultural Critique*, no. 90 (Spring 2015): 165–73.

21. Tiqqun, *This Is Not a Program*, 69–70.

22. George Jackson, *Soledad Brother: The Prison Letters of George Jackson* (Chicago: Lawrence Hill, 2006), 4, 55, 250; Barber, "Creation"; Cheryl I. Harris, "Whiteness as Property," *Harvard Law Review* 106, no. 8 (1993): 1707–91; George Lipsitz, "The Possessive Investment in Whiteness: Racialized Social Democracy and the 'White' Problem in American Studies," *American Quarterly* 47, no. 3 (1995): 369–87.

23. Claire Fontaine, "Human Strike Within the Field of Libidinal Economy," in *Human Strike Has Already Begun and Other Writings* (London: PML, 2013).

24. Gilles Deleuze, *Difference and Repetition*, trans. Paul Patton (New York: Columbia University Press, 1994), 140.

25. Deleuze, 145.

26. Gilles Deleuze, "Vincennes Session of April 15, 1980, Leibniz Seminar," trans. Charles J. Stivale, *Discourse* 20, no. 3 (1998): 79.

27. James Williams, *The Transversal Thought of Gilles Deleuze: Encounters and Influences* (Manchester, England: Clinamen, 2005), 23–24.

28. Gilles Deleuze, *Francis Bacon: The Logic of Sensation*, trans. Daniel W. Smith (Minneapolis: University of Minnesota Press, 2003), 60.

29. Deleuze, xi–xii.

30. Deleuze, "Nomadic Thought," 259.

31. For more elaboration on the Metropolis as the lived experience of contemporary power (through recent theoretical work on logistics and the digital), initially developed as a concept in Italian regional geography and expanded in the last few decades through the political thought of Tiqqun, Michael Hardt and Antonio Negri, Giorgio Agamben and others, see chapters 5, 6, and 8.

32. Fredric Jameson, *Postmodernism, or, the Cultural Logic of Late Capitalism* (Durham, N.C.: Duke University Press, 1991), 47–48.

33. Invisible Committee, *The Coming Insurrection* (Cambridge, Mass.: Semiotext(e), 2009), 108.

34. *Fourth World War*, directed by Rick Rowley, narrated by Michael Franti and Suheir Hammad, (Los Angeles: Big Noise Films, 2003), DVD, 78:00, at 0:04–0:17.

35. *Fourth World War*, 0:21–46.

36. Nanni Balestrini, *The Unseen*, trans. Liz Heron (New York: Verso, 1989), 239–41.

Index

Aarons, Kieran, 110
abolition: and aesthetics, 149; and Blackness, 154; and depression, 96; and fugitivity, 28, 29, 146, 158–62; self-abolition, 110–11, 117–28; and the underground, 155–57
abstraction: and aesthetics of Blackness, 148, 150–53; and anonymity, 32; and cybernetic capitalism, 165; and fugitivity, 11, 157; and guerrilla philosophy, 24–25, 45; and identity politics, 115–16, 156–57; and the Imaginary Party, 58; and imperceptibility, 8, 27; and inclusive disjunction, 83–84; and screencaps, 121; lacking in *Testo-Junkie* (Preciado), 91
affect, 28, 92–93, 94–100, 103–8, 157, 163–64
Afropessimism, 149, 153. *See also* Sexton, Jared; Wilderson, Frank
Agamben, Giorgio, 183n4, 196n29, 204n31
agitation therapy, 102, 106–7, 191n17. *See also* Socialist Patients' Collective
Ahmed, Sara, 97, 98
Alarm, The (Parsons), 48
Allen, Devin, 119
anarchism: anarchist media, 54–55, 57, 119–20, 126–28, 196n30; and anonymity, 27, 31; and the avant-garde, 178n137; and guerrilla philosophy, 24–25; and propaganda by the deed, 47–50; and war, 23. *See also* Autonomia Operaia; Tiqqun
anonymity, 31–33, 163, 164; and abolition, 28–29; 157; and Black rebellion, 28, 119–20; and camouflage, 43–46; and contingency, 70; and guerrilla tactics, 21–23, 52–53; and insinuation, 27, 74; and propaganda by the deed, 49–50; and saturation, 9–10; and surveillance, 81. *See also* affect; camouflage; exposure; imperceptibility; insinuation; redaction; transparency; visibility; withdrawal
antagonism, 66, 67, 100, 103, 107, 126–28. *See also* contingency; clutter; density; inclusive disjunction
Antifa, 22–23, 121
asymmetry, 27, 64–74
authoritarianism, 19, 21, 56, 157
Autonomia Operaia, 13, 22, 23, 26, 117, 183n4. *See also* Berardi, Franco "Bifo"; Negri, Antonio
autonomy: and affect, 157; and anonymity, 32; and guerrilla philosophy, 22–23, 25; and guerrillas, 36, 51–52; and slums, 41; and *2015 Baltimore Uprising*, 117. *See also* anarchism; Autonomia Operaia

avant-garde, the, 11, 16, 24–25, 178n137. *See also* abstraction
Azoulay, Ariella, 135

Babbage, Charles, 2
Bædan, 78. *See also* queerness
Bakunin, Mikhail, 55
Balestrini, Nanni, 167–68
Baltimore uprising, 113–15, 123. *See also* Gray, Freddie; *2015 Baltimore Uprising*
Barchiesi, Franco, 152
Barthes, Roland, 28, 135, 136–38, 197n24
Bash Back!, 77–78
Bataille, Georges, 196n29
becoming: and abolition, 157; and escape, 179–80n15; and exclusive disjunction, 69; and fugitivity, 158; and the guerrilla, 44; and imperceptibility, 8, 9–12, 164–66. See also *Thousand Plateaus, A* (Deleuze and Guattari)
Bee-hive, 54
behaviorism, 3–4, 10
Bell, Derrick, 159
Beller, Jonathan, 137
Benjamin, Walter, 103
Berardi, Franco "Bifo," 26. *See also* Autonomia Operaia
Bernadette Corporation, 89–90
Bersani, Leo, 77, 105
Binger, Louis-Gustave, 136–37. *See also* Barthes, Roland
biopoltics: and abolition, 160, 161; and cybernetics, 10, 38; and Empire, 72, 190n5; and escape, 42, 43; and sex, 84–91. *See also* cybernetics; Empire; pornopower; spectacle
Birds, The (Hitchcock), 104–5
Biswas Mellamphy, Nandita, 6–7

blackface, 115–16, 123
Blackness, 28; and abolition, 159–60; and aesthetics, 144–54, 200n17; and the Baltimore uprising, 113–15; Barthes terms for, 197n24; and the body, 129–31; and captive media, 117–28, 132–38; and counterinsurgency, 18, 19; and escape, 99; and fugitivity, 109–11; and *Invisible Man* (Ellison), 32; and surveillance, 139–43; and unruliness, 115–16. *See also* Black Panther Party; race
Black Panther Party, 12, 25, 160. *See also* Jackson, George
Black Skin, White Masks (Fanon), 151
Black Square (Malevich), 153
Black Sun (Pendleton), 150–51
Bland, Sandra, 140
Blas, Zach, 79–82
body, the: and affective politics, 96, 97–98, 163–64; and Blackness, 109, 110, 129–31, 139–40, 142–43, 144–54; and captive media, 28, 132–38; and cybernetics, 79–81; and liberalism, 5; and pornopower, 84–89. *See also* biopolitics; Blackness
Born in Flames (Borden), 21
B®anded (Thomas), 129. *See also* Thomas, Hank Willis
branding, 129. *See also* Blackness; body, the; capitalism
Brazil, 41–42
Brown, Michael, 117, 130
Browne, Simone, 18, 129, 132, 133, 146
Burglar's Guide to the City, A (Manaugh), 31
Butler, Judith, 87

Call, 24, 177n134
Camera Lucida (Barthes), 136–37
camouflage, 27, 36, 43–46, 73, 164.
See also anonymity; exposure; imperceptibility; opacity; redaction; transparency; visibility; withdrawal
Campt, Tina D., 134–35, 145
capitalism: and the body, 84–85, 88–89; and branding, 129; and "the Common," 160; and cybernetics, 3; false freedoms of, 158; and the guerrilla, 38–39, 42, 51; and illness, 101–2, 104, 105, 106; and imperceptibility, 44–45; and the infrastructure of whiteness, 141, 142–43; and the Metropolis, 66–68, 70, 74, 183n4; and prosecution, 117–19, 121–22, 123; and revolutionary war machines, 203n19; and the Sprawl, 61–63. See also cybernetics; spectacle
captive media, 28, 118–19, 120–26, 132–38, 197n7
Carceral Capitalism (Wang), 62
CCTV, 141–42. See also surveillance
Center for Initiatives for New Free Spaces (CINEL), 26
Châtelet, Gilles, 3
Citizen (Rankine), 117, 139
"Climate, Capitalism, Control" (Paul), 61–63
clutter, 27, 36, 43–44, 70–71, 73. See also anonymity; camouflage; contingency; density
CNN, 114–15
Cohn, Jesse, 25, 178n137
Cole, Ernest, 130–31
Coleman, Philip, 140
colonialism: and guerrilla warfare, 68, 69; and photography, 135–38; and policing, 18, 176n102; and Preciado, 90; and recognition, 5; and visibility, 6, 12
color theory, 146–54
communism, 8, 21, 28–29, 155–68. See also subtraction
Como, Vincent, 153
Concept of Non-Photography, The (Laruelle), 145
Concerto in Black and Blue (Hammon), 150
consciousness, 49, 55, 130
contingency, 27, 36, 38–39, 70–71, 148. See also anonymity; clutter; density
Cooper, D. G., 105–6
Copeland, Huey, 124–25
Coulthard, Glen, 5
counterinsurgency, 17–20, 24, 26–27, 52–53. See also policing; surveillance
criminality, 156–57, 162–64; in anarchist media, 54–55; and Blackness, 120, 129–31; and captive media, 28, 132–38; and queerness, 27–28, 75–78
Croissant, Klaus, 26
CryptoHarlem, 132
Cuba, 21
Cvetkovich, Ann, 97
cyberfeminism, 88–89. See also body, the; feminism
cybernetics: and asymmetry, 64–74; and Blackness, 146; and counterinsurgency, 17–20, 52–53; and fugitivity, 159; and the guerrilla, 32–33, 37, 38–39, 40, 43, 155; and imperceptibility, 8, 10–11, 27, 44–45; and inclusive disjunction, 83–84; and the Metropolis, 183n4; and the perpetual present, 165–66; and queerness, 75, 77, 105; and recognition, 1–5; and

sexual politics, 79–82; and the Sprawl, 60–63; and subtraction, 6, 21; and women's domestic torment, 104. See also biopolitics; capitalism; Metropolis; spectacle
cyberpunk, 60–61

dashcam, 141. See also surveillance
Davis, Natalie, 115
Dean, Aria, 145–46
Debord, Guy, 45, 62, 67
Deleuze, Gilles: on becoming and escape, 179–80n15; on the gaze, 91; and Lacan, 173n51; on Lawrence, 15; and the Metropolis, 66, 67, 69; on philosophy and warfare, 24; political activities of, 25–26; and revolutionary war machines, 203n19; *A Thousand Plateaus* (Deleuze and Guattari), 5–15, 174n70
Demos, T. J., 136
density, 27, 36, 41–42, 70, 71–72. See also anonymity; clutter; contingency
depression, 95–97. See also affect; illness
Deseriis, Marco, 32
Deutsch, Karl, 2
Deutsche Bahn, 101
de Villiers, Nicholas, 196n29
difference: and anonymity, 32, 43; and cybernetics, 2–3, 38, 83–84, 165–66; and cyberpunk, 61; and the Metropolis, 66–69. See also identity; inclusive disjunction; interiority; recognition; subject, the
difference engine, 2
digital culture, 68, 70, 72, 73, 164. See also asymmetry; Metropolis

Discipline and Punish (Foucault), 6, 91
Douglass, Patrice, 147
doxxing, 121
Dyer, Richard, 146
dynamite, 48

ecofeminism, 88. See also body, the; feminism
Ecuador, 119
Edelman, Lee, 89
Edwards, Adrienne, 150–51
elimination, 10–11. See also anonymity; imperceptibility; opacity
Ellison, Ralph, 29, 32
Empire, 70, 72, 95–96, 160, 185n31, 190n5. See also biopolitics; Metropolis; spectacle
English, Darby, 150
escape: and affect, 92–93; and becoming, 179–80n15; and Blackness, 152, 154; and exclusive disjunction, 69; and feminism, 98–100; and fugitivity, 157–62; and guerrilla warfare, 36–37, 39, 40, 42; and illness, 104–8; and imperceptibility, 165–66; from the Metropolis, 61, 67, 72. See also abolition; fugitivity; liberation; marronage
excitement, 83–91. See also biopolitics; pornopower
exclusive disjunction, 69. See also asymmetry; difference; inclusive disjunction
exposure: and Blackness, 109, 111, 130; and the Metropolis, 66, 72; and pornopower, 28, 84–85, 86–91; and surveillance, 139. See also anonymity; body, the; camouflage; imperceptibility;

opacity; pornopower; redaction; transparency; visibility; withdrawal

Fanon, Frantz, 138, 147, 151, 152, 156
Feel Tank Chicago, 95–96, 100
feminism: and affect, 28, 94–100; and asymmetry, 68; and biopolitics, 84, 87–89; and screenshots, 121; after socialism, 21. *See also* gender; women
Floyd, George, 19
focoism, 35–36, 191n11
Fontaine, Claire, 104
Foucault, Michel: and affect, 97; and biopolitics, 84; the *Call* echoing, 177n134; and cybernetics, 4; and guerrilla philosophy, 24; and opacity, 76; police violence against, 26; on power, 16, 20, 57; and presentism, 59; and self-abolition, 91, 120; on visibility, 6
Foxfire (Oates), 92–93, 100
Freud, Sigmund, 85
fugitivity, 109–11, 157–62; and Blackness, 28, 131, 144–54; and Campt on photography, 134–35; and Twitter, 117–18; and *2015 Baltimore Uprising*, 119–20, 125–26. *See also* escape; liberation; marronage

Gaghan, Stephen, 64, 183n1
Galleani, Luigi, 31
Galloway, Alexander R., 68, 148, 149, 154, 196n29
Gamergate, 88, 121, 123
gender: and becoming, 12, 69; and the body, 87; and criminality, 76–77, 78; and cybernetics, 2; femaleness and Blackness, 115–16; and the torment and isolation of home, 103–4; and vanishing, 11, 88–89, 90–91. *See also* feminism; queerness; women
genericness, 145–46, 148, 154. *See also* Blackness; photography; uchromia
Genet, Jean, 12, 21, 75–76, 159
Get Rid of Yourself (Bernadette Corporation), 89–90
Gibson, William, 60–61
Gilman-Opalsky, Richard, 9
Glissant, Éduoard, 11–12, 152, 158
glitches, 69, 70, 71, 74. *See also* asymmetry; contingency
Goldsby, Jacqueline, 134, 138
Goldsmith, Kenneth, 117
Google, 62, 83–84
Graeber, David, 49
Gray, Freddie, 90–91, 113–15, 119, 124. *See also* Baltimore uprising; *2015 Baltimore Uprising*
Great Arab Revolt, 13–14. *See also* guerrilla warfare; Lawrence, T. E.
Guattari, Félix, 5–15, 25–26, 69, 173n51, 174n70
Guerrilla Aesthetics (Mair), 15–16
guerrilla philosophy, 23–27, 155–56; and clutter, 73; and contingency, 70–71; and density, 71–72; and guerrilla warfare, 27, 35–46, 164; and *A Thousand Plateaus* (Deleuze and Guattari), 12–15; white infrastructures read through, 111. *See also* guerrilla warfare
guerrilla warfare: and asymmetry, 68; and focoism, 191n11; and guerrilla philosophy, 27, 35–46,

164; Lawrence on, 13–14, 174n77; as minoritarian form of war, 174n71; Tiqqun on, 22, 177n125; in West Germany, 15–16, 51–53, 175n89. See also guerrilla philosophy
Guevara, Ernesto "Che," 37, 191n11
Guillén, Abraham, 38
Gupta-Nigam, Airban, 146–47, 148

hackers, 32
Hammon, David, 150
happiness, 28, 97–98, 99. See also affect
Haraway, Donna, 62, 87, 88
Hardt, Michael, 64, 160, 183n4, 204n31
Harney, Stefano, 24, 177n134
Hartman, Saidiya, 124, 144, 152, 159
Haymarket Massacre, 48
Hegel, Georg Wilhelm Friedrich, 172n21. See also recognition
History of Sexuality (Foucault), 16
Hitchcock, Alfred, 104–5
Homosexual Revolutionary Action Front (FHAR), 76
Hong Kong, 119
hooks, bell, 123
Hostis, 126–28, 196n30
House of Bondage (Cole), 130–31
How Not to Be Seen (Steyerl), 9–10

identity: and abolition, 161; and abstraction, 115–16; and anonymity, 32, 43; and authoritarian strategy, 56, 157; and authorship, 119–21; and cybernetics, 2–3; and inclusive disjunction, 66; and positionality, 11–12, 174n70; and queerness, 76–78, 105; and recognition, 172n21. See also abolition; difference; interiority; recognition; subject, the
illness, 28, 102, 103–8, 166, 191n17
Imaginary Party, 57–59. See also insinuation; propaganda; Tiqqun
imperceptibility, 6–12, 27–29, 44–45, 155–66. See also abolition; anonymity; camouflage; escape; exposure; fugitivity; opacity; redaction; transparency; visibility; withdrawal
inclusive disjunction, 65–67, 83–84. See also asymmetry; cybernetics; difference; exclusive disjunction; Metropolis
informationalization, 2–3. See also cybernetics
infrapolitics, 203n12. See also Blackness
insinuation, 27, 36, 53, 55–59, 74, 181–82n7. See also propaganda
interiority: and affect, 96–100, 164; and illness, 102, 103–8; and inclusive disjunction, 65–66; and liberalism, 157; queer refusal of, 28, 76. See also abolition; difference; identity; recognition; subject, the
Invisible Man (Ellison), 29, 32
Italy, 13, 22, 26

Jackson, George, 12, 13, 25, 161. See also Black Panther Party; guerrilla philosophy
Jafa, Arthur, 124–25
Jenner, Caitlyn, 90
Johnson, Marsha P., 75
Juhasz, Alexandra, 124, 140

Kelley, Robin D. G., 203n12
killjoys, 98–99. See also affect; feminism

Krafft-Ebing, Richard von, 76
Kurdistan, 119

labor: and Blackness, 131; and the body, 84–85; and capitalism, 158; and consciousness, 55; and cybernetics, 33; excitement and the intensification of, 86; and the hylomorphic model of politics, 156–57; and illness, 106; women's, 89, 104. *See also* slavery
Lacan, Jacques, 173n51
Landauer, Gustav, 49
Lang, Fritz, 64
lantern laws, 18, 109, 132. *See also* Blackness; captive media; counterinsurgency
Laruelle, François, 145, 147–48, 149, 154. *See also* color theory; photography
Latin America, 35–36, 40–42, 51, 90
Lawrence, T. E., 13–14, 15, 24
Lenin, Vladimir, 155–56
liberalism: and affect, 97; and asymmetry, 68, 69; and the closet pact, 76; cyberpunk and liberal existentialism, 61; and exposure, 27; and facts, 56; fugitivity as response to, 159; and inclusive disjunction, 67; and the perpetual present, 59; and plurality, 5; and "politics," 17; and possessive multiculturalism, 149–50, 161; and the state, 7–8, 175n93; and the subject, 4, 157; and transparency, 84, 86–88; weakness paraded as a ritual of, 39. *See also* sovereignty; state, the
liberation: and affect, 92–93, 94–100, 104; and Black aesthetics, 149; guerrillas and the force of, 35–46; liberalism and the promise of queer, 76; persuasion and the poison of national, 56. *See also* abolition; escape; fugitivity; marronage
linear warfare, 13, 174n74
line of flight, 12–13
Listening to Images (Campt), 134–35
Lizius, Gerhard, 48
Long, Crispin, 90, 189n44
Lorde, Audre, 99
Love Is the Message, the Message Is Death (Jafa), 124–25
Lynch, Kevin, 65
lynching, 133–34, 139

Mair, Kimberly, 15–16
Malevich, Kazimir, 153
Mao, 20, 35–36, 37, 68, 191n11
Marcuse, Herbert, 16
marronage, 13, 110, 156. *See also* escape; fugitivity; liberation; slavery; spontaneity
Martinot, Steve, 144
Marx, Karl, 55, 86, 160, 162
Marxism: and asymmetry, 68; and Black aesthetics, 131, 149; and consciousness, 55; and Negri, 13; and politics as war, 20–21; rejection of, 156, 159. *See also* communism; socialism
masks, 6–7, 111, 114–16, 119. *See also* anonymity; imperceptibility; opacity
McDonald, Laquan, 140
Meessen, Vincent, 135–36
Meinhof, Ulrike, 51–52. *See also* Red Army Faction
Metropolis, 35–36, 51, 61, 64–74, 165–66, 183n4. *See also* capitalism; cybernetics
Metropolis (Lang), 64
Mirzoeff, Nicholas, 124, 140

Mitchell, Matthew, 132–33
Mondrian, Piet, 151, 152
Most, Johann, 47–48
Moten, Fred, 24, 131, 151–52, 177n134
Mythologies (Barthes), 135

Nazis, 16, 52, 105–6, 191n10
Negotiations (Deleuze), 24
Negri, Antonio, 13, 26, 64, 160, 183n4, 204n31. See also Autonomia Operaia
Neuromancer (Gibson), 60–61
New Left, the, 16, 23, 102
Newton, Huey P., 21. See also Black Panther Party
Ngai, Sianne, 94
Nietzsche, Friedrich, 6–7, 39, 130
noise. See clutter

Oates, Joyce Carol, 92. See also *Foxfire*
"On the Black Universe" (Laruelle), 147–48
opacity: and Blackness, 146, 152, 154; and imperceptibility, 11–12, 158; lacking in Preciado, 91; and queerness, 76–78, 196n29. *See also* anonymity; camouflage; exposure; imperceptibility; redaction; transparency; visibility; withdrawal
organization, 155–57

Palestine/Palestinians, 21, 26
Parsons, Lucy, 12, 48, 49
Paul, Ian Alan, 61–63
Pendleton, Adam, 150–51
perpetual present: and abolition, 162; and cybernetics, 165–66; and Empire, 96; and the guerrilla, 43–44; and liberalism, 59; and the Metropolis, 67, 69, 73–74. *See also* time
Perry, Sondra, 146
persuasion, 56, 64, 74. *See also* asymmetry; authoritarianism; insinuation
pharmaceuticals, 84–85, 86, 88–89. *See also* pornopower
Philip, M. NourbeSe, 117
Phillips, Utah, 54–55
photography: and the Baltimore uprising, 113–15; and Black aesthetics, 124–26, 139; and Black captivity, 121, 122–23; and Black criminality, 129–31; and Blackness, 28, 145–47, 200n17; and captive media, 132–38, 197n7; and white infrastructure, 139–43
Pisacane, Carlo, 47
policing: in Black aesthetics, 125; and Black death, 113–14, 124, 137, 139–40, 144; and brutality, 16–17; and captive media, 132; Cole's experiences with, 130–31; colonial roots of, 176n102; and cybernetics, 146; and guerrilla warfare, 41–42; and militarization, 26–27; and politics, 4, 18–19; and Twitter, 28, 118–19. *See also* counterinsurgency; surveillance
politics (analytic of power), 16–20. *See also* war (analytic of power)
pornopower, 28, 84–91. *See also* biopolitics
power, analytics of, 16–23. *See also* abolition; affect; asymmetry; biopolitics; politics; pornopower; war
Preciado, Paul B., 84–85, 88–89, 90–91, 189n44
Prison Information Group, 25

propaganda: armed, 35–36, 39, 45; by the deed, 25 47–50; and insinuation, 55–59, 181–82n7 prosecution, 117, 118–19, 120–23. *See also* captive media; policing; surveillance
Proudhon, Pierre-Joseph, 160
Public Feelings, 28, 95. *See also* Feel Tank Chicago; feminism
punk, 89, 120. *See also* queerness

Queer Nation, 77
queerness: and criminality, 27–28, 75–78; and exposure, 88–89, 90–91; and the undoing of identity, 103, 104–5; and imperceptibility, 12; and minstrelsy, 116; and opacity in de Villiers, 196n29; under socialism, 21. *See also* feminism; sex

race, 2, 5, 17, 84, 99. *See also* Blackness; whiteness
Raise Up (Thomas), 130, 131. *See also* Thomas, Hank Willis
Rankine, Claudia, 117, 139
recognition: and authoritarian strategy, 157; dialectic of, 1–5, 172n21; facial, 32, 132–33, 146; rejected by the Imaginary Party, 58; and liberal feminism, 87–88; refusal of, 157–58, 161, 165; and self-abolition, 110–11. *See also* abolition; difference; identity; interiority; subject, the
redaction, 28, 113–14, 117, 120, 124, 139–43. *See also* anonymity; camouflage; exposure; imperceptibility; opacity; transparency; visibility; withdrawal
Red Army Faction (RAF), 15–16, 26, 51–53, 70, 165, 175n89

Red Zora, 10, 52, 53
Reinhardt, Ad, 151
Research and Destroy New York City, 119–20
Revolutionary Cells, 10, 52. *See also* Red Zora; West Germany
Rich, Adrienne, 104
Ritchie, Lionel, 129
Rivera, Sylvia, 75
Rodman, Dennis, 129
Roland Barthes by Roland Barthes (Barthes), 136
Rousse, Paul, 49
Ryan, Paul, 16

Saint-Simon, Henri, 2
Sanbar, Elias, 26
SANCTUM (Blas), 79–82
saturation, 9–10, 70, 71–72. *See also* anonymity
Scenes of Subjection (Hartman), 144
Schiller, Magrit, 191n17. *See also* Socialist Patients' Collective
Schoots-McAlpine, Martin, 19
Scott-Heron, Gil, 1
screencaps, 121, 122–23. *See also* captive media
2 June Movement, 52. *See also* West Germany
Sedgwick, Eve Kosofsky, 94–95, 196n29
self-abolition, 110–11, 117–28. *See also* abolition
sex, 18, 79–82, 83–91. *See also* feminism; queerness
Sexton, Jared, 144, 152–54. *See also* Afropessimism; Wilderson, Frank
Sharpe, Christina, 28, 113, 152
Simians, Cyborgs, and Humans (Haraway), 62
Simpson, Lorna, 146

Simpson, O. J., 129
slavery: and anonymity, 31; Barthes on, 137–38; and Blackness, 148, 149, 151, 153, 154; and branding, 129; capitalism declares itself the enemy of, 158; and captive media, 28, 132, 142; counterinsurgency and slave patrols, 18; and fugitivity, 109–10, 161; and the hylomorphic model of politics, 156–57; and photography, 197n7; policing and colonial, 176n102; whiteness and the extension of, 124, 144. *See also* Blackness; marronage
slot machines, 85–86. *See also* excitement
slums, 41. *See also* terrain
socialism, 8, 20–22, 47, 149. *See also* communism; Marxism; Socialist German Student Union; Socialist Patients' Collective
Socialist German Student Union (SDS), 101
Socialist Patients' Collective (SPK), 28, 102, 105–8, 191n10, 191n17. *See also* illness
Social Rupture (blog), 57
Society of the Spectacle (Debord), 62. *See also* spectacle
South Africa, 130–31
sovereignty: abolition and the refusal of, 110; and fugitivity, 159–60; and the hunt, 31; and recognition, 4; and the state, 7, 59; and "war," 20–21. *See also* liberalism; state, the
spectacle: and abolition, 160; and Black exposure, 109, 111, 114–15, 140, 144, 147; and captive media, 28, 124–25, 133–34; and contingency, 38; and cybernetics, 33, 155, 164–65; and Empire, 72, 190n5; and escape, 42, 43–44; and insinuation, 57, 58, 59; and organization, 157; society of the, 62, 67. *See also* capitalism; cybernetics; Empire
Spinoza, Baruch, 97–98
Sprawl, the, 60–63
spontaneity, 45, 134, 145, 155–57
state, the: and affect, 97; crisis as motor of, 3; and guerrillas in West Germany, 51–53; and imperceptibility, 7–8, 163; and liberalism, 59, 175n93; and "politics," 17–20; and queerness, 75–76; and recognition, 4–5; and reproduction, 43; and "war," 20–22. *See also* counterinsurgency; liberalism; policing; sovereignty
Steyerl, Hito, 9–10
Stop LAPD Spying Coalition, 18
Street Transvestite Action Revolutionaries, 75
subject, the: and abolition, 160, 161–62; and affective politics, 96–98, 100; and anonymity, 32; and authoritarian persuasion, 56; and Black aesthetics, 150–51; and camouflage, 44; and captive media, 121, 124–25, 134–37; and guerrillas, 15–16, 22–23; and illness, 102, 103, 105–8; and the Imaginary Party, 58; and imperceptibility, 9, 10, 11; and liberalism, 157; and propaganda by the deed, 50; and recognition, 4–5, 172n21; and self-exposure, 88–91. *See also* abolition; difference; identity; interiority; recognition

subtraction: and anonymity, 32–33; and Black aesthetics, 139, 146–47; and communism, 21, 28–29; and the underground, 6, 26–27. *See also* communism; opacity; redaction
surveillance: of Blackness, 28, 146; and captive media, 132–33; and counterinsurgency, 19; and guerrilla warfare, 35; and policing, 118–19; and queerness, 77; sex and cybernetic, 79–82; and terrain, 41; and the West German State, 52–53; white infrastructure of, 139–43; and visibility, 6. *See also* counterinsurgency; policing
Syriana (Gaghan), 64, 183n1

Taussig, Michael, 56
Taylor, Cecil, 151
TERFs, 121
terrain, 39–42; and anonymity, 27, 31, 32–33, 157; and camouflage, 43; and counterinsurgency, 18; digital culture as, 164; and density, 45–46, 71–72; and rural guerrillas, 35–36; urban and guerrillas, 36–37
Testo-Junkie (Preciado), 88–89, 91
Thacker, Eugene, 68, 148
Thomas, Hank Willis, 129, 130, 131
Thousand Plateaus, A (Deleuze and Guattari), 5–15, 23, 174n70
Time, 119
time: and cybernetics, 165–66; and Empire, 96; and the guerrilla, 43–44; and insinuation, 59; and the Metropolis, 67, 69, 72, 73–74; and prediction, 1–2; and the Sprawl, 61–63

Tiqqun, 2, 22, 57–58, 160, 177n125. *See also* anarchism
transparency: and criminalization, 76–77; Glissant's challenge to, 12, 158; and liberalism, 84, 86–88; photography's putative, 121, 135, 138; and whiteness, 146–47. *See also* anonymity; camouflage; exposure; imperceptibility; opacity; redaction; visibility; withdrawal
Trotsky, Leon, 156
Twitter, 28, 117–19, 123; and *2015 Baltimore Uprising*, 113–14, 125–26. *See also* captive media
2015 Baltimore Uprising: A Teen Epistolary, The, 113–15, 117, 119–21, 124, 125–26

uchromia, 148, 149, 154. *See also* Blackness; color theory
Uganda, 134
Undercommons (Moten and Harney), 24
Urban Guerilla Concept, The (RAF), 51. *See also* Red Army Faction
U.S. Army, 17–18, 18–19, 19–20, 174n74. *See also* counterinsurgency

Venice School of Architecture, 183n4
visibility: and Blackness, 28, 124, 133, 144–54; and camouflage, 43; and feminism, 87–88; Foucault on, 6; and the Imaginary Party, 58; and the infrastructure of whiteness, 141–43; and the Metropolis, 65, 67; and queerness, 77; and whiteness, 140. *See also* anonymity; camouflage;

exposure; imperceptibility; opacity; redaction; transparency; withdrawal

Vita Nova (Meessen), 135–36

Wang, Jackie, 62

war (analytic of power), 16, 20–23. *See also* guerrilla warfare; politics (analytic of power)

Warren, Calvin 139, 147

WaveNet, 62

West Germany, 101–2; extradition of Croissant, 26; guerrillas in, 10, 15–16, 51–53; and the Socialist Patients' Collective, 105–8, 191n10

What Is Gender Nihilism? (Bash Back!), 78

whiteness, 28; and abolition, 159; and the Baltimore uprising, 114–15; and Black aesthetics, 144, 146, 146–47, 151, 152; and Black captivity, 109–11, 115–16, 117, 120–21, 123, 124; infrastructures of, 133–34, 139–43; and *Invisible Man* (Ellison), 32; and liveliness, 136–37; and other struggles, 193n17. *See also* Blackness

Wilderson, Frank, 147, 149, 159. *See also* Afropessimism; Sexton, Jared

Williams, Sherri, 140

withdrawal, 24, 37, 40, 144–54. *See also* anonymity; camouflage; exposure; imperceptibility; opacity; redaction; transparency; visibility

Wretched of the Earth (Fanon), 152, 156

women: affect as political resource for, 28; and becoming, 12, 69; in *Foxfire*, 92–93; and happiness, 97–100; and home's torment and isolation, 103–4; lynching and white women, 133; online abuse of, 121; and racism, 99; and unruliness, 115–16; and vanishing, 11. *See also* feminism; gender

Zami: A New Spelling of My Name (Lorde), 99

Zong! (Philip), 117

Andrew Culp is professor of media history and theory at the California Institute of the Arts. He is the author of *Dark Deleuze* (Minnesota, 2016).